GREATER WASHINGTON AREA BICYCLE ATLAS

Fourth Edition

Edited by
Charles Baughman
Bonnie Nevel
Bill Silverman

Cover design by Bill Raue
Maps by Cartographics, Inc., Fairfax, Virginia
Typeset by Bill Silverman
Image Set by Publication Technology Corp., Fairfax, Virginia
Printed by Banta Company, Harrisonburg, Virginia

The publishers, editors and authors have done their best to ensure the accuracy of all the information in the *Greater Washington Area Bicycle Atlas*. However, they accept no responsibility for any loss, injury or inconvenience sustained as a result of information or advice contained in the book.

ISBN 0-9614892-3-5
Potomac Area Council of American Youth Hostels
Washington Area Bicyclist Association

Library of Congress Catalog Card Number 91-066429

This book is printed on recycled paper. The co-publishers gladly absorbed the higher cost of using recycled stock.

Printing History	Editor(s)
1st Edition, 1974	Alan Berkowitz
2nd Edition, 1977	Dave Gilbert
3rd Edition, 1985	Ken Moskowitz
3rd Edition Revised, 1987	Sharon Gang
4th Edition, 1992	Charles Baughman, Bonnie Nevel and Bill Silverman

There is more to life than increasing its speed.

-- Mahatma Gandhi

Table of Contents

Introduction

Introduction

This atlas invites you outdoors. It encourages you to discover your surroundings at a more leisurely pace than the mad dash to the office. It entices you to explore the Washington area under your own steam.

Each tour in the atlas offers something special, whether natural, cultural or historical. Spectacular, diverse and interesting, the tours in this atlas are worth exploring without a bike, but are even more special on one.

And what is so special about bicycling? As a sport, it is healthier than most, with aerobic stimulation of the heart, lungs and muscles. Bicycling is also an aesthetic experience: a means of transportation so simple and energy-efficient that the rest of the world seems comparatively busy, noisy and intense. The bicycle allows us to experience the beauty and simplicity of our environment in a clean, economical way. And most of all, it is *fun!*

What Is In This Atlas

Now in its fourth edition, the *Greater Washington Area Bicycle Atlas* dates back to 1974. The first two editions combined commuting and touring routes, compiled when many of the bicycle routes we now take for granted were first established. The third edition (1985) and the revised third edition (1987) added new routes, better maps and more information. More than 100,000 copies were sold, reflecting the popularity of both the sport and the region.

This fourth edition continues the tradition of excellence, and keeps up with the times. During the 1980s, Washington's suburbs were transformed from sleepy towns and dairy farms to office complexes and housing subdivisions. Quiet bicycle routes became a nightmare of delivery trucks and single-occupant automobiles. Roads were built, trails and parks were created (and lost), and land was developed. This new edition introduces routes along today's generation of less-travelled roads, and makes important modifications to old favorites.

This atlas includes everything you need to know about bicycling in the mid-Atlantic region. It describes climate, topography, safety tips and traffic laws. And it suggests equipment and other essentials to help make your trip trouble-free.

Tours range from five to 140 miles in length. Most are 20-40 miles, about a 3-hour ride for recreational cyclists. Where appropriate, tour descriptions include campgrounds, hostels or lodging along the way. Each tour includes a cue sheet, detailing exact directions in a clear, concise style.

A new feature of this edition is a series of rides for the mountain bike enthusiast. Essentially unknown as a product until 1987, the all-terrain mountain bike now accounts for the majority of U.S. bicycle sales. With the new type of bike emerges a new breed of bicyclist: less concerned about long trips on smooth surfaces and more interested in shorter, off-road excursions. The knobby tires, upright handlebars and wide seats of a mountain bike allow bicycle access to almost anywhere, from scenic by-ways to back-country trails.

The appendix contains useful information on bike organizations, government bicycle contacts and more. You will find sources of regional maps and a description of Metro's Bike-on-Rail program, plus information on mountain biking, packing your bicycle for commercial airline flights, and bicycle access to Washington's three major airports.

The index catalogues the routes, points of interest and geographic locations of each tour in an easy-to-use format.

The Mid-Atlantic Region

Mountainous to the west and flat to the east, the mid-Atlantic region includes a variety of terrain that will interest cyclists of every skill level. Maryland's western panhandle has lush forest, steep mountains and broad valleys, while its Eastern Shore features flat farmland and sleepy fishing villages on the spectacular Chesapeake Bay. Virginia's topography ranges from the majestic Blue Ridge Mountains and the historic Shenandoah Valley in the west to the Piedmont region, an elevated rolling plain south of Washington. East of the Piedmont, the flat Tidewater area extends 100 miles inland from the Atlantic Ocean.

Across the region, the spring and fall months are ideal for bicycling. Most bicyclists break out of their winter doldrums and hit the road in March. Summer temperatures reach well into the 90s or higher, usually with heavy humidity. Touring still may be comfortable through November.

The region is steeped in history and includes many important Civil War sites. Barely 100 miles separate Richmond and Washington, the two capitals of the divided nation. Dozens of decisive battles were fought on the Piedmont plain at places like Bull Run, Chancellorsville and Fredericksburg. The fertile Shenandoah Valley was ravaged time after time by numerous campaigns from both sides. In the Tidewater region, the Confederate Army gave ground inch by inch when more than 120,000 Union troops landed near Norfolk to march on Richmond. Sharpsburg, northwest of Washington in Maryland, was the site of America's bloodiest day at the Battle of Antietam. And the Maryland flatland southeast of Washington provided John Wilkes Booth his famous escape route after he shot President Abraham Lincoln at Ford's Theater. Tours in the atlas include these and many other Civil War points of interest -- some famous, some obscure.

Bicycle Safety

All rules of bicycle safety can be summed up in the concept of cautious and defensive cycling with a good bicycle helmet. The hazards of the road for bicyclists are greater than those for car drivers. In addition to other vehicles, cyclists must look out for sewer grates, railroad tracks, road debris, potholes and uneven pavement. On bike paths, many cyclists erroneously discount the danger of collisions with other cyclists.

About 75 percent of all bicyclist accident fatalities result from head injuries. A bicycle helmet can protect your head from serious injury, and is required by law in a growing number of jurisdictions. Wear a helmet that is well-ventilated, fits securely on your head and meets safety standards. There are two U.S. standards for bicycle helmets. The best helmets meet the Snell Memorial Foundation standard -- look for a green or blue Snell sticker inside before buying the helmet. Other helmets may pass the less demanding American National Standards Institute ANSI Z90.4 standard. The Washington Area Bicyclist Association (WABA) publishes a *Consumer's Guide to Bicycle Helmets*. Send $1 and a self-addressed stamped envelope to WABA for a copy of the brochure (see appendix for address).

Bicyclists should cycle as close to the righthand curb as safely possible. This means leaving some room to avoid a pothole or broken glass. If a narrow lane is your only option, bicycle in the center of the lane. Hugging the right side may invite a motorist to squeeze by without leaving enough clearance to pass you safely.

If cars are parked in the curb lane, try to keep at least three feet of clearance to allow for a swinging car door. Do not weave in and out between parked cars. Instead, ride in a straight line in the range of vision of motorists.

Remember that drivers are not expecting bicyclists on the road. For this reason, assume that drivers cannot see you. Allow for unsignaled right turns by cars that might cut you off. Always signal your own turns to alert drivers to your intentions.

Plan to finish your tour before nightfall. If you must cycle during or after dusk, use bicycle lights (as is required by law). A white shirt or reflective clothing makes you more conspicuous, both to other cyclists and to drivers. Also consider adding reflective material to your helmet.

Each year more than 1,000 people in the U.S. -- approximately three per day -- are killed while riding bicycles. Most of these victims are children, and most die without ever receiving a lesson in bicycle safety. Children should take bicycle safety lessons, just as teenagers take driver education courses. Finding a youth bicycle safety course in your community may be a challenge. Begin your search with the non-emergency number of your local police department.

Bicycling and the Law

Bicycles are legally classified as vehicles in the District of Columbia, Maryland and Virginia, which means that bicyclists generally share the same rights and responsibilities as car drivers. Each jurisdiction additionally enforces special bicycling laws that recognize the bicycle's small size, vulnerability and limited speed. The laws are designed for the cyclists' safety, and, although sometimes inconvenient, always should be observed.

Metropolitan Washington area bicyclists should be familiar with the laws of the three jurisdictions, as well as the regulations of the National Capital Region of the National Park Service, which oversees many area parks. Some municipalities also have their own local bicycle ordinances. Even Capitol Hill has its own rules -- and its own police department.

Maryland law prohibits bicyclists from riding on roads with speed limits above 50 mph (though shoulder riding is legal), controlled access highways (with entrance ramps) and in state-run tunnels or over state-run bridges. Bicyclists have the right to use any other roadways unless expressly prohibited.

Maryland and *Virginia* require cyclists to ride as near to the right road edge as is safe, reasonable and practical, unless turning left or passing slower-moving traffic. *Virginia* makes exceptions for various hazards and narrow lanes.

The *District of Columbia* requires only that "slower-moving traffic keep right." The *National Capital Region* of the National Park Service has a similar regulation. The *District of Columbia* also prohibits unnecessary obstruction or impeding of traffic by bicyclists; *Maryland* and *Virginia* laws do not address this issue.

Special situations may exist when an off-road bike path lies adjacent to a road. *Virginia* allows localities to enact ordinances for mandatory use of adjacent paths. *Maryland* requires bicyclists to use a bike lane or shoulder if it is paved to a "comparable surface to the road." The *District of Columbia* does not require the use of bike paths at all. In all of the tours in this atlas where roads adjoin bike paths, bicycling in the roadway is legal, except where the roadway is a limited access highway (e.g., the Mount Vernon Trail and the George Washington Memorial Parkway in Virginia).

Cycling on sidewalks is banned in *Maryland* unless permitted by local ordinance. *Virginia* takes the opposite approach, allowing the use of sidewalks unless forbidden by a locality. The *District of Columbia* allows bicycling on all sidewalks outside the downtown area (roughly defined as Georgetown to the west, Capitol Hill to the east, the waterfront to the south and Dupont Circle and Union Station to the north). When on a sidewalk or in a crosswalk in the *District of Columbia* or *Virginia*, bicyclists have the same rights and duties as pedestrians. Wherever you bicycle on a sidewalk, extend every courtesy to pedestrians, and give an audible warning before passing.

Maryland allows two bicyclists to ride abreast of each other so long as traffic is not impeded. The *District of Columbia* allows riding abreast if "persons are not endangered." *Virginia* and the *National Capital Region* of the National Park Service forbid riding abreast.

In many localities, residents must register their bicycles, usually with the police. For more information on registration, contact the police department or bicycle coordinator in your community (see appendix).

A growing number of jurisdictions have enacted legislation requiring the use of bicycle helmets. Typically, fines collected from offenders provide helmets to low-income families.

Equipment

In the *District of Columbia* and *Maryland*, bicycles must be equipped with a bell or other device capable of giving a signal audible for a distance of 100 feet. *Virginia* has no statewide law, but localities may have such an ordinance.

For night riding, the *District of Columbia, Maryland* and *Virginia* require use of a lamp emitting a white light visible for 500 feet to the front, while the *National Capital Region* of the National Park Service requires simply a "white light." The *District of Columbia* and *Virginia* also require that bicycles used at night have a red reflector or a red light visible from the rear. *Maryland* and the *National Capital Region* of the National Park Service require only a reflector. *Maryland* and *Virginia* laws require that lights must be attached to the bicycle, technically prohibiting battery-operated arm or leg lights.

Requirements for riding with lights sometimes extend into daylight hours. In *Maryland,* lights must be used when persons and vehicles "are not clearly discernible at a distance of 1,000 feet." Therefore, lights and reflectors are unnecessary on some well-lit streets at night, but are required during dark daytime hours. The *National Capital Region* of the National Park Service similarly requires use of lights during periods of low visibility.

For a brochure on local laws pertaining to bicyclists, send $1 and a self-addressed stamped envelope to WABA. You also can read ordinances and state codes in local libraries.

Accidents

If you are involved in an accident on your bicycle, you must stop, identify yourself, and render aid to anyone injured. If death, injury, or substantial property damage has occurred, you must notify the police immediately. These laws apply to motor vehicle operators as well as bicyclists.

You can "be involved" in an accident without having physical contact with a motor vehicle or pedestrian. For instance, if a motorist passes you and collides with an oncoming car, you are legally involved.

If you are involved in an accident that results in death, injury, or substantial property damage, you should notify your homeowner and/or automobile insurance company. Failure to provide notice may give your insurance company the right to refuse to pay a claim. If you are injured by a car collision while bicycling, an automobile insurance policy may cover some medical expenses and wage losses.

A bicyclist who violates a law and causes an accident can be sued, and may be required by a court to pay steep compensation to the injured person. Hence, liability insurance is desirable. Most homeowner or tenant insurance provides liability protection for bicyclists. Automobile insurance policies generally do not provide such protection.

Obeying the law does not insure your safety. You should strive to adopt a philosophy of "defensive cycling," anticipating difficult situations and yielding the road as safety requires.

Touring Tips

Before starting your bike tour, you should quickly check that your bicycle is in good order. Use these helpful steps suggested by the League of American Wheelmen:

- Pinch tires for proper inflation. They should compress slightly on the sides, and feel very hard on the treads.

- Spread a light oil or lubricant on the chain if it squeaks.

- Squeeze your front brakes and push forward (on bikes equipped with front and rear brakes): the rear wheel should rise. Squeeze the rear brakes and push forward: the rear tire should skid. Your brake levers should not touch the handlebars when squeezed with full force.

- Make sure brake pads are in the correct position and brake cables are not frayed.

- Check that quick release wheels are on securely, and that the levers point to the rear of the bicycle to prevent accidental release.

- Spin the wheels. They should rotate evenly and not touch the frame, brakes, or fenders.

- Handlebars, seat, cranks and pedals should be securely fastened.

- Let the bicycle fall from 3-4 inches off the ground, and listen for rattles or loose parts. Check your baggage for loose ends that might enter spokes or other moving parts.

On any trip, you will want to wear a helmet and take a water bottle. A helmet protects your head from injury and is discussed in the "Bicycle Safety" section. A water bottle provides you with quick access to fluids, a necessity to prevent dehydration, particularly in warm, humid conditions. Wear your helmet at all times, drink before you get thirsty and eat before you get hungry.

You always will want to carry some tools and spare parts with you. The size of your tool kit will depend on where you cycle. Tire irons, a patch kit, a frame pump, a small adjustable wrench, pliers and small regular and Phillips-head screwdrivers will handle most roadside emergencies. Newer bikes use hex bolts that require a good set of Allen wrenches. A spare tube will allow you to make a quick change of a flat tire; you can then patch your punctured tube when you return home, rather than on the road. Presta valve users should also carry an adapter that allows use of conventional (Schraeder) air pumps at gas stations.

In addition to the maps and cues from the atlas, you should carry a good bicycle map. The Alexandria Drafting Company (ADC) publishes an excellent bicycle street map of the region showing recommended low-volume streets, and all on- and off-road bicycle routes inside the Capital Beltway. The ADC map is sold in most area convenience stores. Certain jurisdictions also publish their own maps. The appendix contains a complete listing of map sources for the region.

Handlebar bags offer the convenience of reaching food or reading a cue sheet while riding. For longer tours, panniers provide a way to carry your clothing and other essentials. Look for panniers made from rain-resistant materials, with large openings to compartments, covered zippers and reinforced seams. Avoid backpacks, which become uncomfortable on longer trips.

Cycling gloves absorb road shock and protect your hands and wrists from nerve damage. Many cyclists use rear-view mirrors that attach to glasses, helmets, or handlebars. A bicycle bell warns slower traffic ahead of you and is particularly helpful on congested paths (bells are required in some jurisdictions). Odometers simplify following a cue sheet, and help track distance and speed on long tours.

For the occasional cyclist, a 10 mph pace is a good estimate for trip planning. Ride in low gears at about 60 to 70 pedal revolutions per minute to avoid knee damage and maximize the aerobic benefits. Many short rest stops are better than a few long ones, which allow muscles to tighten up and your body to become sluggish.

Clothes for cycling should not restrict leg or arm movement, and colorful cycling jerseys increase visibility. Bicycle shorts are comfortable and constructed to maximize padding where you need it the most. On overnight trips, keep your wardrobe to a minimum to avoid unnecessary weight. A limited wardrobe will go a long way if you take a few minutes in the evening to do laundry.

Bicycle shoes distribute foot pressure evenly over the pedal, but any sneaker with a firm sole is adequate and usually less expensive. Make sure your shoes have a flat bottom if your bicycle has toe clips; otherwise you may have difficulty removing your feet from the pedals.

In wet weather, rain jackets and pants protect you and are less likely to flap around in the wind than ponchos. Fenders effectively keep rain off you (and anyone behind you).

Cycle-camping greatly expands the number of places where you can stay, but requires hauling additional gear. The longer rides in this atlas all offer a choice of hostels, inns, motels, or campgrounds. Hostels are simple dormitory accommodations operated by American Youth Hostels. The state park information offices listed in the appendix have complete brochures on state-operated campgrounds.

Bicycle Groups

Washington is the home to many active bicycle organizations, from touring clubs to advocacy groups to racing clubs to mountain bike clubs. These groups -- and the larger bicycling community -- benefit from the membership, support and involvement of individuals like you.

In addition, several regional and national bicycle organizations such as the League of American Wheelmen and the Rails-to-Trails Conservancy work on a broader scale to improve and support bicycling. The appendix provides a complete listing of these groups.

Using the Atlas

Each tour description in this atlas consists of a general overview, specific information on terrain, distance, food, lodging and points of interest, a map or maps, and a set of directional cues. While en route, bicyclists generally follow the cue sheet, using the map as a back-up reference.

For touring, photocopy the cue sheet and map, and fold them into a pocket or the transparent map case of a handlebar bag. Map cases keep the page open and dry. Some riders clip the map and cues to a brake cable.

The directions on the cue are presented in a simplified, easy-to-read format. While some choose to glance at the cues as they ride, you probably will find it safest to stop your bicycle before you begin navigating.

Each cue sheet is formatted as follows:

START: The location, address or landmark of the beginning of the tour with explicit directions to the starting point from the Capital Beltway or another well-known location. Car parking is available nearby unless indicated. Approximate mileage from the Capital Beltway is given where applicable. Alternate starts and Metro stations near the start or along the tour also are noted.

LENGTH: Total mileage of the tour from start to finish. The lengths of alternate routes, starts, and side trips also are included. Directions for the alternate routes and side trips are found at the end of the tour cues.

TERRAIN: Steepness, hilliness and road surface conditions along the tour. For example, "level" indicates flat or nearly flat for most of the tour; "rolling hills" denotes small hills along the route; "hilly" means at least some steep and difficult hills or mountains.

POINTS OF INTEREST: Highlights, including cultural and historical landmarks, recreational facilities, unique local attractions and natural amenities such as lakes, mountain views and rivers.

FOOD: Restaurants, fast food, cafes, markets and general stores, with mileage to help plan meal stops. Generally, these are grouped into "markets" and "restaurants." Food stops also are listed in the ride cues.

LODGING: Hostels, campgrounds, inns, bed-and-breakfasts and motels.

MAPS (AND INFORMATION): Suggested road and bike maps to supplement the maps in this atlas. Maps are listed from most specific to most general. Where applicable, this listing also contains additional sources of information, such as local Chambers of Commerce and visitor centers.

The cue sheets contain abbreviations and symbols to improve readability. For example, the T symbol refers to an intersection where one road dead-ends into a cross street at a right angle. In cases where a road has more than one name, the most common is listed first, with the alternative name listed parenthetically. Only the names of streets *bicycled on the tours* appear in **boldface**. State route references and U.S. highways are delineated (e.g., VA 28, US 13). Note that "BUS" denotes a *business* route, usually an alternative to a bypass, as in BUS VA 7.

Two or more turns within 0.1-miles are indicated within a single mileage cue.

Each map contains symbols that indicate points of interest, food stops, hostels and Metro stations. The legend on each map includes *all* possible symbols, whether or not they are found on that particular tour.

The following legend pertains to all tour maps:

MAP LEGEND

INTERSTATE ROAD	(95)	METRO STATION	ⓜ
FEDERAL ROAD	(29)	DEFINED PARK AREA	
STATE ROAD	(274)	BIKE ROUTE	▬▬▬
STATE BOUNDARY	— — — —	ALTERNATE ROUTE	▬ ▬ ▬ ▬
COUNTY BOUNDARY	— — —	TRAIL	– – – –
RAILROAD	+—+—+	POINT OF INTEREST	●
RIVER, STREAM		FOOD AVAILABLE	■
FERRY	– – – – –	AMERICAN YOUTH HOSTEL	▲

A regional overview map with all tours depicted is given on the next page. All 71 tours in the atlas are listed at the end of the appendix by length, starting county, Civil War interest, Metro accessibility, family ride suitability and mountain biking opportunities.

Improving the Atlas

While every effort was made to assure the accuracy and utility of the information in this atlas, we would love to hear from you about ways to make future editions even better. Send your comments, corrections and suggestions about the tours to GWABA, c/o Potomac AYH, P.O. Box 28607, Washington, DC 20038.

And Finally...

"When one begins to tell why the bicycle is one of the great inventions of the century, it is hard to begin, because there is so much to say," wrote Philip G. Hubert, Jr. in *Scribner's Magazine* in 1895. These words still ring true. So have a great time! That, of course, is what bicycling is all about.

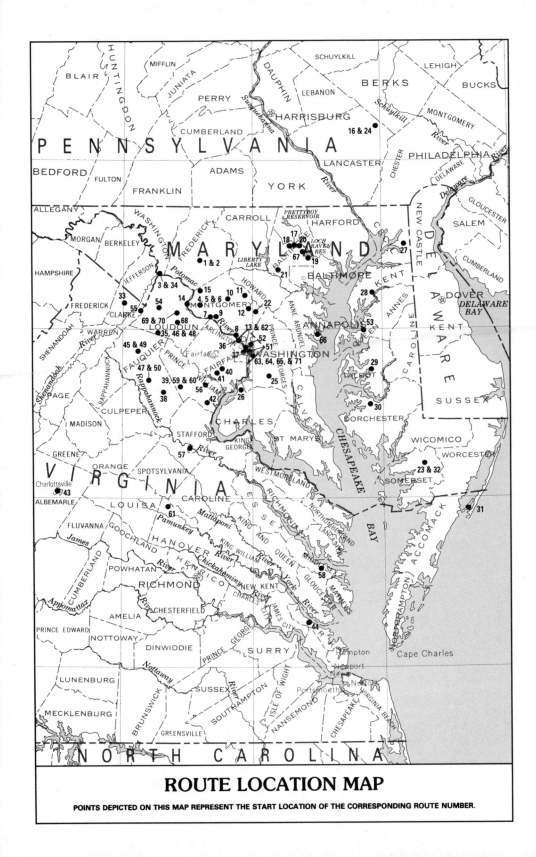

ROUTE LOCATION MAP

POINTS DEPICTED ON THIS MAP REPRESENT THE START LOCATION OF THE CORRESPONDING ROUTE NUMBER.

I. Northwest Passages

1. THREE COVERED BRIDGES

As you bicycle through the scenic valleys of Frederick County with the Blue Ridge Mountains rising in the distance, you will experience the three historic covered bridges that distinguish this tour. Visible along the northern section of the route, the imposing shrine of St. Mary's College (built in 1839) nestled in the mountains further highlights the trip.

*[**Editor's note:** Shortly prior to publication of this atlas, the covered bridges at Loy's Station and on Motters Station Road were damaged. The two bridges are presently out of service to all vehicular traffic and are likely to remain closed through 1993. Check with the Frederick County Tourism Council (301-663-8687) for updates and alternative routes.]*

START: Holiday Inn at the intersection of US 15 and US 40 in Frederick, Md. From the Capital Beltway, take I-270 North and bear left at fork onto US 15 North (to Frederick). Continue two miles to US 40 West; motel is visible before exit. Frederick is 33 miles northwest of the Capital Beltway.

LENGTH: 45.1 miles.

TERRAIN: Gentle hills.

POINTS OF INTEREST: Covered bridges at 10.1, 15.6 and 21.5 miles.

FOOD: Markets at start and 15.3 miles. Restaurants at start and 27.4 miles.

LODGING: In Frederick, Holiday Inn (301-662-5141) at start. In the Frederick area, bed-and-breakfasts include Spring Bank Inn (310-694-0440), Turning Point Inn (301-831-8232), Tyler-Spite House (301-831-4455) and Rosebud Inn (301-845-2221). In Thurmont, Thurmont's Cozy Motel (301-271-4301), at 27.4 miles, welcomes bicyclists.

MAPS AND INFORMATION: *A Frederick Cycling Guide,* available for $3.75 from Frederick County Tourism Council, 19 East Church Street, Frederick, MD 21701-5401 (301-663-8687); Frederick County, Md. road map.

MILES   DIRECTIONS & COMMENTS

0.0   **Right** out of motel parking lot to go north on **BAUGHMANS LANE**.

0.6   **Right** on **SHOOKSTOWN ROAD**.

0.8   **Right** on **ROSEMONT AVENUE**.

0.9   **Immediate left** on **WILSON PLACE**.

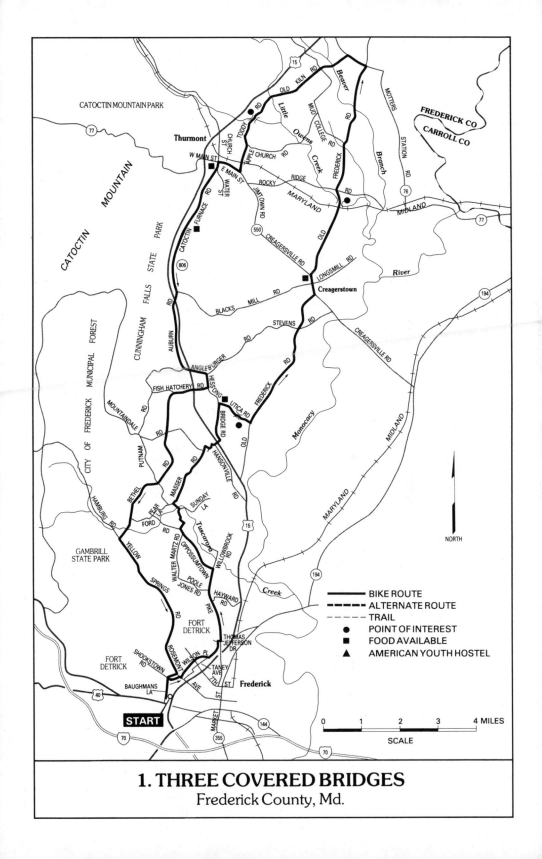

1. THREE COVERED BRIDGES
Frederick County, Md.

1.9   **Left** on **TANEY AVENUE.**

2.4   **Right** on **THOMAS JEFFERSON DRIVE.**

2.5   **Left** on **OPPOSSUMTOWN PIKE.**

4.5   **Bear left** to remain on **OPPOSSUMTOWN PIKE.**

5.9   **Right** at Ford Road to remain on **OPPOSSUMTOWN PIKE.**

6.5   **Left** at Sunday Lane to remain on **OPPOSSUMTOWN PIKE.**

6.7   **Right** on **MASSER ROAD.**

8.4   **Right** on **MOUNTAINDALE ROAD.**

8.8   **Left** on **HANSONVILLE ROAD** (no sign).

9.0   Cross US 15 to **left** on **HESSONG BRIDGE ROAD.**

10.1   **Right** on **UTICA ROAD** over covered bridge.

11.3   **Left** on **OLD FREDERICK ROAD.**

15.3   **Bear left** on **CREAGERSVILLE ROAD** at stop sign. Store on right.

15.6   **Right** to remain on **OLD FREDERICK ROAD.** Covered bridge at Loy's Station Park.

21.6   **Left** at second road after covered bridge on **MOTTERS STATION ROAD** (no sign); red barn on right.

22.2   **Left** on **OLD KILN ROAD** (no sign).

24.7   **Left** on **RODDY ROAD** at T.

26.3   **Straight** on **APPLE CHURCH ROAD.**

26.7   **Right** on **EAST MAIN STREET** (MD 77; no sign).

27.4   **Left** on **WATER STREET** (MD 806). Restaurants.

27.5   **Right** to remain on **MD 806** (Catoctin Furnace Road).

31.4   **Straight** to **AUBURN ROAD** crossing US 15.

33.4   **Left** on **ANGLEBURGER ROAD** crossing US 15.

33.9   **Right** on **HESSONG BRIDGE ROAD.**

34.3   **Right** on **FISH HATCHERY ROAD.** *Caution at US 15.*

35.2   **Left** on **BETHEL ROAD.**

40.0 **Left** on **YELLOW SPRINGS ROAD.** This becomes **ROSEMONT AVENUE.**

44.2 **Right** on **BAUGHMANS LANE.**

45.1 **Left** into motel **PARKING LOT.**

2. FREDERICK ICE CREAM

Pedaling through the small towns and farmland of western Frederick County, you will enjoy many interesting diversions on this invigorating route. Stop at a homemade ice cream parlor, enjoy the hilltop panoramas, glimpse the ruins of a Civil War era estate, and explore antique shops and an aquatic plant garden. Most roads in this area are good for biking, so try your own side trips!

START: Shopping center at intersection of US 15 and South Jefferson Street (US 340) in Frederick, Md. From the Capital Beltway, take I-270 North and bear left at fork onto US 15 North. Continue approximately one-half mile to intersection with South Jefferson Street. Shopping center is on left, across from Bob's Big Boy. Frederick is 33 miles northwest of the Capital Beltway.

LENGTH: 44.0 miles. **ALTERNATE ROUTE:** 48.0 miles

TERRAIN: Hilly; some narrow roads and unpaved segments.

POINTS OF INTEREST: Main's Ice Cream at 11.5 miles; Gathland State Park at 18.4 miles, with museum, historic arch, ruins of mansion; Appalachian Trail at 18.4 miles; and Lilypons Water Gardens (301-874-5133) on 4-mile alternate route.

FOOD: Markets at start and 19.5 miles. Ice cream at 11.5 miles.

LODGING: In Frederick, Holiday Inn (301-662-5141). In the Frederick area, bed-and-breakfasts include Spring Bank Inn (310-694-0440), Turning Point Inn (301-831-8232), Tyler-Spite House (301-831-4455) and Rosebud Inn (301-845-2221). At Gathland State Park (301-293-2420), public campgrounds at 18.4 miles.

MAPS AND INFORMATION: *A Frederick Cycling Guide,* available for $3.75 postpaid from Frederick County Tourism Council, 19 East Church Street, Frederick, MD 21701 (301-663-8687); Frederick County, Md. road map.

MILES   DIRECTIONS & COMMENTS

0.0	**Right** out of parking lot, to go southwest on **US 340.**
0.6	**Take exit** for **MD 180** (Ballenger Creek Pike, Jefferson Pike).
0.8	**Left** on **MD 180** at stop sign.
0.9	**Right** on **BUTTERFLY LANE.**
2.7	**Left** on **MOUNT PHILLIPS ROAD** at stop sign.

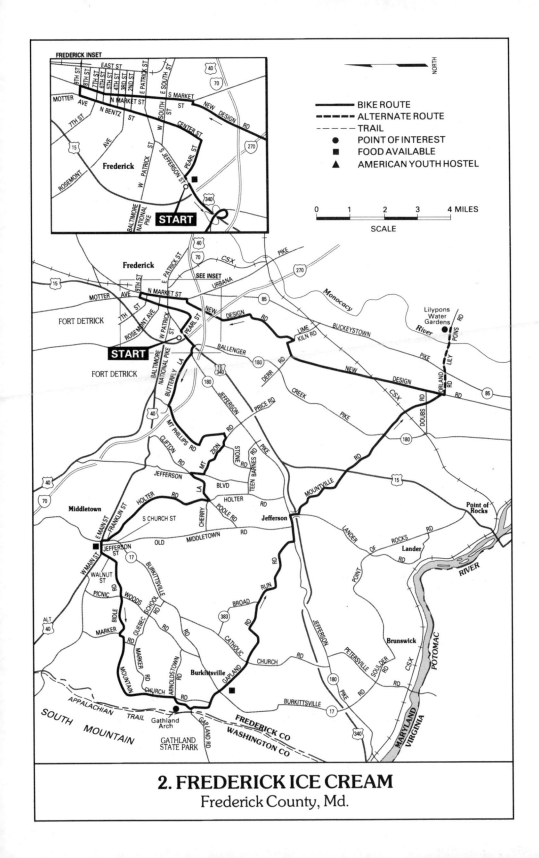

2. FREDERICK ICE CREAM
Frederick County, Md.

5.1   **Right** on **MOUNT ZION ROAD** at T.

5.3   **Keep right** at fork to stay on **MOUNT ZION ROAD**. *Caution: rough road for short stretch.*

6.3   **Right** on **JEFFERSON BOULEVARD** at T.

6.7   **Left** on **CHERRY LANE** at stop sign.

7.7   **Right** on **HOLTER ROAD** at stop sign. This becomes **FRANKLIN STREET** in Middletown.

11.3   **Right** on **SOUTH CHURCH STREET** (MD 17).

11.5   **Left** on **WEST MAIN STREET** at traffic light. Half-block to Main's Ice Cream. Restaurant just past church on left, closed Sundays. Continue on West Main Street, heading toward mountains.

11.7   **Bear left** on **WALNUT STREET,** leaving downtown. This becomes **BIDLE ROAD** at town limits. Packed dirt at 14.3 miles.

14.6   **Merge left** on **MARKER ROAD.**

14.9   **Right** on **MOUNTAIN CHURCH ROAD** (no sign). **Merge right** with **MARKER ROAD.**

17.8   **Right** on **ARNOLDSTOWN ROAD.**

18.4   **Left** on **GAPLAND ROAD** (unmarked) at Gathland State Park sign and Gathland Arch (built in 1896). Museum, ruins of mansion, picnicking, Appalachian Trail.

19.5   General store in Burkittsville (still on Gapland Road).

22.8   **GAPLAND ROAD** becomes **MD 383 SOUTH**. *Caution: one-lane bridge at bottom of steep hill.*

25.3   **Left** on **MD 180 EAST** (Jefferson Pike).

26.0   **First right** on **LANDER ROAD** after leaving town of Jefferson.

26.2   Take bridge over US 340. **Left** on **MOUNTVILLE ROAD** immediately following bridge and highway entrance.

28.1   Cross US 15. *Caution: fast, heavy traffic.*

30.6   Railroad crossing. *Caution: cross at right angle.*

31.7   **Left** on **NEW DESIGN ROAD.** ALTERNATE ROUTE side trip to Lilypons Water Gardens begins here (see end of cues).

36.3   **Bear right** to stay on **NEW DESIGN ROAD** at fork. Derr Road goes left.

36.8   Follow **NEW DESIGN ROAD** around to **left** for 90-degree turn just past electric transformers.

40.4   **Left** on **SOUTH MARKET STREET** at T. Enter Frederick. South Market Street becomes **NORTH MARKET STREET.**

41.7   **Left** on **9TH STREET.**

42.0   **Left** on **MOTTER AVENUE.** Becomes **NORTH BENTZ STREET.**

43.0   Cross West South Street. North Bentz Street becomes **CENTER STREET**, with two-way traffic.

43.5   **Right** on **PEARL STREET.**

44.0   **Arrive** at **SHOPPING CENTER.**

ALTERNATE ROUTE

From end of Mountville Road at 31.7 miles, zig **right,** then **left** on **ORLAND ROAD,** which becomes **LILY PONS ROAD.** Gardens are on left. **Reverse direction** and turn **right** on **NEW DESIGN ROAD**, heading north.

3. ANTIETAM BATTLEFIELD LOOP

Encompassing mountainous inclines, rolling farmlands and scenic canal roads, this ride rolls through the heart of Civil War Maryland.

A tour of Antietam National Battlefield highlights the trip. On September 17, 1862, the bloodiest day of the Civil War, 12,400 Union and 10,300 Confederate soldiers fell on the Antietam fields, slightly less than half of the number of U.S. casualties during the entire Vietnam War. More than 4,770 Confederate soldiers are buried at Antietam National Cemetery.

The Battle of Antietam was the first major attempt by the South to attack in the North. Led by General Robert E. Lee, the Confederates were vastly outnumbered by Union armies under General George McClellan. After his bloody victory at Antietam, McClellan missed an opportunity to crush Lee's army, which slipped across the Potomac River the day after the battle. Despite direct orders from President Abraham Lincoln, McClellan failed to pursue Lee. Exasperated, Lincoln removed McClellan from command. Most historians agree that an aggressive attack by McClellan would have ended the Civil War.

START: Harpers Ferry AYH-Hostel at 19123 Sandy Hook Road in Knoxville, Md. From the Capital Beltway, take I-270 North to Frederick and exit onto US 340 West (toward Charles Town, W.Va.). Continue 16 miles west on US 340 and turn left onto MD 180 (Keep Tryst Road) at blinking yellow light. Continue 0.8 miles and turn right onto Sandy Hook Road. Hostel is first building on left. Knoxville is 48 miles northwest of the Capital Beltway.

LENGTH: 32.1 miles.

TERRAIN: Very hilly up to Sharpsburg. Downhill on the return. The **ALTERNATE ROUTE** avoids C&O Canal Towpath in bad weather.

POINTS OF INTEREST: Antietam National Battlefield (301-432-5124) at 13.8 miles (open daily 8:30 a.m. to 5 p.m.); Antietam Creek Aqueduct at 22.2 miles; and C&O Canal at 22.3 miles.

FOOD: Markets at 7.3 and 13.2 miles. Restaurant at 13.2 miles.

LODGING: Near Harpers Ferry, Harpers Ferry AYH-Hostel, 19123 Sandy Hook Road, Knoxville, Md. (301-834-7652) at start; and Hilltop House (800-338-8319), on Ridge Street, 10 blocks from C&O Canal Towpath. Near Antietam, inns include Gilbert House (304-725-0637), Antietam Overlook Farm (800-878-4241) and Piper House (301-797-1862) in the National Battlefield Park.

MAPS: Washington County, Md. road map.

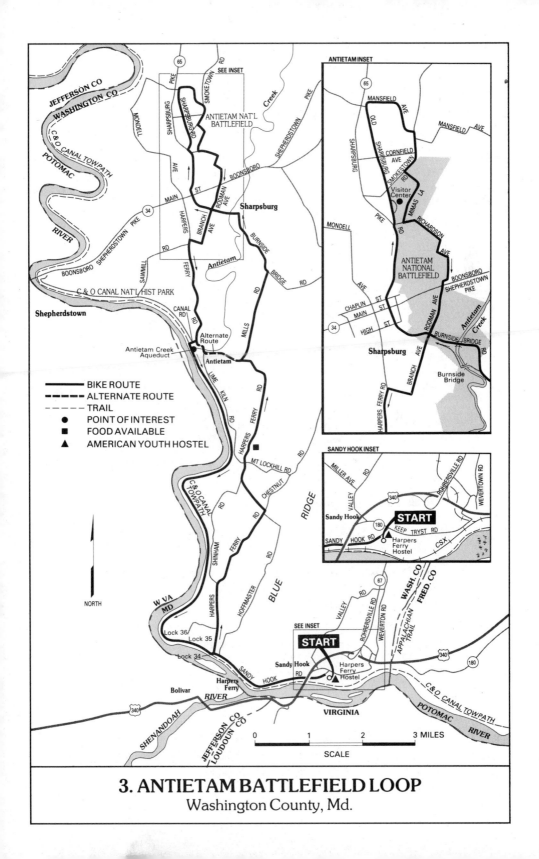

3. ANTIETAM BATTLEFIELD LOOP
Washington County, Md.

MILES   DIRECTIONS & COMMENTS

0.0   **Left** to go south out of Harpers Ferry AYH-Hostel driveway, on **SANDY HOOK ROAD.** This becomes **HARPERS FERRY ROAD.** Steep hills.

5.4   **Bear left** at Chestnut Road to remain on **HARPERS FERRY ROAD.**

6.3   **Bear right** to remain on **HARPERS FERRY ROAD.**

7.3   Food on right.

8.8   **Right** on **MILLS ROAD.**

10.5   **Left** on **BURNSIDE BRIDGE ROAD.** This passes but does not cross Burnside Bridge, where 400 Georgians held for three decisive hours against Union General Ambrose Burnside's 12,500 troops.

13.2   **Straight** on **MD 65,** crossing East Main Street (MD 34) in Sharpsburg.

13.8   **Right** into **ANTIETAM NATIONAL BATTLEFIELD** to Visitor Center. Follow battlefield tour in National Park Service flyer (at Visitor Center), with these recommended changes:

> 1. After turning **right** on **SMOKETOWN ROAD** from Mansfield Avenue, continue **straight** past Cornfield Avenue and take the **first left.**
>
> 2. From **BRANCH AVENUE,** turn **left** on **HARPERS FERRY ROAD** to begin return trip.

20.2   **Left** on **HARPERS FERRY ROAD,** leaving battlefield tour route.

22.2   **Right** on **CANAL ROAD.** Follow markers to C&O Canal. ALTERNATE ROUTE begins here (see end of cues).

22.3   **Left** at Antietam Creek Aqueduct, and **left** on **C&O CANAL TOWPATH.** Camping. *Caution: Mountain bike recommended. Avoid C&O Canal Towpath when wet or snowy.*

30.1   **Left** at **LOCK 34** to leave C&O Canal Towpath. (Canal condition deteriorates south of here.) **Right** on **HARPERS FERRY ROAD** which becomes **SANDY HOOK ROAD.**

32.1   **Arrive** at **HARPERS FERRY AYH-HOSTEL.**

ALTERNATE ROUTE

At 22.2 miles, to avoid C&O Canal Towpath, stay on **HARPERS FERRY ROAD.** all the way back to **HARPERS FERRY AYH-HOSTEL.**

4. AQUEDUCT RIDE

From its start in western Montgomery County to the famous C&O Canal Monocacy Aqueduct, this loop features generally level terrain with plenty of lush greenery. Constructed in 1833 from white quartzite quarried near Sugarloaf Mountain, the aqueduct looms as the highlight of the tour.

START: Poolesville High School on West Willard Road in Poolesville, Md. From the Capital Beltway, take I-270 North and exit onto MD 28 West (Rockville exit). Continue 12 miles and turn left onto MD 107. Continue five miles to West Willard Road. Turn left and continue one block; the school is on left. Alternatively, from the Capital Beltway take River Road west to West Willard Road. Turn right. The school is approximately 3.5 miles on the right. Poolesville is 21 miles northwest of the Capital Beltway.

LENGTH: 27.7 miles.

TERRAIN: Level, with a steep hill on Big Woods Road. Mouth of Monocacy Road to the aqueduct is a gravel surface.

POINTS OF INTEREST: Monocacy Aqueduct at 17.7 miles.

FOOD: Markets near start and at 9.5, 15,9 and 27.3 miles. Restaurants at 9.5, 11.9, 24.9 and 27.3 miles.

MAPS: Montgomery County, Md. road map; Maryland state highway map.

MILES   DIRECTIONS & COMMENTS

0.0   **Left** out of Poolesville High School, to go south on **WEST WILLARD ROAD.**

4.3   **Left** on **RIVER ROAD** at T.

4.7   **Left** on **HUGHES ROAD.** Polo club on left.

8.5   **Right** on **WESTERLY STREET.**

8.7   **Left** on **FISHER AVENUE** (MD 107).

9.5   **Right** on **ELGIN ROAD** (MD 109). Food available in town at markets and restaurant.

9.8   **Stay to left** on **MD 109** (Beallsville Road) when Elgin Road branches to right.

11.9   Cross MD 28. Food at inn.

13.3   **Left** on **BIG WOODS ROAD.**

15.9 **Right** on **DICKERSON ROAD** (MD 28). Food at left, railroad overpass on right.

16.3 **Left** on **MOUTH OF MONOCACY ROAD**.

17.7 **Arrive** at **AQUEDUCT. Reverse direction.**

19.0 **Right** on **DICKERSON ROAD** (MD 28).

20.6 **Right** on **MARTINSBURG ROAD.** Becomes a narrow concrete road, after bearing left.

21.9 **First left** on **WASCHE ROAD.** *Caution: gravel at intersection.*

23.2 **First left** on **WEST HUNTER ROAD.**

24.9 **Right** on **MD 28,** then **immediate right** on **BEALLSVILLE ROAD** (MD 109). Food at intersection.

27.3 **Right** on **FISHER AVENUE.** Food available.

27.4 **Left** on **WEST WILLARD ROAD.**

27.7 **Arrive** at **POOLESVILLE HIGH SCHOOL.**

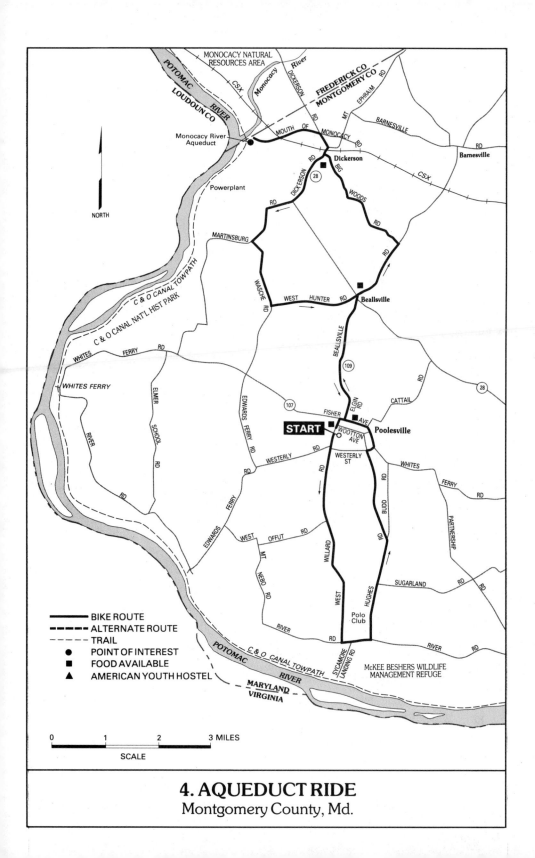

MONOCACY NATURAL
RESOURCES AREA

POTOMAC RIVER

LOUDOUN CO

CSX

Monocacy River

DICKERSON RD

FREDERICK CO
MONTGOMERY CO

RD

MT EPHRAIM RD

BARNESVILLE

RD

Monocacy River
Aqueduct

MOUTH OF MONOCACY RD

Dickerson

BARNESVILLE

Powerplant

DICKERSON RD

28

BIG

WOODS

CSX

C & O CANAL TOWPATH

C & O CANAL NAT'L HIST PARK

MARTINSBURG

WASCHE RD

RD

RD

RD

WEST HUNTER RD

Beallsville

WHITES FERRY RD

ELMER SCHOOL RD

EDWARDS FERRY RD

107

BEALLSVILLE RD

109

CATTAIL

RD

28

NORTH

WHITES FERRY

RIVER

RD

FISHER

ELGIN RD

AVE

START

WOOTTON AVE

Poolesville

WESTERLY

ST

WESTERLY

RD

RD

RD

WHITES

FERRY

RD

RD

PARTNERSHIP

EDWARDS FERRY RD

WEST OFFUT RD

MT NEBO RD

WILLARD RD

BUDD RD

SUGARLAND

RD

RD

RIVER RD

WEST RD

HUGHES RD

Polo
Club

SYCAMORE LANDING RD

RIVER

RD

——— BIKE ROUTE
– – – ALTERNATE ROUTE
- - - TRAIL
● POINT OF INTEREST
■ FOOD AVAILABLE
▲ AMERICAN YOUTH HOSTEL

POTOMAC RIVER

C & O CANAL TOWPATH

MARYLAND
VIRGINIA

McKEE BESHERS WILDLIFE
MANAGEMENT REFUGE

0   1   2   3 MILES

SCALE

4. AQUEDUCT RIDE
Montgomery County, Md.

5. POOLESVILLE - LEESBURG LOOP

Rural roads and historic towns present a diverse experience on this tour. The charming towns of Poolesville and Leesburg are interspersed with farmland scenes of days gone by. An abandoned railroad right-of-way and two crossings of the Potomac River -- one by ferry and one by bridge -- offer additional highlights. This popular tour also includes sweeping vistas of the distant Blue Ridge Mountains.

START: Poolesville High School on West Willard Road in Poolesville, Md. From the Capital Beltway, take I-270 North and exit onto MD 28 West (Rockville exit). Continue 12 miles and turn left onto MD 107. Continue five miles to West Willard Road. Turn left and continue one block; the school is on left. Alternatively, from the Capital Beltway take River Road west to West Willard Road. Turn right. The school is approximately 3.5 miles on the right. Poolesville is 21 miles northwest of the Capital Beltway.

LENGTH: 44.5 miles.

TERRAIN: Hilly. Good shoulder on MD 28.

POINTS OF INTEREST: Whites Ferry (301-349-5200) at 6.3 miles (Leesburg), the only continually operating ferry on the Potomac River ($0.50 for bicycles, 7 days a week); and Point of Rocks, Md. at 29.8 miles on the Potomac River, with restored 19th century railroad station.

FOOD: Markets at start, 10.0, 18.7 (closed Sunday) and 38.4 miles. Restaurants at start and 38.4 miles.

MAPS: Montgomery and Frederick Counties, Md. and Loudoun County, Va. road maps.

MILES DIRECTIONS AND COMMENTS

0.0 **Right** out of Poolesville High School to go north on **WEST WILLARD ROAD. Left** on **WHITES FERRY ROAD** (MD 107).

6.3 Cross Potomac River on Whites Ferry. Go **south** on **VA 655.**

7.6 **Left** on **US 15**. *Caution: trucks and heavy traffic.*

8.8 **Straight** on **BUS US 15**.

10.5 **Right** on **WEST CORNWALL STREET**, just after North Street in Leesburg. Food available in Leesburg.

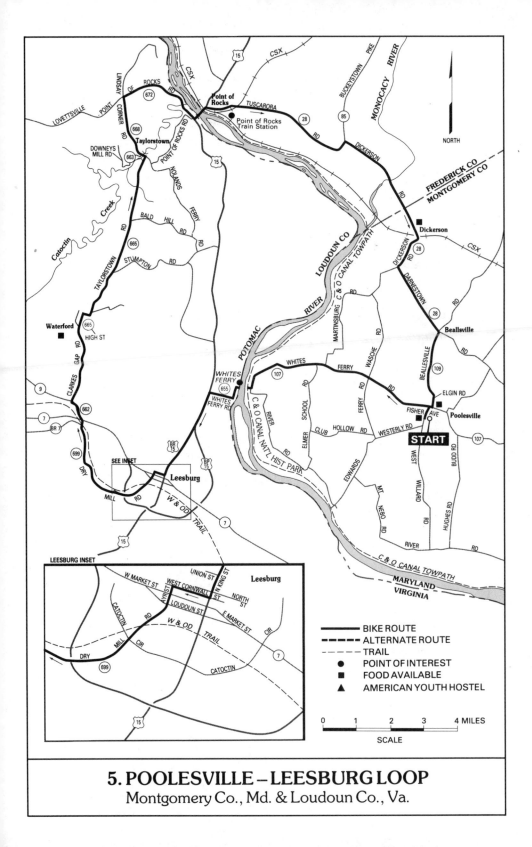

NORTH

LEESBURG INSET

BIKE ROUTE
ALTERNATE ROUTE
TRAIL
● POINT OF INTEREST
■ FOOD AVAILABLE
▲ AMERICAN YOUTH HOSTEL

0   1   2   3   4 MILES

SCALE

5. POOLESVILLE – LEESBURG LOOP
Montgomery Co., Md. & Loudoun Co., Va.

10.9   **Left** on **AYR STREET**. Continue **straight** on **DRY MILL ROAD**, cross W&OD Trail. Pass Loudoun County High School.

12.1   Cross bridge. **Bear right** to stay on **DRY MILL ROAD**.

15.6   Cross VA 7. *Caution: heavy traffic.*

16.3   **Right** on **VA 662**, just before Texaco station.

18.7   **Straight** on **VA 665** (Taylorstown Road) in Waterford. Food available at Waterford Grocery (closed Sunday).

24.6   **Left** on **VA 663** in Taylorstown. Cross bridge.

24.7   **Straight** on **VA 668** (Lindsay Corner Road).

26.7   **Right** on **VA 672** (Lovettsville - Point of Rocks Road).

29.4   **Left** on **US 15**. Cross Potomac River into Maryland.

29.8   **Right** on **MD 28** (Tuscarora Road). Enter Point of Rocks. Restored train station on right.

34.6   **Right** to stay on **MD 28** (Dickerson Road) where MD 85 goes straight.

38.4   Enter Dickerson. Food at general store.

41.8   **Right** on **MD 109** in Beallsville.

44.3   Junction of MD 109 and MD 107 in Poolesville. **Right** on **MD 107**.

44.5   **Left** on **WEST WILLARD ROAD**. **Left** into **POOLESVILLE HIGH SCHOOL**.

6. BACK OF SUGARLOAF

The scenic Sugarloaf Mountain is a "must-cycle" for the Washington area bicycle tourist! Circling the mountain, this tour features quiet roads with views of the Catoctin Mountains to the north. We include a shortcut to leave more time for mountain climbing. An excellent fall colors ride!

START: Poolesville High School on West Willard Road in Poolesville, Md. From the Capital Beltway, take I-270 North and exit onto MD 28 West (Rockville exit). Continue 12 miles and turn left onto MD 107. Continue five miles to West Willard Road. Turn left and continue one block; the school is on left. Alternatively, from the Capital Beltway take River Road west to West Willard Road. Turn right. The school is approximately 3.5 miles on the right. Poolesville is 21 miles northwest of the Capital Beltway.

LENGTH: 49.8 miles. **ALTERNATE ROUTE:** 21.3 miles.

TERRAIN: Well-maintained roads, rolling hills.

POINTS OF INTEREST: Dickerson Regional Park at 5.0 miles; Point of Rocks at 11.2 miles, with restored 19th century railroad station; Lilypons Water Gardens at 23.3 miles, one of the world's largest breeding areas for goldfish and water lilies; Urbana Lake Fish Management Area at 29.1 miles; and Sugarloaf Mountain Park at 38.0 miles.

FOOD: Markets at start, 7.6, 15.5, 26.2 (closed Sunday) and 35.4 miles. Restaurants at start. Only the Dickerson market is on the alternate route.

MAPS: Montgomery and Frederick Counties, Md. road maps.

MILES   DIRECTIONS & COMMENTS

0.0   **Right** out of Poolesville High School to go north on **WEST WILLARD ROAD**.

0.1   **Left** on **WHITES FERRY ROAD** (Fisher Avenue; MD 107).

2.3   **Right** on **WASCHE ROAD**.

5.0   **Right** on **MARTINSBURG ROAD**. Dickerson Regional Park on left.

6.4   **Left** on **DICKERSON ROAD** (MD 28). Grocery in Dickerson at 7.6 miles. ALTERNATE ROUTE begins at 7.6 miles (see end of cues).

11.2   **Left** on **MD 28** at intersection with MD 85. Pass Point of Rocks train station on left, just before town of Point of Rocks. Good snack spot.

16.1   **Right** on **BALLENGER CREEK ROAD**.

19.8   **Sharp right** on **CALICO ROCKS ROAD.**

20.0   **Right** on **DOUBS ROAD**.

20.3   **Left** to stay on **DOUBS ROAD,** just after crossing railroad tracks.

21.3   **Right** on **MOUNTVILLE ROAD.**

21.7   **Right** on **NEW DESIGN ROAD.**

21.8   **Left** on **ORLAND ROAD.**

22.5   **Straight** on **LILY PONS ROAD.**

23.2   Pass Lilypons Water Gardens on left.

24.3   **Left** on **PARK MILLS ROAD** at T.

27.8   **Right** on **FINGERBOARD ROAD.**

29.1   **Right** on **THURSTON ROAD.** Urbana Lake Fish Management Area on left.

34.2   **Right** on **OLD HUNDRED ROAD** (MD 109) at T.

35.4   **Right** on **COMUS ROAD** in Comus. Grocery.

38.0   **Arrive** at **SUGARLOAF MOUNTAIN PARK. Right** to climb mountain; **left** on **MOUNT EPHRAIM ROAD** to continue ride.

40.0   **Left** on **BARNESVILLE ROAD.**

43.0   **Right** on **PEACH TREE ROAD.**

47.0   **Left** on **MD 28** (Darnestown Road).

47.1   **Right** on **CATTAIL ROAD.**

49.2   **Left** on **MD 107** (Fisher Avenue; Whites Ferry Road) in Poolesville.

49.3   **Right** on **WOOTTON AVENUE.**

49.8   **Left** into **POOLESVILLE HIGH SCHOOL.**

ALTERNATE ROUTE

At 7.6 miles in Dickerson, rather than turning left on Dickerson Road, turn **right** on **MOUNT EPHRAIM ROAD.** Follow this 2.7 miles directly to Sugarloaf Mountain. After climb, **reverse direction,** picking up tour at 38.0 miles.

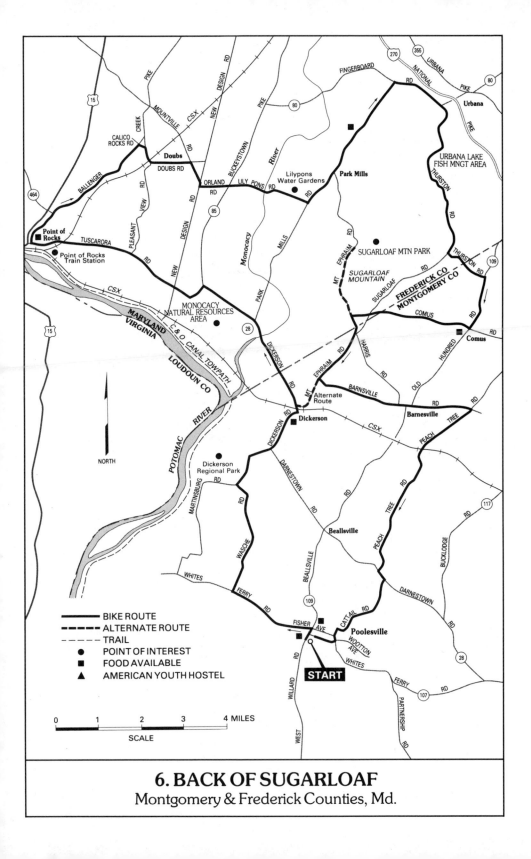

LEGEND

- ━━━━ BIKE ROUTE
- ━ ━ ━ ALTERNATE ROUTE
- – – – TRAIL
- ● POINT OF INTEREST
- ■ FOOD AVAILABLE
- ▲ AMERICAN YOUTH HOSTEL

SCALE
0 1 2 3 4 MILES

NORTH

6. BACK OF SUGARLOAF
Montgomery & Frederick Counties, Md.

7. SENECA - POOLESVILLE LOOP

Enjoy bucolic country scenes and views of Sugarloaf Mountain on this route as you loop between Seneca and Poolesville. Orchards and seasonal fruit stands provide a "taste" of Seneca that should not be missed!

For a brief history of Seneca sandstone, see the description of the Seneca Sandstone Trail (Tour 9).

START: Riley's Lock (Lock 24), abutting the C&O Canal on Riley's Lock Road in Seneca, Md. From the Capital Beltway, take River Road (MD 190) west 11 miles and turn left onto Riley's Lock Road. Follow road to canal parking lot. Seneca is 12 miles northwest of the Capital Beltway.

LENGTH: 33.9 miles.

TERRAIN: Hilly, with a short gravel stretch.

POINTS OF INTEREST: C&O Canal and Seneca Aqueduct at start; and Seneca Creek State Park at 9.7 miles. Fruit stands and numerous views of Sugarloaf Mountain along the route.

FOOD: Markets at 0.7 (closed Sundays), 9.7 and 23.7 miles.

MAPS: *Lower Montgomery County Bicycle Route Map;* Montgomery County, Md. road map.

MILES   DIRECTIONS & COMMENTS

0.0   **Right** out of parking lot to go north on **RILEY'S LOCK ROAD.**

0.7   **Left** on **RIVER ROAD.** Pass Poole's General Store on right. Food available.

1.0   **Right** on **MONTEVIDEO ROAD.**

2.0   Cross narrow bridge.

3.1   **Right** on **SUGARLAND ROAD.** *Caution: narrow pavement for 0.5 miles.*

4.3   Cross Whites Ferry Road (MD 107).

4.9   **Left** on **DARNESTOWN ROAD** (MD 28) at T.

5.0   **Right** on **WHITE GROUNDS ROAD** (MD 121).

6.6   Cross narrow bridge.

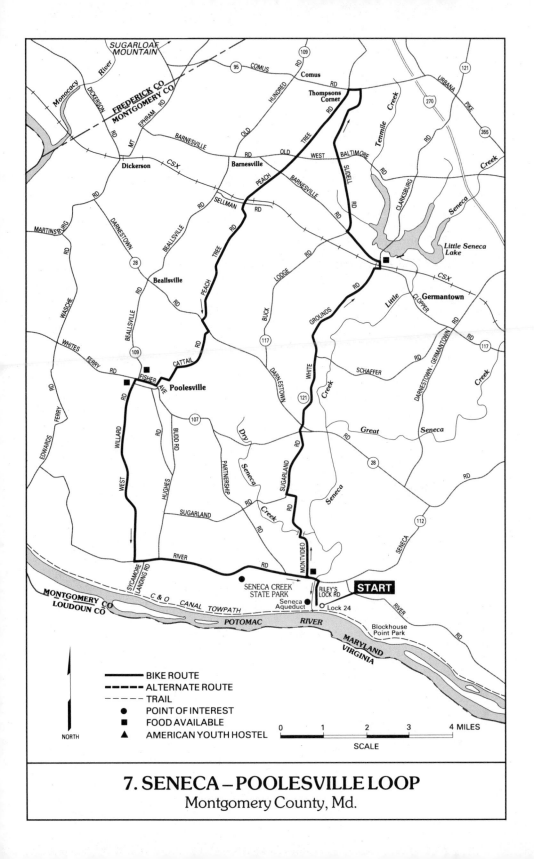

7. SENECA – POOLESVILLE LOOP
Montgomery County, Md.

Legend:
— BIKE ROUTE
--- ALTERNATE ROUTE
- - - TRAIL
● POINT OF INTEREST
■ FOOD AVAILABLE
▲ AMERICAN YOUTH HOSTEL

SCALE: 0 1 2 3 4 MILES

NORTH

8.6   Cross narrow bridge.

9.5   **Right** on **CLOPPER ROAD**.

9.6   **Left** on **CLARKSBURG ROAD**.

9.7   **Left** on **BARNESVILLE ROAD** (MD 117). Go through underpass at railroad and **bear left.** Boyd's Store, with food available. Little Seneca Lake to right.

10.8   **Right** on **SLIDELL ROAD.**

14.5   **Left** on **COMUS ROAD** (MD 95).

14.7   **Left** on **PEACH TREE ROAD.** Pass fruit stands. Sugarloaf Mountain to right.

18.3   Cross narrow bridge, then **bear left** to stay on **PEACH TREE ROAD** at Sellman Road.

21.5   **Left** on **DARNESTOWN ROAD** (MD 28) at T. Fruit stand on left.

21.7   **Right** on **CATTAIL ROAD.**

23.7   **Right** on **FISHER AVENUE** (MD 107). Convenience store in Poolesville.

24.3   **Left** on **WEST WILLARD ROAD.**

28.8   **Left** on **RIVER ROAD** at T.

33.2   **Right** on **RILEY'S LOCK ROAD.**

33.9   **Arrive** at **RILEY'S LOCK.**

8. SENECA TOUR

Taking you from Glen Echo Park in Bethesda, Md. to Seneca Creek State Park, this tour passes rolling horse country and the stylish community of Potomac.

Glen Echo Park preserves the site of the once-popular amusement park and gathering place. For 60 years the Glen Echo amusement park hosted thousands of Washingtonians, who explored the Midway, rode the hand-carved Dentzel Carousel, danced in the Spanish ballroom and swam in the gigantic pool which held 3,000 people. When the amusement park closed in 1968 due to poor attendance, a joint effort by the local community and the federal government preserved the site as a national cultural arts park, dedicated in 1971. Today the antique Dentzel Carousel still entertains children and adults alike, and the park hosts live bands and dances in the large ballroom and arts and community affairs classes in the other refurbished buildings.

START: Glen Echo Park at the corner of Goldsborough Road and MacArthur Boulevard in Bethesda, Md. The park is 2.5 miles northwest of the Washington, D.C. line and just north of the Potomac River. [Glen Echo Park is within the Capital Beltway.]

LENGTH: 34.0 miles.

TERRAIN: Hilly. Final six miles are all either level or downhill. Optional bike paths along MacArthur Boulevard and Falls Road, but narrow and poorly maintained.

POINTS OF INTEREST: Glen Echo Park at start, with antique carousel; Cabin John Bridge at 0.5 miles; Great Falls Park at 6.2 miles; Blockhouse Point Park at 15.1 miles; and Seneca Creek State Park at 18.2 miles. Horse stable and Potomac mansions along the route.

FOOD: Market at 1.5 miles. Restaurants at start, 13.8 and 22.6 miles.

MAPS: *ADC's Washington Area Bike Map; Lower Montgomery County Bicycle Route Map;* Montgomery County, Md. road map.

MILES   DIRECTIONS & COMMENTS

0.0   **Left** to go north out of Glen Echo Park (Oxford Lane) onto **MACARTHUR BOULEVARD.** Narrow, deteriorated bike path on left.

0.5   Cross single-lane Cabin John Bridge, once the world's largest stone arch (220 feet).

1.5   Bethesda Co-op market.

6.2   **Right** on **FALLS ROAD.** Narrow bike path available. Great Falls Park is southwest of the intersection.

8.1   **Left** on **RIVER ROAD** (MD 190).

8.8   **Right** on **NORTON ROAD.**

9.4   **Left** on **SOUTH GLEN ROAD.** Horse stables along road.

10.6   **Left** on **GLEN ROAD,** over bridge, then **left** again to stay on **GLEN ROAD.**

13.8   **Left** on **TRAVILAH ROAD**. Food at corner.

15.1   **Right** on **RIVER ROAD** (MD 190), through Blockhouse Point Park.

18.2   **Right** on **SENECA ROAD** at T. (Seneca Creek State Park is 0.5 miles to left on continuation of River Road.)

19.8   **Right** on **ESWORTHY ROAD.**

21.1   **Left** on **QUERY MILL ROAD.** *Caution: poor road surface.*

21.7   **First right** on **GLEN ROAD** (no sign).

22.6   Cross Travilah Road. Food on right.

24.7   Cross Piney Meetinghouse Road.

25.7   **Right** across bridge, then **right** on **SOUTH GLEN ROAD.**

26.9   **Right** on **NORTON ROAD**.

27.5   **Left** on **RIVER ROAD.** *Caution: heavy traffic.*

28.3   Cross Falls Road.

28.6   **Right** on **PERSIMMON TREE ROAD.**

30.2   Cross Bradley Boulevard, then Capital Beltway.

32.2   **Left** on **MACARTHUR BOULEVARD**.

34.0   **Right** into **GLEN ECHO PARK.**

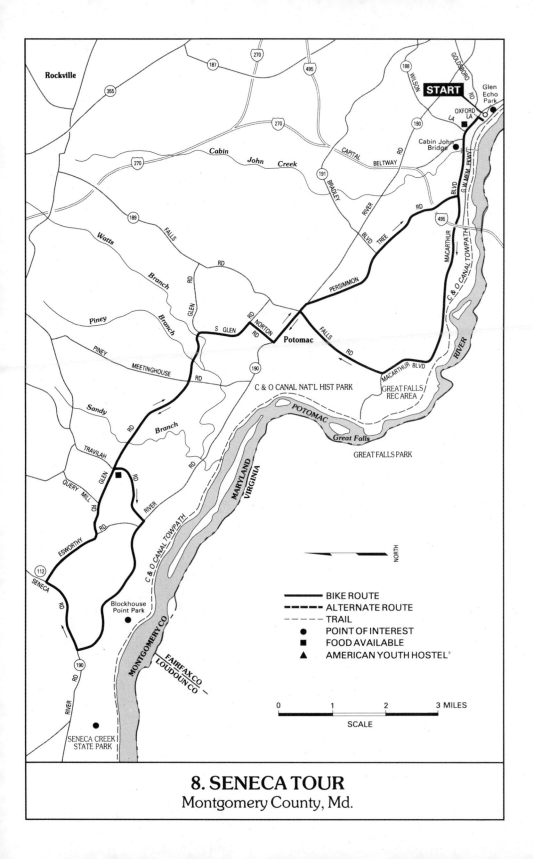

Rockville

Cabin John Creek

Watts Branch

Piney Branch

Sandy Branch

Glen Echo Park

START

Cabin John Bridge

CAPITAL BELTWAY

G. W. MEM. PKWY.

C & O CANAL TOWPATH

MACARTHUR BLVD

PERSIMMON

FALLS RD

BRADLEY BLVD

RIVER RD

TREE RD

Potomac

C & O CANAL NAT'L HIST PARK

GREAT FALLS REC AREA

POTOMAC RIVER

Great Falls

GREAT FALLS PARK

MARYLAND
VIRGINIA

Travilah

Query Mill Rd

Esworthy Rd

Seneca

Blockhouse Point Park

Seneca Creek State Park

MONTGOMERY CO
FAIRFAX CO
LOUDOUN CO

NORTH

BIKE ROUTE
ALTERNATE ROUTE
TRAIL
● POINT OF INTEREST
■ FOOD AVAILABLE
▲ AMERICAN YOUTH HOSTEL

0   1   2   3 MILES
SCALE

8. SENECA TOUR
Montgomery County, Md.

9. SENECA SANDSTONE TRAIL

A path of historic structures, mills, homes and farms of the industrial age marks this tour through Montgomery County, Md. Try this tour in autumn for spectacular colors.

The ride loops through the once-bustling quarry town of Seneca. The sandstone quarried from Seneca was used to construct the Smithsonian "Castle" on the Washington Mall, as well as most of the District of Columbia's other post-Civil War buildings. Once cut, the stone was hauled to town by barge via the C&O Canal.

Seneca's economy declined in the 1920s, as architectural preferences shifted away from sandstone. The C&O Canal faced a similar decline: unable to compete with the railroad, it folded in 1924. The local grist mill also succumbed to the industrial age, and it too closed in 1931.

START: Violet's Lock, abutting the C&O Canal on Violet's Lock Road in Montgomery County, Md. From the Capital Beltway, take River Road (MD 190) west 11 miles and turn left onto Violet's Lock Road. Continue 0.6 miles to Potomac River. Parking on left. Violet's Lock is 12 miles northwest of the Capital Beltway.

LENGTH: 8.6 miles.

TERRAIN: Rolling hills, with dirt roads and hard-packed dirt on the C&O Canal.

POINTS OF INTEREST: Violet's Lock at start (named after Ab Violette, the last lock tender), a lift lock that could raise or lower canal boats eight feet; the remains of a 2,500-foot rock dam, built in 1928 at the head of the Seneca rapids in the Potomac River near start; Seneca Aqueduct (1929) at 0.2 miles, the first of 11 aqueducts between Georgetown and Cumberland, Md., carrying canal boats over Seneca Creek; C&O Canal at 0.3 miles; site of Tschiffely Mill (1780) at 0.8 miles and the narrow-gauge railroad that took mill products to grain boats; Rocklands (1870), an Italianate showplace of the agrarian community; Sandstone School House (1863) at 6.2 miles, built of Seneca sandstone; and Montevideo (1825) at 6.5 miles, built for J.P.C. Peters, owner of the quarry and great-grandson of Martha Custis Washington.

FOOD: Market at 0.8 miles (closed Sundays).

MAPS AND INFORMATION: Montgomery County, Md. road map. The Montgomery County Parks and Planning Commission (301-495-4600) offers a complete guide to this tour.

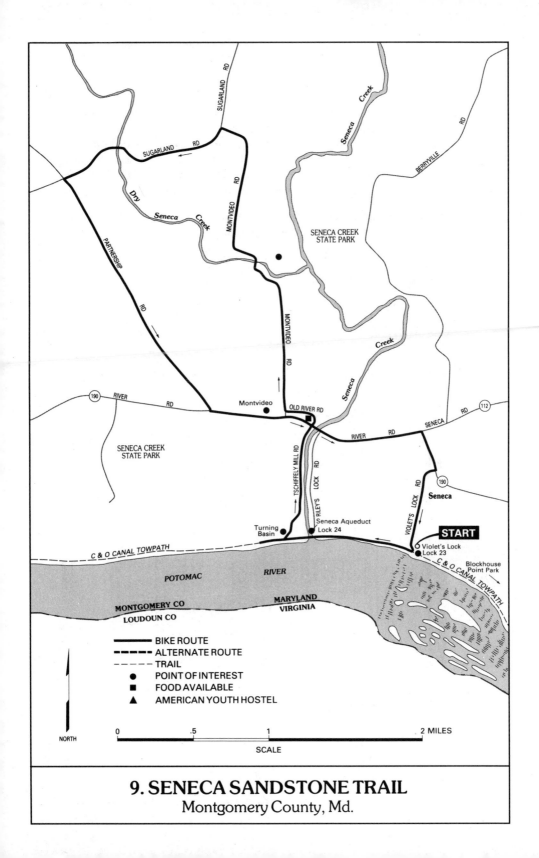

9. SENECA SANDSTONE TRAIL
Montgomery County, Md.

MILES DIRECTIONS & COMMENTS

0.0 From Violet's Lock parking lot, go **west** (upstream) on the **C&O CANAL TOWPATH.** Note remains of 1928 rock dam at head of Seneca rapids. **Cross** Seneca Creek on **AQUEDUCT. Continue** on **TOWPATH** north to turning basin, where 90-foot canal boats turned around. **Reverse direction.** Follow **TSCHIFFELY MILL ROAD** away from canal. Remains of Seneca Stone Mill are on left.

0.8 **Straight** on **OLD RIVER ROAD,** crossing River Road (MD 190). Tschiffely Mill on right, Poole's General Store on left.

1.0 **Right** on **MONTEVIDEO ROAD.**

3.2 **Left** on **SUGARLAND ROAD.**

4.4 **Left** on **PARTNERSHIP ROAD.**

6.2 **Left** on **RIVER ROAD** (MD 190). *Caution: traffic.* Sandstone School House on right.

6.5 Montevideo house on left. Smaller buildings are Overseers House and the slaves' quarters.

7.7 **Right** to stay on **RIVER ROAD.**

7.9 **Right** on **VIOLET'S LOCK ROAD.**

8.6 **Arrive** at **VIOLET'S LOCK.**

10. GAITHERSBURG GETAWAY

You will pedal through new subdivisions and old farm country on this diverse route. It also takes you through the scenic towns of Damascus and Laytonsville.

START: Behind the Roy Rogers/Hardee's in Montgomery Village Shopping Mall at the corner of Montgomery Village Avenue and Club House Road in Gaithersburg, Md. From the Capital Beltway, take I-270 North for 11 miles and exit at Montgomery Village Avenue. Continue east for approximately two miles to shopping mall. Start from corner of service road behind Roy Rogers/Hardee's and Club House Road. Gaithersburg is 12 miles north of the Capital Beltway. **METRO START:** The ride starts approximately five miles from the Shady Grove Metro station (Red Line). From the station, exit onto Frederick Avenue (MD 355) and turn right. Bear right onto North Summit Avenue. Turn left on Centerway Road. Turn right at Montgomery Village Avenue. Club House Road is one block away.

LENGTH: 35.6 miles.

TERRAIN: Hilly at first, then rolling hills.

POINTS OF INTEREST: Town of Laytonsville at 8.5 miles; Rachel Carson River Regional Park at 9.0 miles; and town of Damascus at 22.2 miles.

FOOD: Markets at 8.5, 17.8 and 22.2 miles. Fast food restaurants at start.

MAPS: Montgomery County, Md. road map.

MILES   DIRECTIONS & COMMENTS

0.0   **Left** to go west on **CLUB HOUSE ROAD** (away from Montgomery Village Avenue).

0.2   **Right** on **WATKINS MILL ROAD** at T. Hills for next three miles.

1.8   **Right** on **BLUNT ROAD.**

3.4   **Right** on **BRINK ROAD** (MD 420) at stop sign.

3.7   **Bear left** to stay on **BRINK ROAD** at stop sign.

4.7   **Right** on **GOSHEN ROAD** at T.

5.4   **Left** on **WARFIELD ROAD** at stop sign.

8.5   **Left** on **LAYTONSVILLE ROAD** at T. Enter Laytonsville. Food and antique shops.

9.0   **Right** on **SUNDOWN ROAD** at traffic light. Notable old homes. Pass Rachel Carson Regional Park on right, just past Mount Zion Road.

13.1   **Sharp left** on **DAMASCUS ROAD** at stop sign.

17.8   **Straight** on **MD 108** (Damascus Road). Country store.

22.2   **Left** on **WOODFIELD ROAD** (MD 124) at traffic light in Damascus. Supermarket just ahead.

28.7   Woodfield Road becomes **BURNHAM ROAD.**

29.7   **Right** on **WARFIELD ROAD.**

32.5   **Sharp left** on **WIGHTMAN ROAD.**

33.6   **Right** on **GOSHEN ROAD.**

34.9   **Right** on **CENTERWAY ROAD.**

35.6   **Arrive** at **MONTGOMERY VILLAGE.**

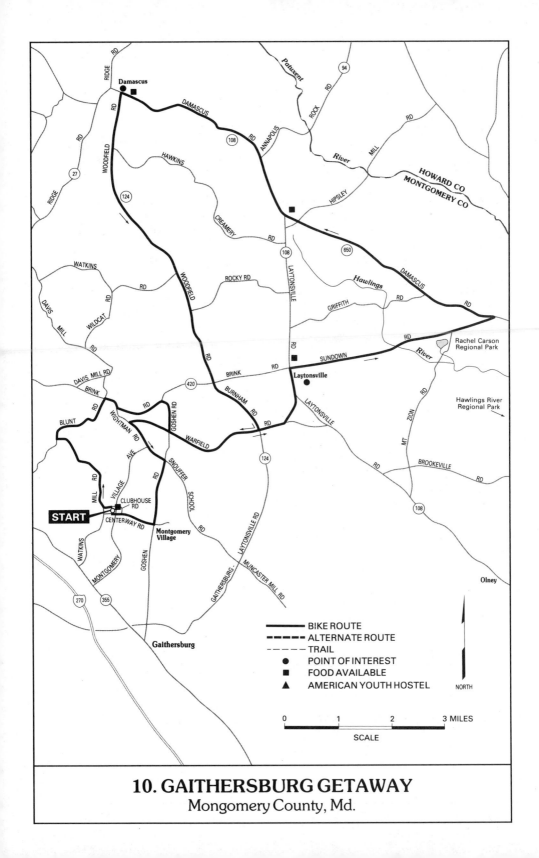

RIDGE RD

Damascus

DAMASCUS RD

108

ANNAPOLIS

Pattuxent

94

ROCK RD

River

RD

MILL RD

HOWARD CO
MONTGOMERY CO

WOODFIELD RD

RIDGE

27

RD

124

HAWKINS RD

CREAMERY RD

108

LAYTONSVILLE RD

HIPSLEY RD

650

Hawlings

DAMASCUS RD

WATKINS RD

DAVIS MILL

WILDCAT RD

WOODFIELD RD

ROCKY RD

GRIFFITH RD

RD

DAVIS MILL RD

BRINK

420

BRINK RD

WIGHTMAN RD

BURNHAM RD

SUNDOWN RD

Laytonsville

River

Rachel Carson
Regional Park

Hawlings River
Regional Park

BLUNT RD

MILL RD

GOSHEN RD

WARFIELD RD

LAYTONSVILLE RD

124

MT ZION RD

BROOKEVILLE RD

108

VILLAGE AVE

SNOUFFER SCHOOL RD

CLUBHOUSE RD

START

CENTERWAY RD

Montgomery
Village

GOSHEN RD

GAITHERSBURG - MUNCASTER MILL RD

Olney

WATKINS

MONTGOMERY

270

355

Gaithersburg

——— BIKE ROUTE
––––– ALTERNATE ROUTE
– – – TRAIL
● POINT OF INTEREST
■ FOOD AVAILABLE
▲ AMERICAN YOUTH HOSTEL

NORTH

0   1   2   3 MILES

SCALE

10. GAITHERSBURG GETAWAY
Mongomery County, Md.

11. TRIADELPHIA TROT

This scenic jaunt around the Triadelphia Reservoir in Patuxent River State Park provides a short but strenuous workout. The route crosses Brighton Dam and passes through hilly countryside with occasional thick forests and glimpses of the reservoir. There are no towns along the route.

START: Corner of Georgia Avenue (MD 97) and New Hampshire Avenue (MD 650) in Montgomery County, Md. From the Capital Beltway, take Georgia Avenue north 17 miles to its intersection with New Hampshire Avenue. Parking at start and at Brighton Dam. The starting point is 17 miles north of the Capital Beltway.

LENGTH: 18.1 miles.

TERRAIN: Hilly, especially first half.

POINTS OF INTEREST: Triadelphia Reservoir; Patuxent River State Park (301-924-2127); Brighton Dam (301-774-9124) at 4.1 miles. Picnic grounds at various stops along the reservoir at the end of Triadelphia Mill Road.

FOOD: Market at start, but often closed. Bring lunch or snack.

MAPS: *ADC's Washington Area Bike Map;* Montgomery and Howard Counties, Md. road maps.

MILES   DIRECTIONS & COMMENTS

0.0   Go **southeast** on **NEW HAMPSHIRE AVENUE** (MD 650).

3.0   **Left** on **BRIGHTON DAM ROAD.**

4.1   Cross Brighton Dam. Picnic area, toilet facilities, soda machines, information.

5.7   **Left** on **HIGHLAND ROAD.**

7.0   **Left** on **TRIADELPHIA MILL ROAD.**

8.8   **Right** and **immediate left** at **GREEN BRIDGE ROAD** to stay on **TRIADELPHIA MILL ROAD.**

10.3   Picnic ground and reservoir on left.

12.5   **Left** on **ROXBURY ROAD** at bottom of steep hill.

14.1   **Left** on **DORSEY MILL ROAD** at T.

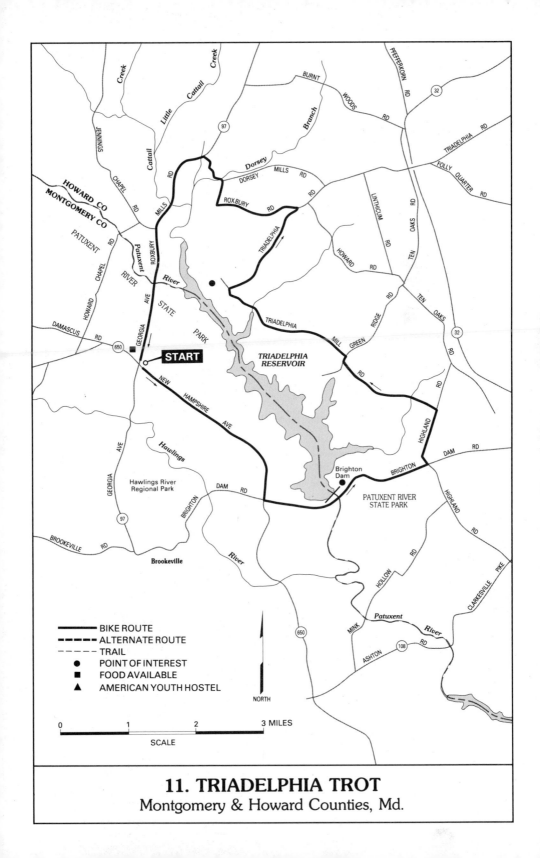

START

TRIADELPHIA RESERVOIR

Brighton Dam

PATUXENT RIVER STATE PARK

Hawlings River Regional Park

Brookeville

HOWARD CO
MONTGOMERY CO

PATUXENT RIVER

Patuxent River

Hawlings River

Patuxent River

Little Cattail Creek

Cattail Creek

Burnt Branch

Dorsey

Brighton Dam Rd

Brighton Dam Rd

Roads and labels:
JENNINGS, CHAPEL RD, MILLS RD, ROXBURY, GEORGIA AVE, STATE PARK, NEW HAMPSHIRE AVE, DAMASCUS RD, HOWARD CHAPEL RD, GEORGIA AVE, BRIGHTON DAM RD, BROOKEVILLE RD, ROXBURY RD, DORSEY MILLS RD, TRIADELPHIA, TRIADELPHIA, MILL GREEN RD, HOWARD RD, RIDGE RD, LINTHICUM RD, TEN OAKS RD, TEN OAKS RD, FOLLY QUARTER RD, TRIADELPHIA RD, PREFFERBORN RD, WOODS RD, HIGHLAND, HIGHLAND RD, CLARKSVILLE PIKE, MINK HOLLOW RD, ASHTON RD, 97, 97, 650, 650, 32, 32, 108

LEGEND
— BIKE ROUTE
--- ALTERNATE ROUTE
- - - TRAIL
● POINT OF INTEREST
■ FOOD AVAILABLE
▲ AMERICAN YOUTH HOSTEL

NORTH

SCALE
0   1   2   3 MILES

11. TRIADELPHIA TROT
Montgomery & Howard Counties, Md.

14.7   **Left** on **MD 97** (Roxbury Mills Road, then Georgia Avenue) at T.

17.0   Cross Patuxent River into Montgomery County.

18.1   **Arrive** at **MD 650** intersection (Damascus and New Hampshire Avenues).

12. AWAY TO OLNEY

Beginning and ending in the quaint town of Olney, this quiet ride takes you through rural Montgomery and Howard Counties, Md.

START: Sherwood Elementary School on Olney-Sandy Spring Road in Olney, Md. From the Capital Beltway, take Georgia Avenue north 10 miles and turn right onto MD 108 (Olney-Sandy Spring Road). Continue 1.2 miles; school is on left. Olney is 12 miles north of the Capital Beltway.

LENGTH: 35.2 miles.

TERRAIN: Moderately hilly, with good surfaces.

POINTS OF INTEREST: Olney Ale House at start; and Olney Theater, across the street from the Ale House.

FOOD: Markets at 1.1, 9.3, 28.0 and 34.9 miles. Restaurants at start and 8.9 miles.

MAPS: *ADC's Washington Area Bike Map;* Howard and Montgomery Counties, Md. road maps.

MILES DIRECTIONS & COMMENTS

0.0   **Left** out of Sherwood Elementary School parking lot to go east on **MD 108** (Olney-Sandy Spring Road). Olney Ale House serves food.

1.1   **Straight** on **ASHTON ROAD,** crossing New Hampshire Avenue (MD 650).

1.9   **Left** on **MINK HOLLOW ROAD.**

2.8   Cross Patuxent River.

5.1   **Left** on **HIGHLAND ROAD** at T.

7.4   **Bear left** on **TEN OAKS ROAD.**

8.9   **Bear right** to stay on **TEN OAKS ROAD** at Marshall's Pub. Food here and at convenience store 0.4 miles farther.

11.2   **Left** on **BURNT WOODS ROAD** at MD 32.

13.2   **Right** on **HOBBS ROAD** (no sign).

14.5   **Left** on **McKENDREE ROAD** at T.

15.0   **Left** on **MD 97** (Roxbury Mills Road).

15.6   **Right** on **UNION CHAPEL ROAD.**

18.3   **Straight** on **ED WARFIELD ROAD**, crossing Daisy Road.

19.0   **Bear right** on **FLORENCE ROAD.**

20.4   **Sharp left** on **JENNINGS CHAPEL ROAD.**

24.9   **Right** on **HOWARD CHAPEL ROAD.**

27.0   **Left** on **DAMASCUS ROAD** (MD 650).

28.0   **Straight** on **NEW HAMPSHIRE AVENUE,** crossing Georgia Avenue. Food on left.

32.1   **Right** on **GOLD MINE ROAD.**

32.5   **Left** on **CHANDLEE MILL ROAD.**

33.8   **Right** on **BROOKE ROAD** at T.

34.9   **Right** on **MD 108.** Food on right.

35.2   **Right** into **SHERWOOD ELEMENTARY SCHOOL.**

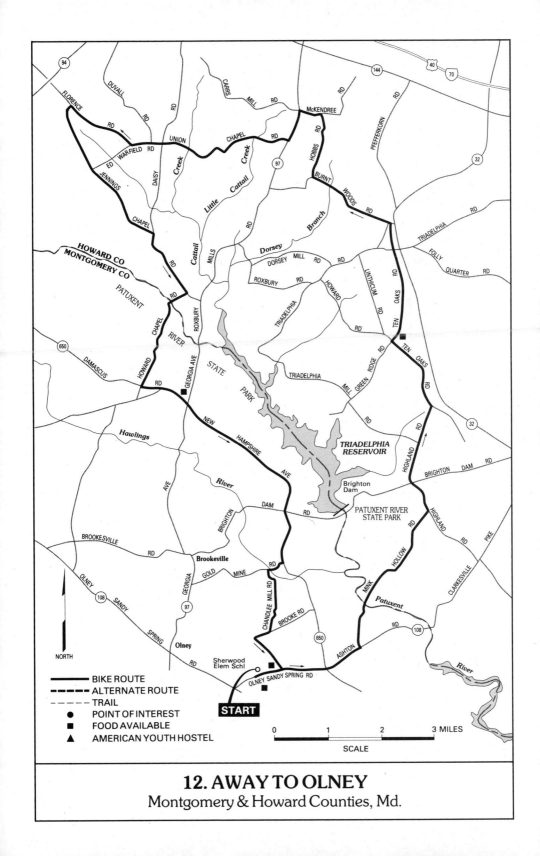

12. AWAY TO OLNEY
Montgomery & Howard Counties, Md.

13. MONUMENTS MEANDER

With the Washington Mall as its centerpiece, this short tour passes many of the major parks, monuments, museums, government buildings and national landmarks in downtown Washington. The only hill you will climb is Capitol Hill.

The Washington Mall accentuates the grand design of the city laid out by the French engineer Pierre Charles L'Enfant in 1791. The dozens of museums, monuments and statues tell their own stories. In addition, the headquarters of many federal agencies and departments are located on this route. Consult a tourist guidebook for detailed information about the Mall sites and surrounding attractions.

The second half of the tour predominantly follows busy city streets. Watch out for both vehicular and pedestrian traffic. Try to schedule your trip on a weekend and avoid the bustle of federal workers. Bring a good lock so you can leave your bike and explore the sites.

Washington is famous for its springtime cherry blossoms, which make a fleeting but memorable appearance in April. They most notably grace the Tidal Basin with their fragile blossoms and lingering aroma.

START: Lincoln Memorial (the side facing the Mall and White House) at the corner of Constitution Avenue NW and 23rd Street NW in Washington, D.C. This point is also the southern terminus of the Rock Creek Trail, and is just across the Potomac River (via Memorial Bridge) from the Mount Vernon Trail. Parking nearby in Potomac Park. [The starting point is within the Capital Beltway.] **METRO STARTS:** The route passes or is close to most downtown D.C. Metro stations: Federal Triangle Metro station (Blue and Orange Lines), Smithsonian Metro station (Blue and Orange Lines) and Union Station Metro station (Red Line) lie along the route; Foggy Bottom Metro station (Blue and Orange Lines) is six blocks north of start on 23rd Street NW; and Arlington Cemetery Metro station (Blue Line) is near start, just across the Memorial Bridge in Virginia.

LENGTH: 11.7 miles.

TERRAIN: Level. Surface includes bike paths, city streets and sidewalks.

POINTS OF INTEREST: Lincoln Memorial at start; Tidal Basin and cherry trees at 0.8 miles; Potomac Park at 1.7 miles; Hains Point and "The Awakening" sculpture at 3.1 miles; Jefferson Memorial at 5.2 miles; Bureau of Engraving and site of Holocaust Museum at 5.6 miles; Washington Monument, Smithsonian Castle and Hirshhorn Museum with Sculpture Garden at 5.7 miles;

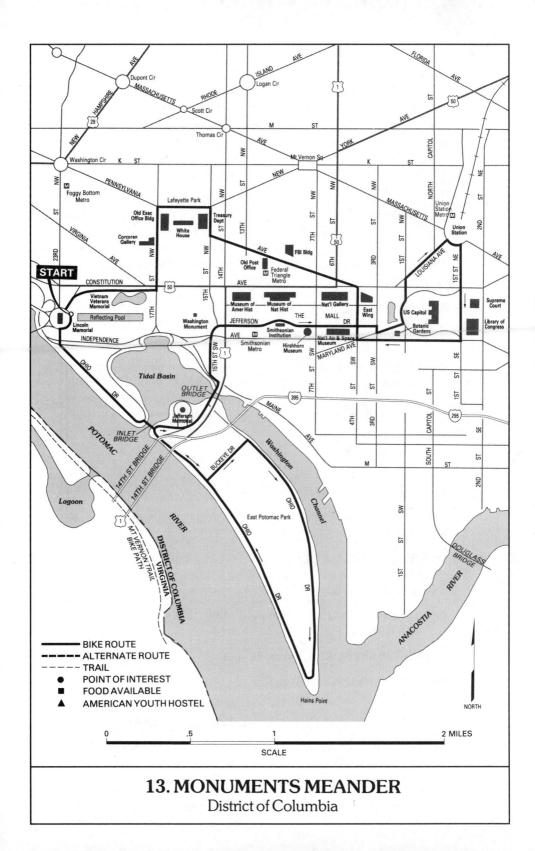

13. MONUMENTS MEANDER
District of Columbia

National Air and Space Museum at 6.7 miles; Botanical Garden at 6.9 miles; U.S. Capitol, Taft Memorial, and Garfield and Peace statues at 7.1 miles; former District of Columbia Main Post Office and Union Station at 7.7 miles; Senate Office Buildings, Supreme Court and Library of Congress at 7.8 miles; House Office Buildings at 8.3 miles; National Gallery of Art (East and West Wings) at 8.9 miles; National Archives, J. Edgar Hoover Building (FBI Headquarters), Ford's Theater, site of President Abraham Lincoln's assassination, and National Museum of American History at 9.2 miles; Old Post Office Pavilion and District Building (D.C. City Hall) at 9.8 miles; Treasury Building at 10.2 miles; White House and Lafayette Park at 10.3 miles; Renwick Gallery, Old Executive Office Building, Corcoran Gallery of Art and Organization of American States building at 10.6 miles; and Vietnam Veterans Memorial at 11.1 miles.

FOOD: Restaurants at 7.7 and 9.8 miles. Hot dog vendors around the Mall. Cafeterias at 6.7 and 8.2 miles. On weekdays, the cafeterias of many government buildings are open to the public.

LODGING: Many hotels of all types. For out-of-town bicyclists, try the Washington International AYH-Hostel, 1009 11th Street NW, Washington, D.C. (202-737-2333). Some city universities offer rooms, but not short-term. Nearest campground is Greenbelt Park, Md. (301-344-3943), eight miles northeast.

MAPS: *ADC's Washington Area Bike Map.*

MILES   DIRECTIONS & COMMENTS

0.0   Go clockwise one-fourth of the way around Lincoln Memorial, to go **left** (south) on **23RD STREET SW.**

0.2   **Straight** on **OHIO DRIVE SW** (West Potomac Park). Use sidewalk or street. Planned site of Franklin Delano Roosevelt Memorial on left, across playing fields.

0.8   **Right** over **INLET BRIDGE,** then **right** again, to stay on **OHIO DRIVE SW** (East Potomac Park). Tidal Basin on left.

1.3   **Left** on **BUCKEYE DRIVE SW** (mandatory).

1.7   **Right** on **OHIO DRIVE SW** at T.

3.1   End of East Potomac Park at Hains Point. "The Awakening" sculpture. Round point and pass cherry trees. **Do not cross** Inlet Bridge again.

5.2   **Cross left** over to **bike path** in front of Jefferson Memorial. *Caution: traffic; no crosswalk.*

5.4 **Bear left** over **OUTLET BRIDGE.**

5.6 **Cross** with traffic light on **15TH STREET SW.** Use sidewalk. Bureau of Engraving and future site of Holocaust Museum on right.

5.7 Cross Independence Avenue SW and travel diagonally across park. Washington Monument on left. **Bear right** on **JEFFERSON DRIVE SW** path. Smithsonian Castle and Hirshhorn Museum. Smithsonian Metro station (Orange and Blue Lines).

6.7 National Air and Space Museum with cafeteria (often crowded) on right.

6.9 **Right** on **3RD STREET SW** at T, then **first left** on **MARYLAND AVENUE SW.** Pass Botanical Garden on right.

7.1 **Left** on **1ST STREET SW,** by going counter-clockwise three-quarters of the way around Garfield statue. U.S. Capitol on right. **Straight** on **1ST STREET NW** by going counter-clockwise half-way around Peace statue. Taft Memorial visible on left (carillon).

7.4 **Bear right** on **LOUISIANA AVENUE NW.**

7.7 **Right** on **MASSACHUSETTS AVENUE NE.** District of Columbia Post Office on left. Union Station, recently renovated with restaurants, food court, shops and Metro on left.

7.8 **Second right** on **1ST STREET NE.** Pass Senate Office Buildings, Supreme Court, U.S. Capitol, Library of Congress.

8.3 **Right** on **INDEPENDENCE AVENUE SE** at traffic light. House Office Buildings on left. Steep downhill.

8.9 **Right** on **4TH STREET SW.** Cross Mall, pass National Gallery of Art on left, and its East Wing on right. Cafeteria on lower level.

9.2 **Bear left** on **PENNSYLVANIA AVENUE NW,** along Inaugural Parade route. Pass National Archives on left at 7th Street NW and FBI Headquarters (J. Edgar Hoover Building) on right at 9th Street NW. Ford's Theater is one block north at 511 10th Street NW. The National Museum of American History, with excellent Civil War artifacts, is one block south (left) of route on the Mall at 14th Street NW and Constitution Avenue NW.

9.8 Old Post Office Pavilion on left with food court, restaurants and souvenir shops. District Building (D.C. City Hall) on left.

10.2 **Right** on **15TH STREET NW.** Treasury Building on left.

10.3   **Left** on **PENNSYLVANIA AVENUE NW.** White House on left, Lafayette Park on right.

10.6   **Left** on **17TH STREET NW.** Renwick Gallery on right, Old Executive Office Building on left. Corcoran Gallery of Art two blocks south on right. Organization of American States building with indoor garden and museum next to Corcoran on south side.

11.1   **Right** on **PATH** after crossing Constitution Avenue NW. Pass pond on left. Vietnam Veterans Memorial on right. [Note: bicycling through the Vietnam Memorial grounds is *strictly* prohibited. Lock your bicycle beyond the memorial grounds and walk.]

11.7   **Arrive** at **LINCOLN MEMORIAL.**

14. POTOMAC RIVER RAMBLE

Crisscrossing the Potomac River five times, this picturesque route features a variety of historic river towns and one of the East Coast's most scenic river valleys. It starts with a ferry ride from Whites Ferry, Md. to Leesburg, Va. The tour then passes through Waterford, Va., a village founded by the Quakers in the 18th century which is now on the National Register of Historic Places. The route also takes you through Brunswick, Md., a typical C&O Canal settlement, and Harpers Ferry, W.Va., where John Brown met his fate. After viewing the confluence of the Potomac and Shenandoah Rivers, there is a steep climb up to Purcellville, Va., where a general store with tasty provisions awaits you.

START: Whites Ferry parking lot on MD 107 in Whites Ferry, Md. From the Capital Beltway, take I-270 North and exit onto MD 28 West (Rockville exit). Continue 12 miles and turn left onto MD 107. Continue 11 miles to Whites Ferry Parking Area. Whites Ferry is 29 miles northwest of the Capital Beltway.

LENGTH: 61.8 miles.

TERRAIN: Hilly.

POINTS OF INTEREST: Whites Ferry (301-349-5200) at start, the only continually operating ferry on the Potomac River ($0.50 for bicycles, 7 days a week); Leesburg at 2.5 miles; Waterford at 8.9 miles; and Harpers Ferry with Harpers Ferry National Historical Park (304-535-6223) at 29.0 miles.

FOOD: Markets at 18.4, 28.6 and 47.2 miles.

LODGING: Near Harpers Ferry, Harpers Ferry AYH-Hostel, 19123 Sandy Hook Road, Knoxville, Md. (301-834-7652); and Hilltop House (800-338-8319), on Ridge Street, 10 blocks from C&O Canal Towpath. In Leesburg area, choices include Cornerstone Inn (703-882-3722), Laurel Brigade Inn (703-777-1010) and Norris House Inn (703-777-1806). In Purcellville, Purcellville Inn (703-338-2850).

MAPS: Montgomery County, Md. and Loudoun County, Va. road maps; Virginia and Maryland state highway maps.

MILES   DIRECTIONS & COMMENTS

0.0   Cross Potomac River into Virginia on **WHITES FERRY**. Go **south** on **VA 655.**

1.3   **Left** on **US 15**. *Caution: trucks and heavy traffic.*

2.5   **Straight** on **BUS US 15**. Enter Leesburg. BUS US 15 becomes **NORTH KING STREET.**

4.2   **Right** on **WEST MARKET STREET**.

4.3   **Left** on **WIRT STREET**.

4.4   **Right** on **LOUDOUN STREET SW**.

4.7   **Left** on **DRY MILL ROAD** (VA 699).

4.9   **Right** onto **W&OD TRAIL.**

8.3   **Right** on **VA 9** west at top of hill (cross over VA 7).

8.9   **Right** on **VA 662** (Clarks Gap Road) to Waterford.

11.3   **Left** to remain on **VA 662** (Factory Street; becomes 2nd Street).

11.7   **Left** on **MAIN STREET** (VA 698) at T.

12.1   Cross bridge over creek.

12.2   **Right** on **VA 681** (Fannie Wilson Hill Road).

16.6   **Left** on **VA 673** (Milltown Road).

17.9   **Straight** on **VA 672** at stop sign.

18.4   **Right** on **VA 287** north (Berlin Turnpike). *Caution at Potomac River bridge to Brunswick.* Restaurants in Brunswick.

21.4   **Right** on **B STREET** (first ramp after bridge).

21.5   **Right** on **MARYLAND AVENUE**.

21.6   **Right** on **POTOMAC AVENUE**. Becomes **KNOXVILLE AVENUE** (MD 478).

23.9   **Left** on **MD 180**.

24.1   **Left** on **US 340 WEST**. *Caution: traffic.*

26.3   **Left** on **SANDY HOOK/KEEP TRYST ROAD** (MD 180) at blinking light.

26.5   **Right** on **SANDY HOOK/HARPERS FERRY ROAD** (steep hill).

28.6   **Left** to cross small **footbridge** over the C&O Canal. Go 0.4 miles on Canal Towpath, then cross Potomac River on large railroad bridge to Harpers Ferry. Bicycle parking near provost office. Food available.

29.0   **Right** out of Harpers Ferry onto **SHENANDOAH STREET**.

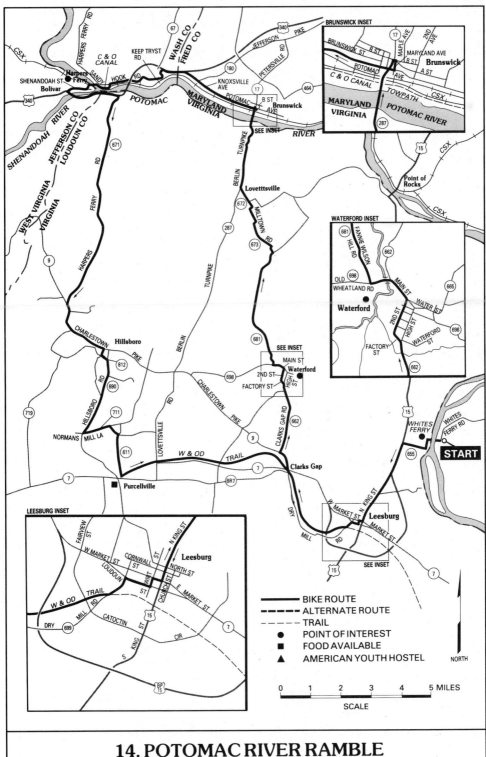

14. POTOMAC RIVER RAMBLE
Montgomery County, Md. & Loudoun County, Va.

29.8 **Left** on **US 340.** *Caution: traffic.* Cross Potomac River back into Virginia. *Use caution at bridge; road shoulder after bridge has gravel and slopes down and to the right.*

31.7 **Right** on **VA 671** (Harpers Ferry Road).

39.4 **Left** on **VA 9**.

41.6 **Right** on **VA 812**.

41.8 **Bear left** to remain on **VA 812**.

42.1 **Right** on **VA 690**.

44.7 **Left** on **VA 711** (Normans Mill Lane).

46.0 **Right** on **VA 611**, which becomes **HATCHER AVENUE.**

47.2 **Left** onto **W&OD TRAIL.** General store, inn in Purcellville.

56.9 **Left** on **DRY MILL ROAD**.

57.1 **Right** on **LOUDOUN STREET SW**.

57.4 **Left** on **WIRT STREET**.

57.5 **Right** on **WEST MARKET STREET**.

57.6 **Left** on **NORTH KING STREET**. This becomes BUS US 15 and US 15 north. *Caution at blinking light.*

60.5 **Right** on **WHITES FERRY ROAD**.

61.8 Board ferry for return trip to Maryland.

15. MONOCACY MADCAP

This moderately hilly ride passes through farmlands and several small towns in Montgomery and Frederick Counties, Md. A tasty break in Middletown for homemade ice cream should not be missed! Later you will visit Lilypons Water Gardens, an enjoyable respite for bird watchers and aquatic plant lovers.

START: Monocacy Elementary School on Barnesville Road in Montgomery County, Md. From the Capital Beltway, take I-270 North 22 miles and exit onto MD 109 South (Old Hundred Road) toward Barnesville. Continue 5.3 miles and turn right at T onto Barnesville Road. Continue one mile; school is on the right. The starting point is 28 miles northwest of the Capital Beltway.

LENGTH: 58.2 miles.

TERRAIN: Hilly.

POINTS OF INTEREST: Main's Ice Cream Parlor at 26.8 miles; and Lilypons Water Gardens (301-874-5133) at 49.3 miles.

FOOD: Markets at 26.8 and 42.9 miles.

MAPS: Montgomery and Frederick Counties, Md. road maps.

MILES   DIRECTIONS AND COMMENTS

  0.0   **Right** on **BARNESVILLE ROAD**.

  1.3   **Left** on **MOUNT EPHRAIM ROAD**.

  1.9   **Right** on **MOUTH OF THE MONOCACY ROAD**.

  2.2   **Right** on **MD 28** (Dickerson Road). Cross Monocacy River.

  4.0   **Right** on **PARK MILLS ROAD**.

  9.4   **Left** on **FLINT HILL ROAD**.

 10.5   **Left** on **MD 80** (Fingerboard Road) at stop sign. Cross Monocacy River.

 12.1   **Right** on **MD 85** (Buckeystown Pike).

 12.9   **Left** on **MANOR WOOD ROAD**.

 15.6   **Right** on **BALLENGER CREEK ROAD**.

 17.1   **Left** on **SOUTH RENN ROAD**.

18.5   **Left** on **ELMER DERR ROAD**.

19.1   **Right** to remain on **ELMER DERR ROAD**.

19.3   **Left** on **MD 180** (Jefferson Pike) after crossing US 340/US 15.

20.6   **Right** on **HOLTER ROAD**.

26.8   **Left** on **ALT US 40** in Middletown. Main's Ice Cream Parlor.

27.9   **Left** on **MARKER STREET**.

29.6   **Left** on **MARKER STREET**.

31.4   **Right** on **QUEBEC SCHOOL ROAD** at T.

33.1   **Left** on **MOUNT CHURCH ROAD**.

35.0   **Left** on **GAPLAND ROAD** at T.

36.1   **Left** on **MD 17**. Becomes **POTOMAC AVENUE** in town.

37.4   **Right** on **BROAD RUN ROAD**.

39.2   **Left** on **GAPLAND ROAD**.

42.2   **Left** on **MD 180** (Jefferson Pike).

42.9   Store with food available on left.

43.1   **Right** on **LANDER ROAD**.

43.3   **Left** on **MOUNTVILLE ROAD** just after overpass.

49.3   **Right and left dogleg** on **ORLAND ROAD**. Becomes **LILY PONS ROAD** after Buckeystown Pike. Lilypons Water Gardens on left.

52.4   **Right** on **PARK MILLS ROAD** at T.

54.2   **Left** on **MD 28** (Dickerson Road).

56.0   **Left** on **MOUTH OF THE MONOCACY ROAD**.

56.3   **Left** on **MOUNT EPHRAIM ROAD**.

56.9   **Right** on **BARNESVILLE ROAD**.

58.2   **Left** into **MONOCACY ELEMENTARY SCHOOL**.

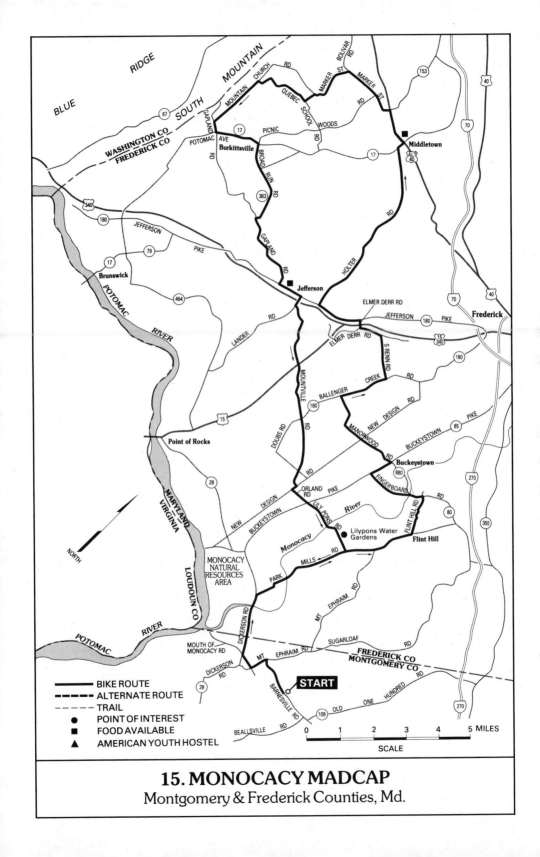

15. MONOCACY MADCAP
Montgomery & Frederick Counties, Md.

II. Back East

16. PENN DUTCH TREAT

Pennsylvania Dutch Country, a region of cultural contrasts and beautiful cycling opportunities, offers some of the best cycling in the mid-Atlantic area. The misnomer "Dutch" finds its roots in the early settlement of the area by German-speaking Amish immigrants, who described their heritage as "Deutsche." The religious and social customs of the large Amish population include a rejection of modern technology and a devotion to a simpler agrarian lifestyle. For the bicycle tourist the Amish countryside offers a unique excursion into the past.

In addition to the route described here, develop your own tours to places like the Ephrata Cloister and nearby Green Dragon Farmers Market, Lancaster and Bird in Hand. See Ephrata Effervescence (Tour 24) for directions to Ephrata Cloister from Bowmansville AYH-Hostel.

START: Bowmansville AYH-Hostel on PA 625 in Bowmansville, Pa. (13 miles south of Reading). From the Baltimore Beltway, take I-83 North to York, Pa. and exit onto US 30 East (toward Lancaster). Take PA 23 East (toward New Holland) and turn left onto PA 625 North. Continue four miles; hostel is on right. Bowmansville is 152 miles north of the Capital Beltway.

LENGTH: 40.7 miles.

TERRAIN: Easy hills.

POINTS OF INTEREST: Lancaster Cheese Factory at 12.0 miles; Hayloft Candles at 13.5 miles, with ice cream and gift shop; and Ebersol's Chair Shop at 18.5 miles. Picturesque Amish farmlands and communities, grist mills, hex signs (to frighten evil spirits), and horses and buggies along the route.

FOOD: Restaurant at 19.0 miles (closed Sundays). Penn Dutch dinners are served to groups at the following farms: Amos King, 229 Hammertown Road, Narvon, PA 17555, 215-445-6005 (near Churchtown, six miles from hostel, no weekend service); Paul Stoltzfus, 2747 Main Street, Morgantown, PA 19543, 215-286-5609 (in Berks County, service by appointment only and no Sunday service).

LODGING: In Bowmansville, Bowmansville AYH-Hostel, 1252 Reading Road, Bowmansville, Pa. (215-445-4831) at start. [Note: Hostel is closed for renovations until summer, 1993.] In Geigertown (15 miles east of Bowmansville), Shirey's AYH-Hostel (215-286-9537). In Bird in Hand, Greystone Manor (717-393-4233). In Ephrata, Historic Smithton Inn (717-733-6094). In Lancaster, Whitmer's Tavern (717-299-5305). In Lititz, Sutter Inn (717-626-2115). In Mount Joy, Cameron Estate (717-653-1773).

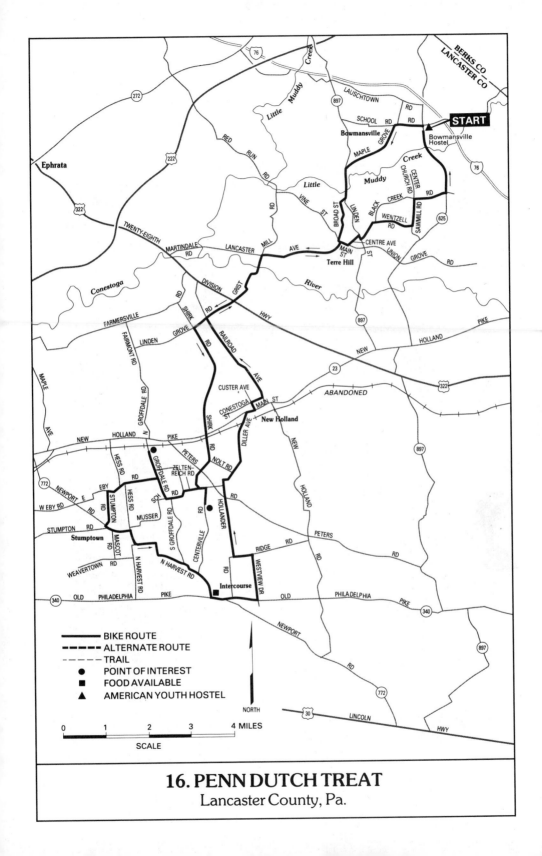

16. PENN DUTCH TREAT
Lancaster County, Pa.

MAPS AND INFORMATION: *Lancaster County Bicycle Tours,* available for $8.50 (postpaid) from the Lancaster Bicycle Club, P.O. Box 535, Lancaster, PA 17603 (717-394-8220). Pennsylvania Dutch Visitors Bureau (717-299-8901).

MILES   DIRECTIONS & COMMENTS

0.0   **Straight** out of hostel to go west on **MAPLE GROVE ROAD.**

0.6   **Bear left** to stay on **MAPLE GROVE ROAD.** Cross School Road and continue **left** on **MAPLE GROVE ROAD** up the hill.

2.2   **Left** on **PA 897** (Broad Street). Stay **straight** on **PA 897** to Terre Hill.

4.1   Arrive Terre Hill. **Left** on **MAIN STREET,** then **first right** on **LANCASTER AVENUE.**

6.1   **Left** on **GRIST MILL ROAD. Straight** on **LINDEN GROVE ROAD,** crossing US 322.

8.2   **Left** on **SHIRK ROAD** (may be unsigned). *Caution: heavy traffic.*

10.5 Cross PA 23, then railroad tracks. *Caution: heavy traffic.* **Bear right** to stay on **SHIRK ROAD,** where Nolt Road goes left. Cross Peters Road.

12.0 **Left** on **ZELTENREICH ROAD,** then **first right** on **CENTERVILLE ROAD,** to Lancaster County Cheese Factory. **Retrace route** to **ZELTENREICH ROAD,** turning **left** to continue.

12.5 **Left** on **MUSSER SCHOOL ROAD.**

13.0 **Right** on **GROFFDALE ROAD.** (Do not take South Groffdale Road, which precedes Groffdale Road and goes left.) Pass East Eby Road and go 0.5 miles to Hayloft Candles on right (closed Sundays).

13.7 **Retrace route.** Right on **EAST EBY ROAD.** Pass Hess Road and cemetery on right.

15.2 **Left** on **STUMPTON ROAD.**

16.1 **Left** on **NEWPORT ROAD** (PA 772).

16.8 **Right** on **HESS ROAD.**

17.0 **Left** on **NORTH HARVEST ROAD** (PA 772 east).

18.5 **Bear right** on **PA 772.** Pass Ebersol's Chair Shop at junction with Centerville Road. *Caution: traffic heavy into Intercourse.*

19.0 Arrive Intercourse. Kitchen Kettle Restaurant (closed Sundays) on left. **Left** on **OLD PHILADELPHIA PIKE** (PA 340) in Intercourse. *Caution: heavy traffic for 0.5 miles.*

19.2 **Bear left** to stay on **PA 340** (Old Philadelphia Pike) at fork.

20.0 **Left** on **WEST VIEW DRIVE.**

20.9 **Left** on **RIDGE ROAD.**

21.4 **Right** on **HOLLANDER ROAD.**

25.2 **Straight** on **DILLER AVENUE.**

25.5 Cross railroad tracks and enter New Holland.

25.8 **Right** on **MAIN STREET** (PA 23).

26.0 **Left** on **CUSTER AVENUE.**

26.1 **Right** on **CONESTOGA STREET.**

26.3 **Left** on **RAILROAD AVENUE.**

28.6 **Right** on **LINDEN GROVE ROAD.** Becomes **GRIST MILL ROAD.**

30.9 **Right** on **LANCASTER AVENUE.**

34.3 **Right** on **MAIN STREET** in Terre Hill.

34.4 **Left** on **CENTRE AVENUE.**

34.9 **Right** on **LINDEN STREET.** Go 200 feet, then **left** on **WENTZELL ROAD**.

36.1 **Left** on **SAW MILL ROAD.**

36.8 **Right** on **BLACK CREEK ROAD**.

37.7 **Left** on **PA 625** at T (to Bowmansville).

40.7 **Right** into **HOSTEL.**

17. PRETTYBOY PRANCE

If you are in search of hills, this tour is for you. The route follows old, narrow roads bordered by cornfields as it circles the Prettyboy Reservoir.

The reservoir, which supplies water to Baltimore County, has many inlets that pop up along the loop. Steep declines lead to panoramas of sparkling water and tall pines. The reservoir dam, shortly before the 10-mile ride back to the start, offers a good lunch stop.

START: Commuter parking lot on corner of Shawan Road and Western Run Road in Baltimore County, Md. From the Baltimore Beltway, take I-83 North for six miles and exit onto Shawan Road (exit 20). Continue west for 0.6 miles; lot is on the left, just west of I-83. The starting point is 51 miles north of the Capital Beltway. **ALTERNATE START:** At 9.4 miles. Park at intersection of Yeoho Road and Mount Carmel Road, and just loop the reservoir.

LENGTH: 36.8 miles. From **ALTERNATE START:** 27.4 miles.

TERRAIN: Steep hills. Several short stretches of bad surfaces.

POINTS OF INTEREST: Prettyboy Reservoir with Prettyboy Dam at 23.2 miles. Scenic countryside along the route.

FOOD: Markets near start, but none along the route. Buy food near start or pack your own.

MAPS: *Baltimore Area Bike Map;* Baltimore County, Md. road map.

MILES	DIRECTIONS & COMMENTS
0.0	**Right** on **WESTERN RUN ROAD.**
3.7	**Right** on **TANYARD ROAD.** Very narrow old road.
5.1	**Left** on **BELFAST ROAD** at T.
5.3	**Right** on **YEOHO ROAD.**
9.4	**Left** on **MOUNT CARMEL ROAD** at T. ALTERNATE START begins here.
10.0	**Right** on **FORESTON ROAD.**
12.4	**Bear left** on **GEORGES CREEK ROAD.**
13.2	**Right** on **GUNPOWDER ROAD** at T.
14.8	**Right** on **BECKLEYSVILLE ROAD.**

18.2 **Right** on **SPOOKS HILL ROAD.** Steep downhill to reservoir.

23.2 **Right** on **PRETTYBOY DAM ROAD** at T.

24.4 Cross Prettyboy Dam. Toilet and water facilities.

26.9 **Right** on **MOUNT CARMEL ROAD.** Church straight ahead.

27.5 **Left** on **YEOHO ROAD.**

31.5 **Left** on **BELFAST ROAD** at T.

31.7 **Right** on **TANYARD ROAD.**

33.1 **Left** on **WESTERN RUN ROAD** at T.

36.8 **End ride** at **COMMUTER PARKING LOT.**

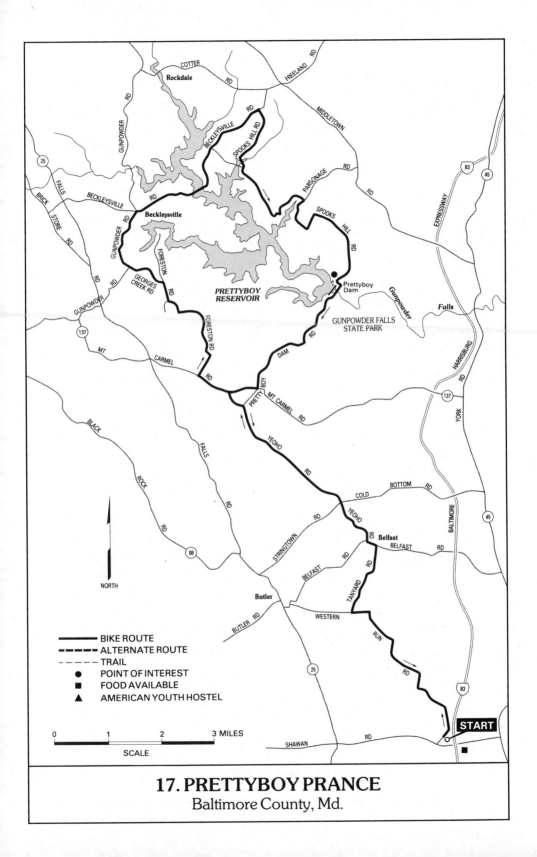

17. PRETTYBOY PRANCE
Baltimore County, Md.

18. SHAWAN SHAKE

Wandering through rolling Maryland farmland and horse country north of Baltimore, this pleasant tour features rolling hills and opportunities for swimming and picnicking.

START: Commuter parking lot on corner of Shawan Road and Western Run Road in Baltimore County, Md. From the Baltimore Beltway, take I-83 North for six miles and exit onto Shawan Road (exit 20). Continue west for 0.6 miles; lot is on the left, just west of I-83. The starting point is 51 miles north of the Capital Beltway.

LENGTH: 14.1 miles.

TERRAIN: Rolling hills.

POINTS OF INTEREST: Side trip to Oregon Ridge Park at 1.0 miles, with picnic area and theater.

FOOD: Markets at 3.8 and 11.8 miles. Fast food restaurants at start.

MAPS: *Baltimore Area Bike Map;* Baltimore County, Md. road map.

MILES	DIRECTIONS & COMMENTS
0.0	**Right** from parking lot on **SHAWAN ROAD** toward I-83.
1.0	**Left** on **CUBA ROAD.** *Caution: road is narrow and rough in places.* [Turn right here for side trip to Oregon Ridge Park.]
3.1	**Left** on **WESTERN RUN ROAD** at T.
3.6	**Bear left** across bridge to stay on **WESTERN RUN ROAD.**
3.7	**Right** on **FALLS ROAD.**
3.8	**Left** on **BUTLER ROAD.** General store on right.
6.2	**Bear left** to stay on **BUTLER ROAD,** where Dover Road bears right.
7.9	**Left** on **BELMONT ROAD.**
9.6	**Left** on **TUFTON AVENUE.**
11.1	**Left** on **DOVER ROAD,** then **quick right** to stay on **TUFTON AVENUE.**
11.8	**Straight** on **SHAWAN ROAD.** Cross Falls Road. General store on left.
14.1	**Arrive** at **COMMUTER PARKING LOT.**

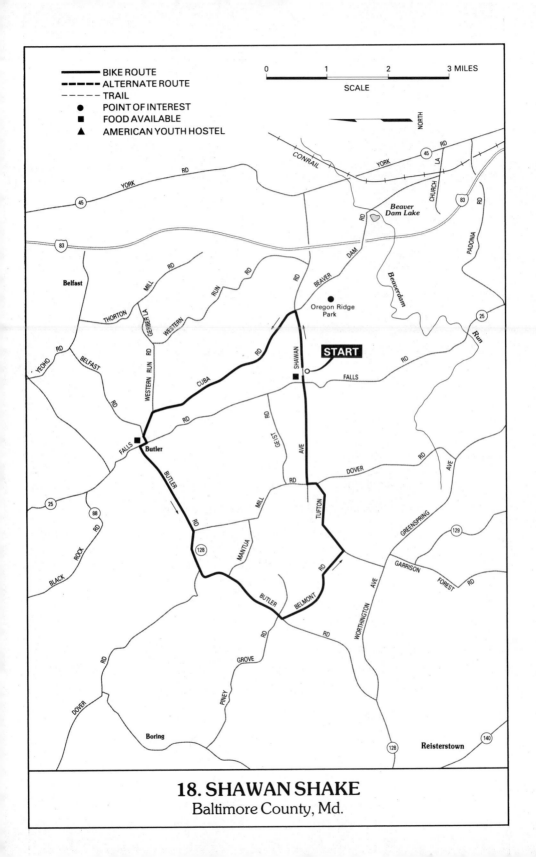

LEGEND
— BIKE ROUTE
----- ALTERNATE ROUTE
- - - - TRAIL
● POINT OF INTEREST
■ FOOD AVAILABLE
▲ AMERICAN YOUTH HOSTEL

0   1   2   3 MILES
SCALE

NORTH

START

Oregon Ridge Park

Beaver Dam Lake

Belfast

Butler

Boring

Reisterstown

18. SHAWAN SHAKE
Baltimore County, Md.

19. LOCH RAVEN LOOP

The rolling hills and scenic woodland watershed of Loch Raven Reservoir set the tone of this tour. Created for novice bicyclists, the tour offers three routes for exploring the area. Along the way you will find quaint farmland and a welcome ice cream stop, but little traffic.

START: Loch Raven Dam parking lot on Loch Raven Road in Baltimore County, Md. From the Baltimore Beltway, take Cromwell Bridge Road (exit 29) north for two miles and turn left onto Loch Raven Road. Continue one mile to parking lot. The starting point is approximately 40 miles northeast of the Capital Beltway.

LENGTH: 19.9 miles. **ALTERNATE ROUTES:** 18.8 miles and 13.1 miles.

TERRAIN: Rolling hills.

POINTS OF INTEREST: Loch Raven Reservoir and Pearce Plantation at 3.8 miles.

FOOD: Markets at 4.2 and 10.2 miles. Ice cream shop at 18.9 miles.

MAPS: *Baltimore Area Bike Map;* Baltimore County, Md. road map.

MILES   DIRECTIONS & COMMENTS

0.0   **Left** out of parking lot to go northwest on **LOCH RAVEN ROAD.**

3.8   **Right** on **DULANEY VALLEY ROAD.** Pass Pearce Plantation.

4.2   Food available at country store.

6.3   **Left** on **MANOR ROAD** at T. 13.1-mile ALTERNATE ROUTE begins here (see end of cues).

6.5   **Right** on **CARROLL MANOR ROAD.**

8.0   **Right** on **SWEET AIR ROAD** (MD 145) at T.

8.6   **Bear right** on **PATTERSON ROAD.**

10.2   **Right** on **LONG GREEN PIKE** at T. General store. 18.8-mile ALTERNATE ROUTE begins here (see end of cues).

11.1   **Right** on **HYDES ROAD.**

13.5   **Left** on **MANOR ROAD** at T.

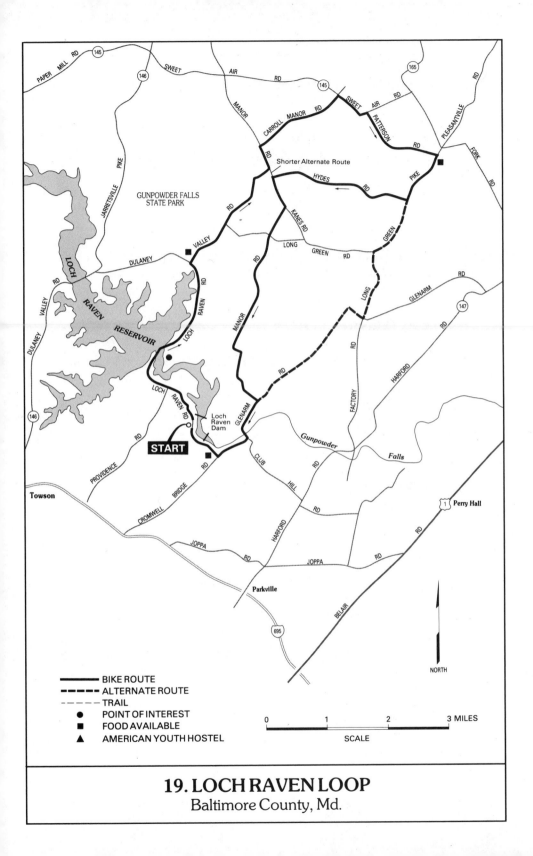

19. LOCH RAVEN LOOP
Baltimore County, Md.

BIKE ROUTE
ALTERNATE ROUTE
TRAIL
● POINT OF INTEREST
■ FOOD AVAILABLE
▲ AMERICAN YOUTH HOSTEL

0   1   2   3 MILES
SCALE

NORTH

14.2   **Bear right** to stay on **MANOR ROAD.**

17.7   **Right** on **GLENARM ROAD**.

18.5   **Right** on **CROMWELL BRIDGE ROAD.**

18.9   **Right** on **LOCH RAVEN ROAD.** Ice cream at Cloverland Dairy.

19.9   **Arrive** at **PARKING LOT.**

18.8-MILE ALTERNATE ROUTE

At 10.2 miles, after **right** on **LONG GREEN PIKE,** do not turn on Hydes Road. Turn **right** on **GLENARM ROAD** at 13.8 miles and pick up cues at 18.5 miles, for an 18.8-mile ride.

13.1-MILE ALTERNATE ROUTE

At 6.3 miles, go **right** on **MANOR ROAD** at T, then pick up cues at 14.2 miles for a 13.1-mile ride.

20. SWEET AIR SWING

A colorful ramble through eastern Baltimore and western Harford Counties, this ride boasts scenic roads, pretty farm country and parks.

START: Commuter parking lot on corner of Shawan Road and Western Run Road in Baltimore County, Md. From the Baltimore Beltway, take I-83 North for six miles and exit onto Shawan Road (exit 20). Continue west for 0.6 miles; parking lot is on the left, just west of I-83. The starting point is 51 miles north of the Capital Beltway.

LENGTH: 29.5 miles

TERRAIN: Rolling hills.

POINTS OF INTEREST: Loch Raven Reservoir at start and Gunpowder Falls State Park at 15.0 miles.

FOOD: Market at 11.6 miles.

MAPS: *Baltimore Area Bike Map;* Baltimore and Harford Counties, Md. road maps.

MILES   DIRECTIONS & COMMENTS

0.0   **Left** out of parking lot to go east on **SHAWAN ROAD.**

1.2   **Right** (south) on **YORK ROAD** (MD 45).

1.5   **Left** on **ASHLAND ROAD** (MD 145), which becomes **PAPER MILL ROAD.**

6.5   **Left** on **OLD YORK ROAD.** Scenic rest stop.

9.0   **Merge left** on **MANOR ROAD.**

9.3   **Right** on **HESS ROAD.**

11.6   Cross Jarretsville Pike (MD 146). Country stores.

13.4   **Right** on **FALLSTON ROAD** (MD 152).

15.0   **Right** on **BALDWIN MILL ROAD.** Pass Gunpowder Falls State Park on left.

18.9   **Right** on **LONG GREEN PIKE.**

20.0   **Right** on **HYDES ROAD.**

22.3   **Right** on **MANOR ROAD.**

24.3 **Left** on **SWEET AIR ROAD.**

25.7 Cross Jarretsville Pike at blinking light. **Straight** on **PAPER MILL ROAD** (MD 145), which becomes **ASHLAND ROAD.**

28.0 **Right** on **YORK ROAD** (MD 45).

28.3 **Left** on **SHAWAN ROAD**.

29.5 **Arrive** at **PARKING LOT.**

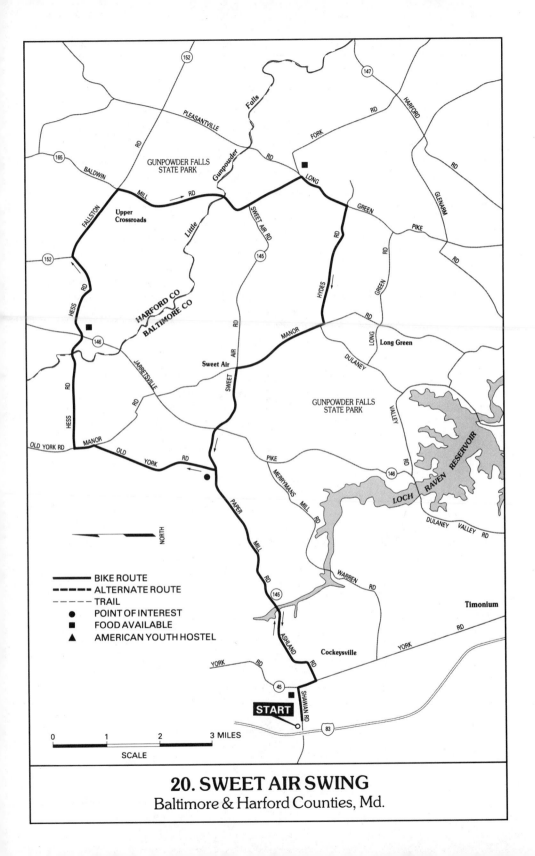

20. SWEET AIR SWING
Baltimore & Harford Counties, Md.

21. ELLICOTT CITY LOOP

The historic town of Ellicott City, on the south bank of the Patapsco River, marks the midpoint of this loop. The city was established in 1774 with the construction of George Ellicott's grist and flour mill. The town flourished with the laying of the Cumberland Road and the arrival of the B&O Railroad in 1830. Some of the old remaining granite buildings wedged into the rocky hillside attest to the history of the area. Today, Ellicott City hosts America's oldest remaining railroad station, built in 1831 and now the home of the B&O Railroad Museum.

START: Baltimore County Library (Randallstown Branch) on Liberty Road in Baltimore County, Md. From the Baltimore Beltway, take Liberty Road (exit 18) west. Continue two miles; library is on right after intersection with Old Court Road. The starting point is 34 miles north of the Capital Beltway.

LENGTH: 23.0 miles.

TERRAIN: Hilly.

POINTS OF INTEREST: In Ellicott City (410-992-2027) at 12.5 miles: B&O Railroad Museum, open daily (except Monday) spring through fall and on weekends during winter (410-461-1944 for directions and information); Tongue Row; 1840s houses, converted into shops; Town Hall; Patapsco Female Institute (1835) on Church Road, overlooking the city; craft and antique shops; and Patapsco River State Park.

FOOD: Markets at start and 12.1 miles. Restaurants at start, 6.1, 12.1 and 14.5 miles.

LODGING: At Patapsco River State Park (410-461-5005), public campgrounds.

MAPS: *Baltimore Area Bike Map;* Baltimore and Howard Counties, Md. road maps.

MILES   DIRECTIONS & COMMENTS

0.0   Go **right** (southwest) on **OLD COURT ROAD.**

6.1   **Straight** on **WOODSTOCK ROAD** (MD 125), crossing Patapsco River. Restaurant on left.

7.4   **Left** on **MD 99** (Old Frederick Road) at T.

10.3   **Right** on **ST. JOHNS LANE.**

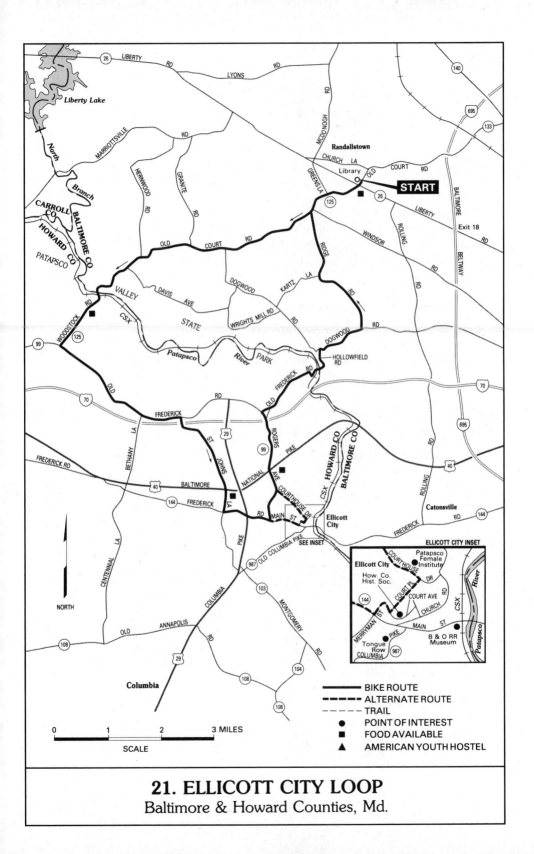

21. ELLICOTT CITY LOOP
Baltimore & Howard Counties, Md.

12.1   Cross US 40. Grocery store and restaurant.

12.5   **Left** on **FREDERICK ROAD** (MD 144) and enter Ellicott City.

13.5   **Left** on **ROGERS AVENUE.**

To see more of Ellicott City, do not turn on Rogers Avenue. Continue on Frederick Road for one mile. To leave Ellicott City and return to the route, from Main Street heading toward the river, turn left on Merryman Street (street sign on right). Turn right on unmarked street at Howard County Historical Society. Turn left on Court Place. Turn left on Courthouse Drive. Merge right on Rogers Avenue to continue route.

14.5   Cross US 40. Restaurant.

15.4   **Left** to stay on **ROGERS AVENUE** (MD 99) at T.

15.8   **Right** on **OLD FREDERICK ROAD,** just past I-70.

17.4   **Straight** on **HOLLOWFIELD ROAD,** crossing Patapsco River.

17.9   **Right** on **DOGWOOD ROAD** at T.

19.0   **Left** on **RIDGE ROAD.**

21.8   **Right** on **OLD COURT ROAD** (MD 125).

23.0   **Left** into **LIBRARY.**

22. HOWARD'S HILLS

After the steep hills of the first leg, this tour settles down to rolling countryside. The miles of corn fields, punctuated by an occasional pumpkin patch and horse ranch, charm you as you leave behind the bustle of the metropolitan area. If you begin the ride early in the day, you will find few cars on the first five miles of the route along New Hampshire Avenue (except on Sundays when churchgoers attend services in the area).

START: Safeway at the corner of New Hampshire Avenue (MD 650) and Briggs Chaney Road, in Cloverly, Md. From the Capital Beltway, take New Hampshire Avenue north for 6.5 miles. Safeway is on the right, past Briggs Chaney Road. Cloverly is six miles north of the Capital Beltway.

LENGTH: 45.4 miles. **ALTERNATE ROUTE:** 30.6 miles.

TERRAIN: Hilly.

POINTS OF INTEREST: Brighton Dam at 8.2 miles. Vegetable stands on New Hampshire Avenue and open countryside along the route.

FOOD: Markets at start, 3.5, 13.1, 18.7 and 27.0 miles. Pub at 12.0 miles.

MAPS: *Lower Montgomery County Bicycle Route Map;* Howard and Montgomery Counties, Md. road maps.

MILES   DIRECTIONS & COMMENTS

0.0   Turn **right** out of parking lot to go north on **NEW HAMPSHIRE AVENUE** (MD 650).

3.5   Cross MD 108. Grocery store at right.

5.0   **Right** on **HAVILAND MILL ROAD.**

8.2   **Right** on **BRIGHTON DAM ROAD** at T. (Brighton Dam is one mile to the left from this intersection.)

8.7   **Left** on **HIGHLAND ROAD.**

10.4   **Bear left** on **TEN OAKS ROAD** at stop sign.

12.0   **Right** to stay on **TEN OAKS ROAD.** Pub on right.

13.1   **Left** on **TRIADELPHIA ROAD.** General store on right. ALTERNATE ROUTE begins here (see end of cues).

13.4   **Right** on **IVORY ROAD.**

14.1 **Right** on **BURNT WOODS ROAD,** then **immediate left** on **MD 32.** *Caution: traffic.*

14.4 **Left** on **PFEFFERKORN ROAD.**

16.4 **Left** on **MD 144** (Frederick Road) at T.

18.7 **Left** on **MD 97** (Roxbury Mills Road). General store on right. Site of Civil War skirmish on left.

20.0 **Left** on **McKENDREE ROAD.**

20.4 **Right** on **HOBBS ROAD.**

21.7 **Bear left** on **SHADY LANE.**

23.3 Shady Lane becomes **SHARP ROAD.** Do not turn left on Sharp Road!

25.6 **Left** on **TRIADELPHIA ROAD.**

27.0 Cross Ten Oaks Road at stop sign. General store on right.

27.4 **Bear right** on **FOLLY QUARTER ROAD.**

30.4 **Right** on **SHEPPARD LANE,** where Folly Quarter Road goes left.

33.2 **Left** on **MD 108** (Clarksville Pike) at T.

33.9 **Right** on **TROTTER ROAD.**

36.7 **Left** on **MD 32** (Guilford Road) at T.

36.9 **Right** on **HALL SHOP ROAD**.

38.5 **Bear left** on **BROWNS BRIDGE ROAD.**

39.5 Cross MD 216. Stables to right. Browns Bridge Road becomes **EDNOR ROAD,** crossing Patuxent River.

43.2 **Left** on **NEW HAMPSHIRE AVENUE** (MD 650) at traffic light.

45.4 **Left** into **SAFEWAY.**

ALTERNATE ROUTE

At 13.1 miles, turn **right** instead of left on **TRIADELPHIA ROAD,** then pick up cues at 25.3 miles.

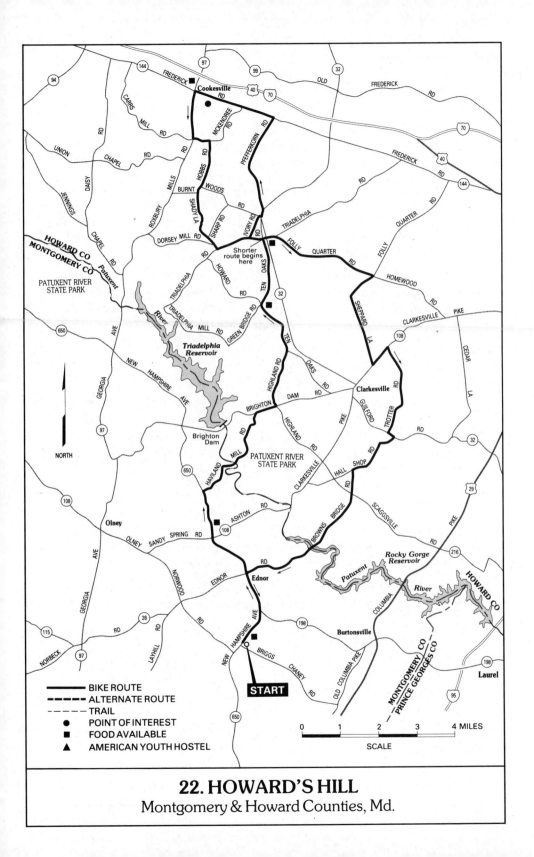

——	BIKE ROUTE
- - - -	ALTERNATE ROUTE
– – – –	TRAIL
●	POINT OF INTEREST
■	FOOD AVAILABLE
▲	AMERICAN YOUTH HOSTEL

START

NORTH

0   1   2   3   4 MILES

SCALE

22. HOWARD'S HILL
Montgomery & Howard Counties, Md.

23. NASSAWANGO NATURAL

Passing through historic Princess Anne and the Wellington Wildlife Management Area, this flat, circular route on the Maryland Eastern Shore affords almost no traffic. Princess Anne is the seat of Somerset County and contains lovely pre-Revolutionary houses and buildings. The Wellington Wildlife Management Area displays a splendid example of bog and swamp ecology.

The route can be combined with the Ferry Flat Tour (Tour 32) for a relaxing weekend trip.

START: Washington Hotel on Somerset Avenue (MD 675) in Princess Anne, Md. From the Capital Beltway, take US 50 East over the Bay Bridge and continue to Salisbury. Turn south onto US 13 and continue 11 miles to the Princess Anne turn-off (on the left). Continue two miles to the center of town; Washington Hotel is on Somerset Avenue, on the right. Princess Anne is 130 miles southeast of the Capital Beltway.

LENGTH: 38.1 miles.

TERRAIN: Level.

POINTS OF INTEREST: In Princess Anne (410-651-2968) at start, with Washington Hotel (1774), Prince William Street, Teackle Mansion ($2 admission, open Sundays 2 p.m. to 4 p.m.), old jail (one block behind Washington Hotel); Beach-to-Bay Indian Trail (part of route from Princess Anne to Furnacetown) from 0.1 to 13.9 miles; Nassawango Furnacetown at 13.9 miles, a renovated 1830s iron smelting village (open 11 a.m. to 5 p.m. daily, April to October, admission $1, 410-632-2032); and Millburn Landing State Park at 22.0 miles. Also Pocomoke State Forest, Pocomoke River Wildlife Management Area and Milburn Landing State Park along the route.

FOOD: Market at 29.8 miles. Restaurant at start (Washington Hotel has an excellent dining room). Snacks in Furnacetown at 13.9 miles.

LODGING: In Princess Anne, Washington Hotel (410-651-2525) at start, Elmwood Inn (410-651-1066), bed-and-breakfasts on Prince William Street, motels on US 13. Just north of Princess Anne, Princess Anne Campground on US 13 (410-651-1520). Near Snow Hill, inns include Chanceford Hall (410-632-2231) and Snow Hill Inn (410-632-2102).

MAPS AND INFORMATION: Somerset and Worcester Counties, Md. road maps. Princess Anne Information Center (410-651-2968); Worcester County Tourism (410-632-3617).

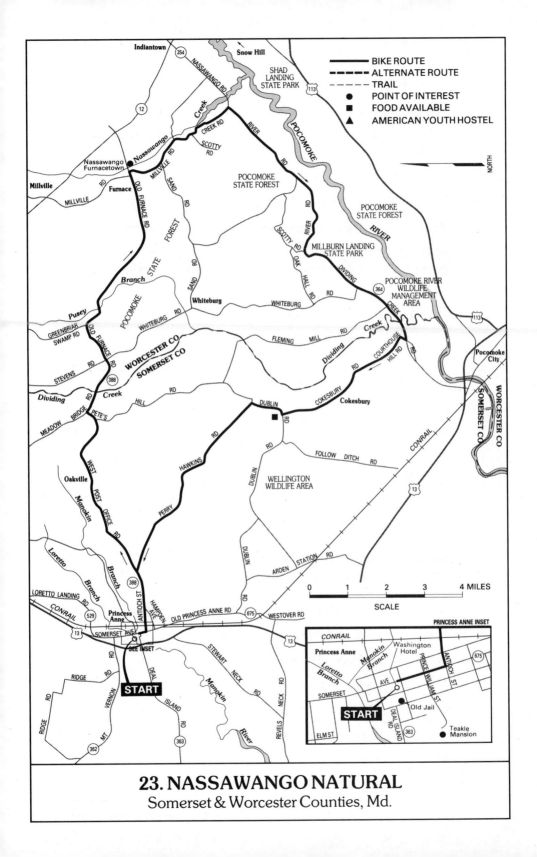

23. NASSAWANGO NATURAL
Somerset & Worcester Counties, Md.

MILES   DIRECTIONS & COMMENTS

0.0   **Right** from front of hotel onto **SOMERSET AVENUE** (MD 675).

0.2   **Left** on **ANTIOCH STREET** (MD 388). Becomes **WEST POST OFFICE ROAD.**

0.3   Cross railroad tracks.

6.3   **Left** at T on **PETE'S HILL ROAD** toward Snow Hill.

6.6   **Right** at T on **MEADOW BRIDGE ROAD**, still toward Snow Hill.

7.2   Cross Dividing Creek on wood bridge. Enter Worcester County. Meadow Bridge Road becomes **OLD FURNACE ROAD.**

8.2   Cross Stevens Road.

9.9   Cross Pusey Branch on wood bridge.

13.8   Cross Millville Road.

13.9   Nassawango Furnacetown. Visit village and walk the nature trail before **reversing direction.** Food available in town.

14.0   **Left** on **MILLVILLE ROAD**. *Caution: poor surface.*

14.9   **Straight** on **PAVED ROAD** at intersection with Sand Road.

15.5   **Right** on **CREEK ROAD** (Viewtrail 100) at T.

15.8   **Bear left** on **CREEK ROAD** at intersection with Scotty Road.

17.3   **Right** on **RIVER ROAD/NASSAWANGO ROAD**.

22.0   Pass Millburn Landing State Park on left.

22.7   **Left** (south) on **DIVIDING CREEK ROAD** (MD 364).

25.3   Cross bridge into Somerset County.

25.7   **Right** on **COURTHOUSE HILL ROAD** (becomes Cokesbury Road).

29.8   **Right** on **DUBLIN ROAD** at T. Store.

30.6   **Left** on **PERRY HAWKINS ROAD.**

36.3   **Bear left** on **WEST POST OFFICE ROAD.**

37.8   Cross railroad tracks.

37.9   Enter Princess Anne. **Right** on **MD 675** (Somerset Avenue).

38.1   **Left** into **HOTEL.**

24. EPHRATA EFFERVESCENCE

Looping through the Pennsylvania Dutch country of Lancaster County, Pa., this short trip starts and ends at the Bowmansville AYH-Hostel. Highlights include several covered bridges and the lovely Ephrata Cloisters.

START: Bowmansville AYH-Hostel on PA 625 in Bowmansville, Pa. (13 miles south of Reading). From the Baltimore Beltway, take I-83 North to York, Pa. and exit onto US 30 East (toward Lancaster). Take PA 23 East (toward New Holland) and turn left onto PA 625 North. Continue four miles; hostel is on right. Bowmansville is 152 miles north of the Capital Beltway.

LENGTH: 30.0 miles.

TERRAIN: Easy hills.

POINTS OF INTEREST: Covered bridges at 8.3, 18.7 and 25.1 miles; and Ephrata Cloisters (717-733-6600) at 12.6 miles.

FOOD: Restaurants and markets in Ephrata at approximately 12.0 miles. Penn Dutch dinners are served to groups at the following farms: Amos King, 229 Hammertown Road, Narvon, PA 17555, 215-445-6005 (near Churchtown, six miles from hostel, no weekend service); Paul Stoltzfus, 2747 Main Street, Morgantown, PA 19543, 215-286-5609 (in Berks County, service by appointment only and no Sunday service).

LODGING: In Bowmansville, Bowmansville AYH-Hostel, 1252 Reading Road, Bowmansville, Pa. (215-445-4831) at start. [Note: Hostel is closed for renovations until summer, 1993.] In Geigertown (15 miles east of Bowmansville), Shirey's AYH-Hostel (215-286-9537). In Bird in Hand, Greystone Manor (717-393-4233). In Ephrata, Historic Smithton Inn (717-733-6094). In Lancaster, Whitmer's Tavern (717-299-5305). In Lititz, Sutter Inn (717-626-2115). In Mount Joy, Cameron Estate (717-653-1773).

MAPS AND INFORMATION: *Lancaster County Bicycle Tours,* available for $8.50 (postpaid) from the Lancaster Bicycle Club, P.O. Box 535, Lancaster, PA 17603 (717-394-8220). Pennsylvania Dutch Visitors Bureau (717-299-8901).

MILES   DIRECTIONS & COMMENTS

0.0   **Right** (north) from hostel on **PA 625**.

0.5   **Left** on **LAUNCHTOWN ROAD** just before Pennsylvania Turnpike (I-76).

2.6   Cross PA 897.

4.1 **Right** on **KRAMER MILL ROAD** at T.

5.9 **Right** on **PFEIFFER HILL ROAD** at T. Cross under US 222.

6.5 **Left** on **MAIN STREET** into Reamstown.

7.9 **Right** on **COCALICO CREEK ROAD.**

8.2 **Left** on **UNMARKED ROAD**.

8.3 Cross Cocalico Creek on covered bridge.

8.6 Cross PA 272. Road becomes **PFAUTZ HILL ROAD.**

9.2 **Left** on **STEVENS ROAD**. Cross railroad tracks ahead. Enter Stevens.

9.6 **Left** on **LINE ROAD**. This becomes **STEVENS ROAD,** then **ACADEMY DRIVE** at 12.0 miles in Ephrata.

12.4 **Left** on **MAIN STREET** (US 322).

12.5 Cross under PA 272.

12.6 Ephrata Cloisters on right.

12.9 **Bear right** on **FULTON STREET**.

14.3 **Right** on **BETHANY ROAD**.

15.3 **Left** on **FARMERSVILLE ROAD**. Becomes **NORTH ROAD** and passes under US 222.

17.5 **Left** on **COVERED BRIDGE ROAD**.

18.7 **Left** on **CIDER MILL ROAD** (unmarked). Covered bridge.

18.9 **Right** on **CONESTOGA CREEK ROAD**.

19.8 Foot bridge on right.

20.4 **Right** on **US 322** (28th Division Highway).

20.7 **Left** on **MARTINDALE ROAD** (Lancaster Avenue).

21.8 **Left** on **KURTZ ROAD** (Napierville Road).

22.8 **Jog left** on **LANDIS ROAD**.

23.7 **Right** on **MARTIN ROAD** (Fivepointville Road).

24.5 **Right** on **RED RUN ROAD**.

25.1 **Left** on **MARTIN CHURCH ROAD** before covered bridge.

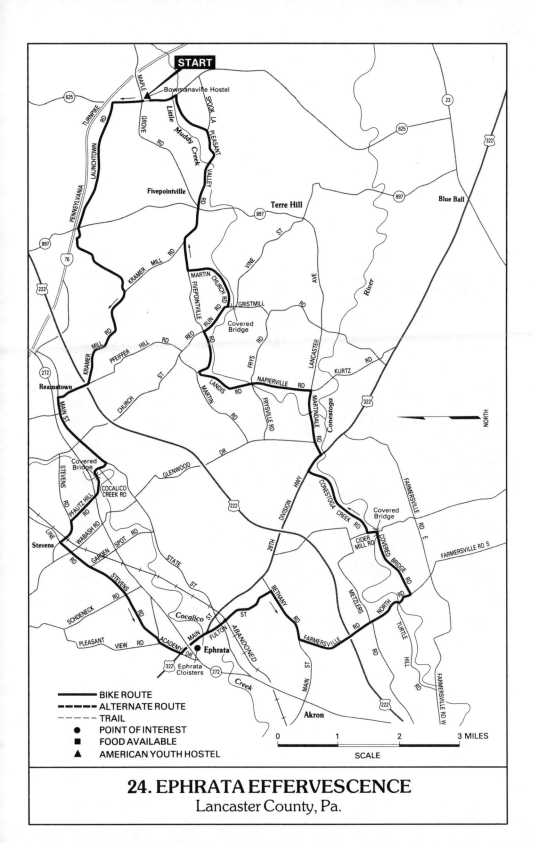

24. EPHRATA EFFERVESCENCE
Lancaster County, Pa.

26.2 **Right** on **FIVEPOINTVILLE ROAD**. This becomes **PLEASANT VALLEY ROAD** at 27.3 miles in Fivepointville.

29.5 **Left** on **PA 625**.

30.0 **Right** into **HOSTEL**.

25. NONEXISTENT NOTTINGHAM

This relaxing and refreshing loop uncovers the once-prosperous city of Nottingham in Prince Georges County, Md. Nottingham, a late colonial era town, once thrived on the Patuxent River.

The British camped at Nottingham after landing at Benedict (approximately 14 miles downriver) during the War of 1812. They burned the city before marching on to Washington. No trace of Nottingham remains today.

Nottingham Road, the straight main roadway into the former town, was popular in its early days as a race track and was frequented by George Washington.

The Surratt House Historic Site is about one mile northeast of the start/finish. After shooting President Abraham Lincoln, John Wilkes Booth fled here. The owner, Mary Surratt, was arrested and convicted for her role in the assassination and became the first woman executed by the U.S. government. For a route to the Surratt House, see end of cues.

START: Southern Maryland Hospital Center on Surratts Road in Clinton, Md. From the Capital Beltway, take exit 7A, Branch Avenue (MD 5) south for six miles. Turn left onto Surratts Road, at the fifth traffic light. Hospital is on right. Clinton is seven miles southeast of the Capital Beltway.

LENGTH: 24.6 miles.

TERRAIN: Rolling hills. Good roads with light traffic.

POINTS OF INTEREST: Surratt House Historic Site (301-868-1121) near start, at 9118 Brandywine Road in Clinton; and former site of the town of Nottingham at 12.1 miles. Also tobacco farms and forests along the route.

FOOD: Markets at 3.7, 9.2 and 20.9 miles.

MAPS: Prince Georges County, Md. road map.

MILES   DIRECTIONS & COMMENTS

0.0   **Right** out of hospital parking lot, to go east on **SURRATTS ROAD.** Pass through Boys Village reform school.

3.4   **Right** on **FRANK TIPPETT ROAD** at T.

3.7   **Left** on **US 301.** *Caution: traffic.* Grocery store at corner.

4.1   **Right** on **OLD INDIAN HEAD ROAD.**

4.6 **Right** on **VAN BRADY ROAD.** Cross railroad tracks.

4.8 **Bear right** to stay on **VAN BRADY ROAD**.

7.5 **Left** on **MOLLY BERRY ROAD** at T.

8.1 **Right** on **CROOM ROAD** at T.

9.2 **Left** on **NOTTINGHAM ROAD.** Buy food at grocery store here for a picnic in Nottingham.

12.0 **Left** on **WATERSHED DRIVE** at T.

12.1 **Arrive** at Nottingham and Patuxent River. *Caution: use care on old pier.*

12.3 **Reverse direction. Right** on **NOTTINGHAM ROAD.**

13.0 **Left** on **CANDY HILL ROAD.**

14.8 Cross Croom Road.

16.0 **Right** on **MOLLY BERRY ROAD** at T.

16.5 **Left** on **NORTH KEYS ROAD.**

17.4 **Right** on **CROSS ROAD TRAIL.**

20.6 **Right** on **US 301** at T.

20.9 **Left** on **FRANK TIPPETT ROAD.** Last grocery stop.

21.2 **Left** on **SURRATTS ROAD** at sign for "Boys Village."

24.6 **Left** into **HOSPITAL.** To get to the Surratt House after the ride, continue past the Southern Maryland Hospital Center on Surratts Road to Brandywine Road (Old Branch Avenue), and turn right. The Surratt House is one-half mile ahead on the right.

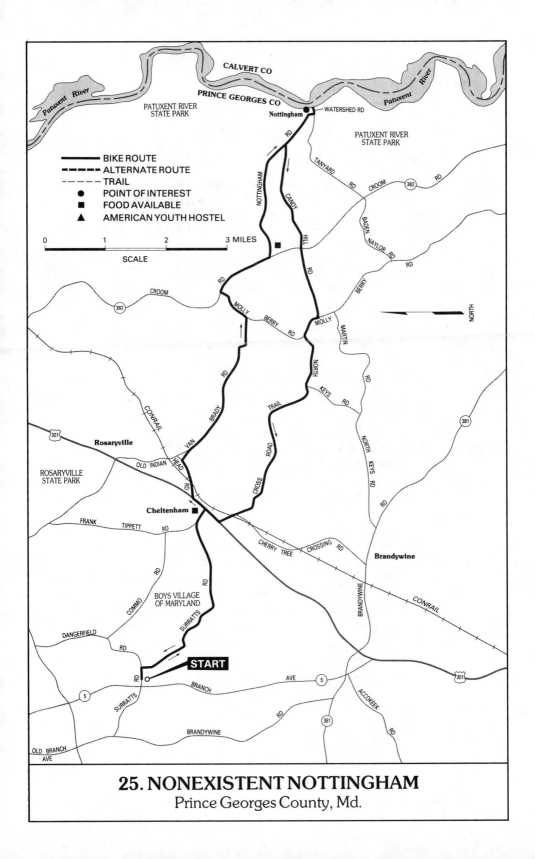

BIKE ROUTE
ALTERNATE ROUTE
TRAIL
● POINT OF INTEREST
■ FOOD AVAILABLE
▲ AMERICAN YOUTH HOSTEL

0   1   2   3 MILES
SCALE

25. NONEXISTENT NOTTINGHAM
Prince Georges County, Md.

26. PORTSIDE PACER

Enjoy historic Charles County, Md. on this tour through the towns of Port Tobacco and La Plata.

Port Tobacco was once an important river port and the designated Charles County seat. However, by 1895 the Port Tobacco River filled with so much silt that ships could no longer reach the town. Trade collapsed and Charles County moved its seat to La Plata. Today, both Port Tobacco and La Plata boast historic churches and courthouses, with a museum in Port Tobacco that recounts its local history.

The tour runs primarily on roads with broad shoulders and little traffic. Along the way, road markers tell the histories of Dr. Gustavus Brown (a surgeon and friend of George Washington) and the flight of John Wilkes Booth after the assassination of President Abraham Lincoln.

Stop at the National Colonial Farm for a rewarding side trip. Just north of the ride's starting point, the farm, with its staff dressed in period costume and its assortment of colonial crops, takes you back to life during colonial times.

START: Bryans Road Shopping Center at the intersection of MD 210 and MD 227, in Charles County, Md. From the Capital Beltway, exit onto MD 210 (exit 3A, Indian Head Highway), east of Wilson Bridge. Continue south into Charles County, to junction of MD 210 and MD 227 (Marshall Hall Road). The starting point is 16 miles south of the Capital Beltway.

LENGTH: 32.2 miles.

TERRAIN: Easy hills.

POINTS OF INTEREST: Port Tobacco at 10.0 miles, with museum, historic courthouse (301-475-2467), marina and restaurant on Port Tobacco River; St. Ignatius Church at Chapel Point with a famous river view at 13.5 miles, the oldest continuously active Catholic parish in America; Chapel Point State Park at 13.5 miles; colonial-era Episcopal Church, courthouse with undulating brick wall, and farmers market in La Plata at 21.1 miles; and Myrtle Grove Wildlife Refuge at 25.6 miles, an 800-acre scenic reserve. Also many tobacco farms along the route.

FOOD: Markets at start, 15.9, 21.1 and 22.1 miles. Restaurant at start. Barbecue stand at 9.7 miles.

MAPS: Charles County, Md. road map.

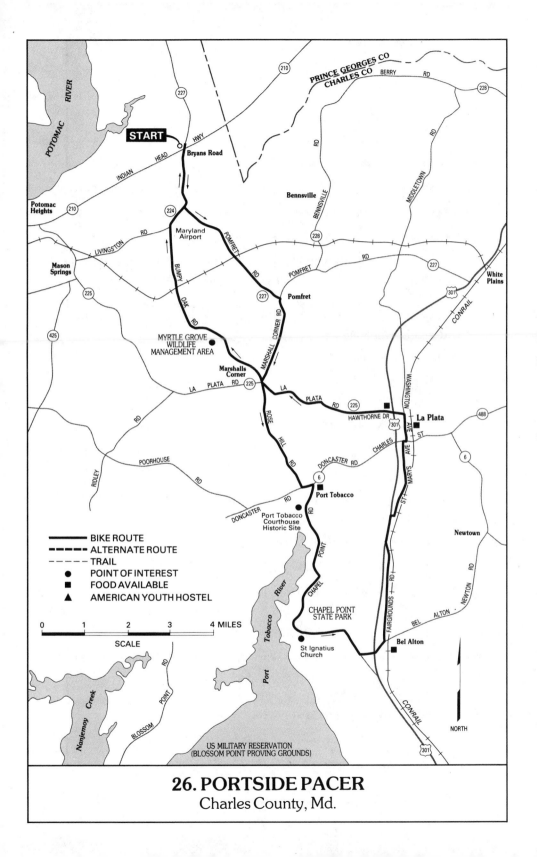

START

Bryans Road

PRINCE GEORGES CO
CHARLES CO

BERRY RD

POTOMAC RIVER

Potomac Heights

Bennsville

INDIAN HEAD HWY

Maryland Airport

Mason Springs

BUMPY OAK RD

LIVINGSTON RD

Pomfret

MYRTLE GROVE WILDLIFE MANAGEMENT AREA

Marshalls Corner

MARSHALL CORNER RD

POMFRET RD

LA PLATA RD

La Plata

HAWTHORNE DR

ROSE HILL RD

POORHOUSE RD

RIDLEY RD

DONCASTER RD

CHARLES ST

WASHINGTON AVE

ST MARYS AVE

Port Tobacco

Port Tobacco Courthouse Historic Site

BIKE ROUTE
ALTERNATE ROUTE
TRAIL
POINT OF INTEREST
FOOD AVAILABLE
AMERICAN YOUTH HOSTEL

CHAPEL POINT RD

Chapel Point River

Newtown

NEWTON RD

0   1   2   3   4 MILES
SCALE

Port Tobacco

CHAPEL POINT STATE PARK

St Ignatius Church

FAIRGROUNDS RD

BEL ALTON RD

Bel Alton

BLOSSOM POINT RD

Nanjemoy Creek

US MILITARY RESERVATION
(BLOSSOM POINT PROVING GROUNDS)

CONRAIL

NORTH

White Plains

Bennsville

Middletown

26. PORTSIDE PACER
Charles County, Md.

MILES DIRECTIONS & COMMENTS

0.0   Cross MD 210 at stop sign to go **southeast** on **MD 227.** Restaurant.

1.4   **Left** to stay on **MD 227** (Pomfret Road).

4.6   **Right** on **MARSHALL CORNER ROAD.**

6.7   **Straight** on **ROSE HILL ROAD.** Historical marker. Cross MD 225.

9.4   **Left** on **MD 6** (Doncaster Road).

9.7   **Right** on **CHAPEL POINT ROAD.** Barbecue stand, store.

10.0   Port Tobacco Courthouse Historical Site and Museum on right. Water from pump in front yard.

13.5   St. Ignatius Church with scenic river view. **Left** to stay on **CHAPEL POINT ROAD.** Water available from spigot in front of church. Chapel Point State Park on left.

13.8   Historical marker, St. Ignatius Church.

15.9   **Straight** on **BEL ALTON-NEWTOWN ROAD,** crossing US 301. Convenience store.

16.2   **Left** on **FAIRGROUNDS ROAD.** Pass historical marker.

18.6   **Straight** on **US 301** (shoulder).

19.2   **Right** on **ST. MARYS AVENUE.**

21.1   **Right** on **CHARLES STREET** in La Plata. Historical courthouse and Episcopal church. Farmers market and supermarket one block away.

21.2   **Left** on **WASHINGTON AVENUE.**

21.8   **Left** on **HAWTHORNE DRIVE.**

22.1   **Straight** on **MD 225** (La Plata Road), crossing US 301. Fast food, convenience store.

25.5   **Right** on **MARSHALL CORNER ROAD.**

25.6   **Left** on **BUMPY OAK ROAD.** Pass Myrtle Grove Wildlife Refuge on left, Maryland Airport on right. Refuge entrance is on MD 225, 2.2 miles west of Bumpy Oak Road.

30.2   **Right** on **MD 224** (Livingston Road, no sign).

30.7   **Merge left** on **MD 227.**

32.2   **Arrive** at **BRYANS ROAD SHOPPING CENTER.**

27. DELAWARE-MARYLAND FLATLAND

On this ride you will explore picturesque farm country of the northern Delmarva Peninsula while traveling on sparsely trafficked roads through old towns and the Silver Run State Wildlife Management Area. Look forward to flocks of ducks, geese and swans to accompany you on your trip.

If you are making good time, a stop in Odessa provides a rewarding diversion. The small town contains part of Winterthur, the country estate of H.F. duPont, scion of the Delaware industrial family. A museum and two historic houses preserve treasures of 18th century Americana. The town was a leading commercial center until the mid-19th century and is now on the National Register of Historic Places.

START: Bohemia Manor High School on MD 213, one mile south of Chesapeake City in Cecil County, Md. From the Capital Beltway, take US 50 East, cross the Bay Bridge and continue north on US 301. Turn left onto MD 313, at sign for Galena. This becomes MD 213 in Cecil County. School is on left, largely obscured by trees. Opposite is a Texaco Station and Jack and Helen's Restaurant. Chesapeake City is 88 miles northeast of the Capital Beltway.

LENGTH: 48.2 miles. Tour can easily be shortened (for example: cut out loop to canal by staying straight at 16.8 miles).

TERRAIN: Level.

POINTS OF INTEREST: Historic towns of Chesapeake City (410-885-5233) at start; C&D Canal and Museum at 2.1 miles (open daily except Sundays in the winter); colorful town of Port Penn, Port Penn Museum (302-834-7525) and Augustine State Wildlife Management Area at 24.6 miles; swimming at Augustine Beach at 25.6 miles, just across the Delaware River from the Salem, N.J. Nuclear Power Plant; Silver Run State Wildlife Area at 27.7 miles; and Winterthur (302-654-1548) at 31.4 miles, including museum and gardens, Corbit-Sharp House (1774) and Wilson-Warner House (1769) (admission charged, 302-378-2681).

FOOD: Groceries at 1.6, 24.9 and 32.5 miles. Restaurants at start.

LODGING: At Lums Pond State Park (302-368-6989), campgrounds on the northern shore of C&D Canal on DE 71 in Kirkwood, Del.

MAPS AND INFORMATION: Newcastle County, Del. and Cecil County, Md. road maps; Delaware and Maryland state highway maps. Chesapeake City Visitors Center (410-885-5233).

MILES   DIRECTIONS & COMMENTS

0.0   **Left** (north) on **MD 213.**

1.2   **Right** on **MD 286** just before bridge.

1.6   **Right** to stay on **MD 286** (second street). Groceries at Pyles Store.

2.1   **Right** to stay on **MD 286** at T. C&D Canal Museum and picnic area on left.

3.4   Cross Old Telegraph Road.

5.4   **Left** on **CHOPTANK ROAD** (DE 433) at T.

6.3   **Right** on **DE 71/896.** *Caution: fast traffic; use shoulder.*

7.0   **Left** on **ROAD 63.** Sign is before left-turn lane.

7.6   **Right** on **ROAD 412** (no sign), just past Summit United Methodist Church on left, in Summit Bridge. Summit railroad bridge (Conrail) visible to left from Road 412.

8.9   Cross railroad tracks.

9.7   **Right** on **ROAD 414.** Tree windbreaks, planted in lines to prevent wind erosion of soil, on both sides of road.

11.2   **Left** on **ROAD 896** (no sign) at T. *Caution: busy road; use shoulder.*

14.2   **Straight** on **ROAD 420,** crossing US 13. *Caution: busy intersection.*

16.8   **Sharp left** on **ROAD 2.** [Note: continue straight here into Port Penn for a shortcut. Pick up cues at 24.6 miles.]

18.1   **Right** on **ROAD 417** (no sign). Pass modern houses, then tidal marshes. C&D Canal on left.

20.8   **Right** to stay on **ROAD 417.** Sand road goes straight.

21.8   **Right** on **SOUTH REEDY POINT ROAD.**

22.6   **Right** on **DE 9** at stop sign. *Caution: 50 mph, two-lane road with no shoulder, but little traffic.*

24.6   **Left** on **MARKET STREET** at T to stay on **DE 9.** Port Penn Museum on right. Augustine State Wildlife Management Area on left.

24.8   **Right** on **CONGRESS STREET** at T to stay on **DE 9.** Grocery on right at 24.9 miles.

25.6   Augustine Beach and picnic area on left. Salem Nuclear Power Plant across Delaware River in New Jersey.

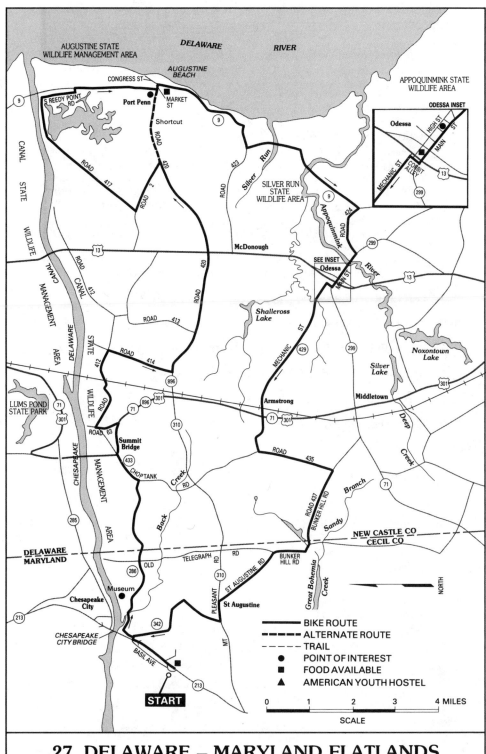

27. DELAWARE – MARYLAND FLATLANDS
Cecil County, Md. & New Castle County, Del.

27.7   **Left** to stay on **DE 9,** where Road 423 goes straight. Pass through Silver Run State Wildlife Area. Tall reed grasses abound. Cross bridge at 28.6 miles.

31.0   **Right** on **ROAD 424** at stop sign.

31.4   **Right** on **DE 299** (Main Street; no sign) at T. Enter historic town of Odessa at 32.0 miles. Winterthur Museum on right, provides directions to historic Corbit-Sharp House and Wilson-Warner House.

32.5   Cross US 13, north and south segments. Grocery store on right. **Straight** on **DE 299** for one-half block, then **right** on **CORBIT ALLEY.**

32.6   **First left** on **MECHANIC STREET** (DE 429). Descend hill, cross one-lane bridge.

36.2   **Straight** on **ROAD 429,** crossing US 301 (DE 71, Road 39).

37.1   **Left** on **ROAD 435** (no sign) at T. Pass horse farms.

38.9   **Right** on **ROAD 437** at T. More horse farms. Re-enter Maryland.

40.7   **Right** on **BUNKER HILL ROAD** at fork and stop sign. Cross creek.

41.6   **Bear left** on **ST. AUGUSTINE ROAD** at fork.

43.3   **Left** on **MD 310** (Mount Pleasant Road; no sign) at T.

43.9   **Sharp right** on **MD 342.** Church on left.

46.7   **Left** at stop sign.

46.8   Pass under Chesapeake City Bridge. Follow signs for MD 213 South.

47.0   **Left** (south) on **MD 213.**

48.2   **Right** into **HIGH SCHOOL.**

28. ROCK HALL RAMBLE

Looping through two wildlife refuges, this tour is a must for the outdoor enthusiast and especially for bird-watching bicyclists. The Eastern Neck Island National Wildlife Refuge is home to herons and egrets year-round. You also can spot bald eagles, woodpeckers, osprey, quail and doves. Earthbound creatures include deer, rabbits and possum. Remington Farms, the other nature preserve, holds acres of ponds, marshes, fields and woodlands with over 20,000 waterfowl.

Between October and early April the region serves as a feeding and resting ground for migratory waterfowl, such as ducks, swans and geese, as they travel along the Eastern Shore flyway.

Do not miss the Chestertown "tea party" at the end of May, the wildlife in November, and the walking tour sponsored by the Kent County Chamber of Commerce. There is also a farmers' market Saturday mornings in the town park, from June to October.

START: Waterfront at High and Water Streets in Chestertown, Md. From the Capital Beltway, take US 50 East, crossing the Bay Bridge to the Eastern Shore. Take US 301 North, and turn left onto MD 213. Turn left onto Cross Street in Chestertown, and left onto Water Street to High Street. Chestertown is 73 miles northeast of the Capital Beltway.

LENGTH: 49.2 miles. **ALTERNATE ROUTE:** 32.7 miles (eliminates leg to Eastern Neck Island Wildlife Refuge).

TERRAIN: Level. Good ride for novices.

POINTS OF INTEREST: In Chestertown (410-778-0416) at start: Custom House, Buck-Bacchus Store Museum, Geddes Piper House, Bikeworks (410-778-6940), Washington College (1782), historic houses, Old St. Paul's Church (1692) with Tallulah Bankhead grave site (c.1778). Remington Farms at 9.2 miles; Eastern Neck Island National Wildlife Refuge at 21.5 miles, with trails and boat rentals; and Rock Hall at 31.3 miles, a maritime community with a rich history.

FOOD: Markets at start, 11.7 and 31.1 miles. Snack bar and restaurant at start and 37.6 miles.

LODGING: In Chestertown, motels, bed-and-breakfasts and inns include the Imperial (410-778-5000), Mitchell House (410-778-6500) and the White Swan Tavern (410-778-2300). South of Chestertown, Courtyard Inn (410-778-2755) on MD 213 and Duck Neck Campground (410-778-3070). In Rock Hall, Mariner's Motel (410-639-2291).

MAPS AND INFORMATION: Kent County, Md. road map. Kent County Chamber of Commerce, 400 High Street (410-778-0416).

MILES   DIRECTIONS & COMMENTS

0.0   Go **northwest** away from river on **HIGH STREET.** Custom House at corner.

0.2   **Left** on **QUEEN STREET** (MD 289).

1.4   Pass Chester River Yacht and Country Club on right, and go **straight** on **QUAKER NECK ROAD.**

3.1   **Right** on **LANGFORD-POMONA ROAD** at T. Sign on post at grocery just before intersection.

4.6   **Straight** on **RICAUDS BRANCH LANGFORD ROAD,** crossing Broad Neck Road (MD 446).

9.0   Pass Old St. Paul's Episcopal Church and Tallulah Bankhead grave site on right.

9.2   Remington Farms.

9.7   **Left** on **MD 20** (Rock Hall Fairlee Road) at T.

11.7   Store.

13.7   **Left** on **MAIN STREET** (MD 445) in Rock Hall.

13.8   **Right** on **SHARP STREET**. 0.5 miles to docks. **Reverse direction**. Turn **right** on **MD 445** to continue south to Eastern Neck. ALTERNATE ROUTE begins here (see end of cues).

20.7   Cross Eastern Neck Island Bridge.

21.5   Observation Trail on right.

22.0   **Left** on **BOGLES WHARF ROAD** to landing at 22.8 miles. Views of lower Chester River. Portable toilets. **Reverse direction** for return to Rock Hall on **MD 445.**

31.1   **Straight** on **MD 445** (Main Street), crossing MD 20 in Rock Hall. Groceries available.

36.7   **Left** on **MD 21** (Tolchester Beach Road).

37.6   Tolchester Beach on Chesapeake Bay. Snack bar, restaurant, marina. **Reverse direction.**

38.5   **Left** on **BAYSHORE ROAD.**

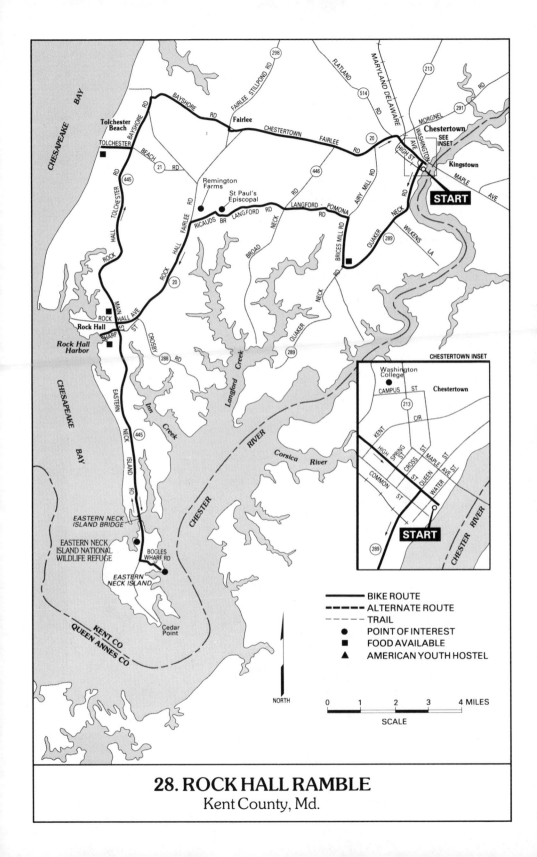

28. ROCK HALL RAMBLE
Kent County, Md.

42.7   **Right** on **MD 298** (unmarked) at T in Fairlee. Go 100 yards, then **first left** on **UNMARKED STREET.**

42.9   **Bear left** on **UNMARKED STREET** in Fairlee.

43.2   **Left** on **MD 20** (Chestertown Fairlee Road).

48.7   **Straight** on **HIGH STREET** in Chestertown. *Caution: grates in road.*

49.2   **Arrive** at **WATER STREET.**

ALTERNATE ROUTE

At approximately 13.8 miles, turn **left** instead of right on **MD 445** for shorter tour. Pick up cues at 36.7 miles.

29. ST. MICHAELS SCRAMBLE

This delightful, popular ride loops through the quaint towns of Oxford and St. Michaels and takes you through some of the mid-Atlantic's best cycling and bird watching territory. Most of the Delmarva Peninsula is worth exploring by bicycle, so use this route as a base to discover the area on your own.

In St. Michaels you will enjoy parks, antique shops and the Chesapeake Bay Maritime Museum. The Oxford-Bellevue ferry, established in 1683, departs every 20 minutes from Oxford (it does not operate from mid-December to February). Oxford also has a nice park, beach and shops, including a unique hardware-gourmet-bicycle shop that should not be missed.

If you continue past St. Michaels, you reach the fishing community of Tilghman Island. Seemingly cut off from the 20th century, Tilghman Island is the home of the Chesapeake Skipjack Fleet (410-822-2807).

START: YMCA on MD 333 in Easton, Md. From the Capital Beltway, take US 50 East, cross the Bay Bridge and continue to Easton on Maryland's Eastern Shore. In Easton, bear right onto MD 322, and continue 3.5 miles. Turn left onto MD 333. The YMCA is on the right. Do not turn onto MD 33! Easton is 74 miles east of the Capital Beltway.

LENGTH: 28.9 miles.

TERRAIN: Level, with signed, on-road bike lanes most of the way.

POINTS OF INTEREST: Easton at start, with waterfowl festival in early November, Historic District (410-822-0773) with museum and tours; Oxford at 9.6 miles, with beach, park, shops and Oxford-Bellevue ferry (410-745-9023; $1.50 for bicycles); St. Michaels at 17.0 miles, with parks, shops, the famous Crab Claw Restaurant (410-745-2900) and the Chesapeake Bay Maritime Museum (410-745-2916) at 17.4 miles. Fishing and sailing areas along the route.

FOOD: Markets at start, 9.6, 12.8 and 17.0 miles. Restaurants at start, 9.6 and 17.0 miles.

LODGING: In Easton, four motels, a tourist home and the Tidewater Inn (410-822-1300). In Royal Oak, Pasadena Conference Center (410-745-5053), with bountiful home-cooked food and special care for bicyclists. In Oxford, Robert Morris Inn (410-226-5111). In St. Michaels, inns include Tarr House (410-745-3419), Kemp House (410-745-2243), Two Swan Inn (410-745-2929) and Wades Point Inn (410-745-2500).

MAPS AND INFORMATION: Talbot County, Md. road map; Maryland state highway map. St. Michaels Visitor Center (410-745-2916).

MILES   DIRECTIONS & COMMENTS

0.0   **Left** out of YMCA parking lot, to go southwest on **MD 333** (Peach Blossom Road). Bike lane on road.

9.6   Enter Oxford. Bike shop, delicatessen and restaurant on right, and park and beach on left. Stay on **MD 333** (Morris Street) to Oxford-Bellevue ferry across Tred Avon River.

9.8   In Bellevue, take **BELLEVUE ROAD** toward Royal Oak.

12.8   **Left** on **MD 329** at T. General store, antiques shop. Pass Pasadena Conference Center on right.

13.8   **Left** on **MD 33** at T. *Caution: fast-moving traffic.* Signed on-road bike lane.

17.0   Enter St. Michaels. Inns, restaurants, antique shops.

17.3   **Right** on **MILL STREET**. Pass historic homes.

17.4   **Arrive** at maritime museum, gift shops and the famous Crab Claw restaurant near end of street. **Reverse direction.**

17.5   **Left** on **MD 33.** (A right turn here will take you to Tilghman Island, at the end of MD 33 in 13 miles.)

27.4   **Right** on **MD 322** in Easton.

28.8   **Left** on **MD 33** (Peach Blossom Road). *Caution: traffic.*

28.9   **Right** into **YMCA PARKING LOT.**

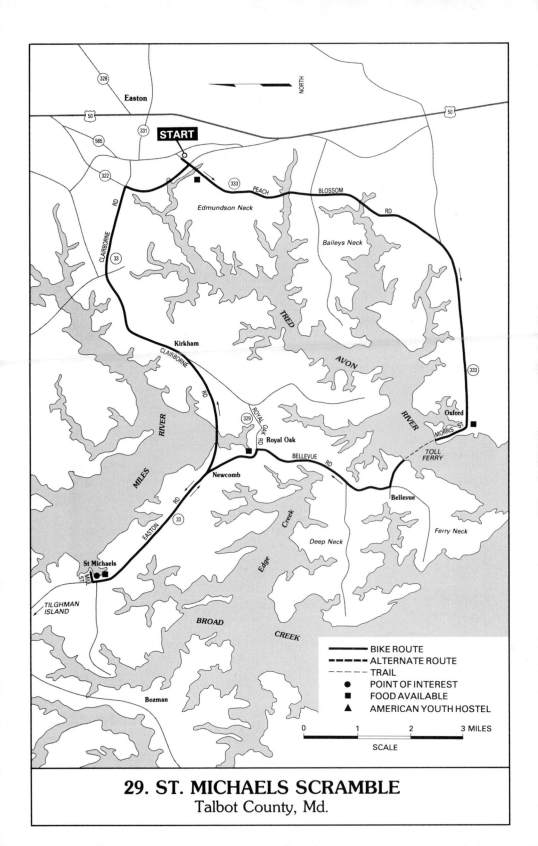

29. ST. MICHAELS SCRAMBLE
Talbot County, Md.

30. BLACKWATER WILDLIFE REFUGE RIDE

Starting from the town of Cambridge, Md., this ride swings through Blackwater National Wildlife Refuge. Famous for its flocks of geese and ducks, the refuge also is home for muskrat, deer and many other animals. A visit in fall, winter and early spring avoids the hot summer months when flying insects can be a nuisance.

Historic High Street in Cambridge features old Victorian homes. For extended touring, try MD 343, which travels west of Cambridge and has a bike lane. So does MD 16, which takes you to Taylors Island. Or you may want to take MD 335 west from mile 24.9 to Hooper Island, with its fishing villages and splendid views of the Chesapeake Bay. Many bicycling opportunities exist in this area -- stay off US 50 and you won't go wrong!

START: South Dorchester High School at the corner of Church Creek Road (MD 16) and Maple Dam Road (Race Street) in Cambridge, Md. From the Capital Beltway, take US 50 East across the Bay Bridge to Cambridge. Turn right in town onto Washington Street, then left onto Race Street. School is just past Church Creek Road on the right. Cambridge is 90 miles southeast of the Capital Beltway.

LENGTH: 42.1 miles.

TERRAIN: Level.

POINTS OF INTEREST: Picturesque town of Cambridge (410-228-3234) at start, with High Street, museums, Meredith House (1760), beachfront areas and a bike shop at Race and Elm Streets; Blackwater National Wildlife Refuge Visitor Center at 33.2 miles, with 20-minute movie and exhibits, observation tower and two-mile Wildlife Drive (15 mph speed limit).

FOOD: Markets at 23.0 and 29.0 miles. Best to bring lunch with you.

LODGING: In Cambridge, Quality Inn (410-228-6900) at US 50 and Crusader Road.

MAPS AND INFORMATION: Dorchester County, Md. road map. Cambridge Visitor Center (410-228-3234).

MILES   DIRECTIONS & COMMENTS

0.0   **Right** out of parking lot, to go south on **MAPLE DAM ROAD.** Pass through Blackwater National Wildlife Refuge.

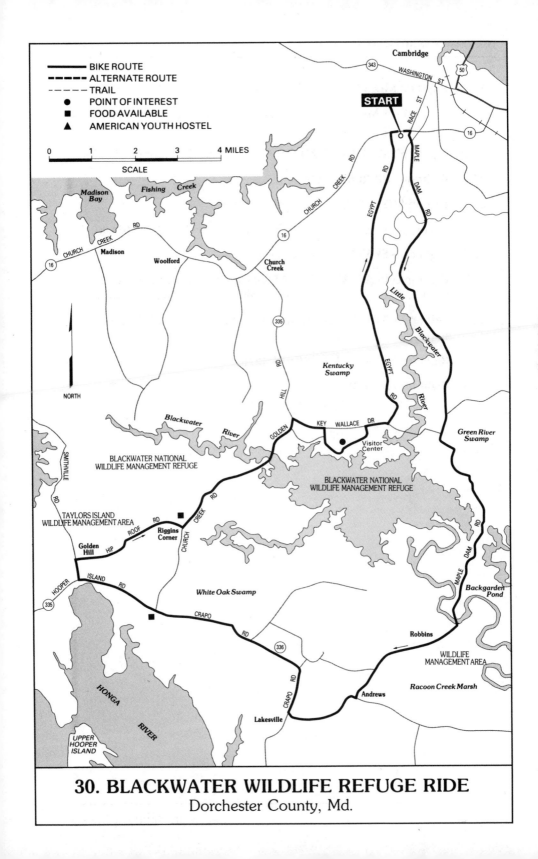

30. BLACKWATER WILDLIFE REFUGE RIDE
Dorchester County, Md.

18.1 **Right** on **MD 336** (Crapo Road) at T.

23.0 **Straight** on **MD 335** (Hooper Island Road) at Church Creek Road. Marina with food available.

24.9 **Right** on **SMITHVILLE ROAD.** (Straight here for Hooper Island.)

25.4 **Right** on **HIP ROOF ROAD**.

28.3 **Left** on **MD 335** (Church Creek Road) at T.

29.0 Small general store on left. MD 335 becomes **GOLDEN HILL ROAD.**

32.2 **Right** on **KEY WALLACE DRIVE.**

33.2 **Right** into **BLACKWATER NATIONAL WILDLIFE REFUGE.** Visitors Center, with water. Exit Refuge, **right** on **KEY WALLACE DRIVE.**

34.5 **Left** on **EGYPT ROAD.** (Straight here to beginning of Wildlife Drive in 0.2 miles, with Observation Tower.)

41.7 **Right** on **MD 16** (Church Creek Road).

42.1 **Right** into **SCHOOL.**

31. GHOST TOWN GAMBOL

Passing through wildlife refuges, open countryside and desolate swamps, this tour explores the picturesque Delmarva Peninsula. Discover the 17th century fishing town of Chincoteague, Va., whose early inhabitants reportedly prospered by salvaging shipwrecks from nearby Assateague Island.

The tour visits Greenbackville, a charming town of retired farmers, and the ghost town of Franklin City, established in 1876 as the terminus of the Eastern Shore Railroad. For 40 years, Chincoteague Bay oysters were shipped north by rail to urban "foreigners." Franklin City's prosperity abruptly ended with the construction of the Chincoteague causeway.

START: Refuge Motor Inn at the intersection of VA 175 and VA 679 in Chincoteague, Va. From the Capital Beltway, take US 50 East across the Bay Bridge and continue to Salisbury, Md. Turn onto US 13 South into Virginia, and then turn left onto VA 175. Continue five miles to VA 679. Chincoteague is 168 miles southeast of the Capital Beltway. **ALTERNATE START:** At 10.0 miles, begin the tour at the grocery store at the intersection of VA 679 and VA 175.

LENGTH: 61.4 miles. From **ALTERNATE START:** 41.4 miles.

TERRAIN: Level.

POINTS OF INTEREST: Chincoteague National Wildlife Refuge (804-336-6161) near start and adjacent Assateague Island National Seashore, connected by bicycle trail (both with famous wild ponies); Wallops Island National Wildlife Refuge at 1.5 miles; Franklin City at 20.5 miles; Greenbackville at 21.8 miles; Vaughn Wildlife Management Area at 23.8 miles.

FOOD: Markets near start, at 10.0, 28.4 (0.3 miles off route) and 43.5 miles.

LODGING: In Chincoteague, motels include Refuge Motor Inn (804-336-5511) at start, campgrounds, four bed-and-breakfasts: Year of the Horse Inn, 3583 Main Street (804-336-3221); Channel Bass Inn, 6228 Church Street (804-336-6148); Little Traveler Inn, 4160 Main Street (804-336-5436); Miss Molly's Inn, 4141 Main Street (804-336-6686). For general bed-and-breakfast information call 804-627-1983.

MAPS AND INFORMATION: Accomack County, Va. and Worcester County, Md. road maps; *ADC Chesapeake Bay Regional Map.* For information on Chincoteague and Assateague, call 804-336-6161. For information on a 100-mile Worcester County loop, contact: Worcester County Extension Service, P.O. Box 219, Snow Hill, MD 21863-0219 (410-632-1972). Worcester County Tourism (410-632-3617).

MILES   DIRECTIONS & COMMENTS

0.0   **Left** out of Refuge Motor Inn parking lot on **MADDOX BOULEVARD.**

1.0   **Left** on **MAIN STREET** (VA 175) at T.

1.5   **Right** on **VA 175** causeway. May be windy. Wallops Island National Wildlife Refuge on left.

10.0 **Right** on **VA 679.** Grocery. ALTERNATE START begins here.

15.5 **Right** to stay on **VA 679** at T.

20.0 **Arrive** at **FRANKLIN CITY**, end of road. **Reverse direction.**

20.5 **Right** on **GREENBACKVILLE ROAD.** Enter Maryland.

21.8 **Right** to stay on **GREENBACKVILLE ROAD** at fork.

23.8 **Right** on **GEORGE ISLAND LANDING ROAD** (MD 366). Vaughn Wildlife Management Area on left. **Arrive** at **PARKER BAY**, end of road. **Reverse direction.**

28.4 **Straight** on **POCOMOKE STOCKTON ROAD**, crossing MD 12. Pettit's on MD 12, 0.3 miles to left.

33.4 **Left** on **BOSTON ROAD.**

34.7 **Right** on **SHEEPHOUSE ROAD.** May be unmarked.

35.1 **Left** on **BUCK HARBOR ROAD** (Boston Schoolhouse Road).

36.6 **Left** on **BRANTLEY ROAD** (may be unmarked).

36.8 **Right** on **PAYNE ROAD.**

38.1 **Bear left** on **CRITCHER ROAD** (may be unmarked).

38.9 **Right** on **MD 711** (may be unmarked). Re-enter Virginia.

39.4 **Left** on **VA 710** at T.

39.8 **Left** on **VA 712.**

43.5 **Right** on **VA 679.** Grocery store.

48.9 **Left** on **VA 175.** Ride from alternate start ends.

56.9 **Left** on **MAIN STREET.**

60.4 **Right** on **MADDOX BOULEVARD.**

61.4 **Right** into **REFUGE MOTOR INN.**

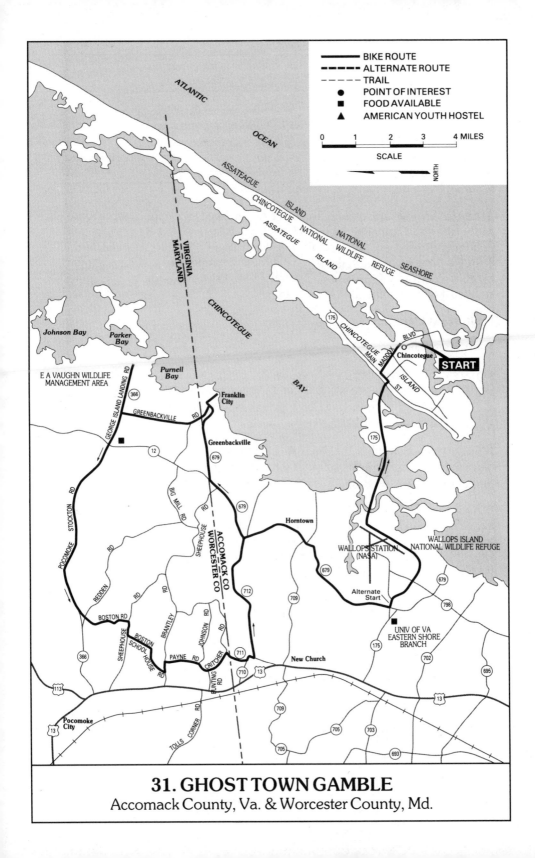

31. GHOST TOWN GAMBLE
Accomack County, Va. & Worcester County, Md.

32. FERRY FLAT TOUR

On this Eastern Shore loop you will experience lightly trafficked roads in scenic rural areas, punctuated by two river crossings on cable-ferries. The ferries transport up to six passengers at no charge. This trip is recommended for early in the season and can be combined with the Nassawango Natural (Tour 23) for a memorable bicycling weekend.

START: Washington Hotel on Somerset Avenue (MD 675) in Princess Anne, Md. From the Capital Beltway, take US 50 East over the Bay Bridge and continue to Salisbury. Turn south onto US 13 and continue 11 miles to the Princess Anne turn-off (on the left). Continue two miles to the center of town; hotel is on Somerset Avenue, on the right. Princess Anne is 130 miles southeast of the Capital Beltway.

LENGTH: 35.5 miles.

TERRAIN: Level.

POINTS OF INTEREST: Princess Anne (410-651-2968) at start, with Washington Hotel (1774), Prince William Street, Teackle Mansion ($2 admission, open Sundays 2 p.m. to 4 p.m.), old jail (one block behind Hotel); Mount Vernon Wharf at 9.4 miles; and cable-ferries at 14.0 and 24.2 miles.

FOOD: Markets at start, 28.2 (may be closed) and 23.9 miles (five miles east of route in Salisbury). Restaurants at start (Washington Hotel has an excellent dining room), 9.4 miles and 23.9 miles (five miles east of route in Salisbury).

LODGING: In Princess Anne, Washington Hotel (410-651-2525) at start, Elmwood Inn (410-651-1066), bed-and-breakfasts on Prince William Street, motels on US 13. Just north of Princess Anne, Princess Anne Campground on US 13 (410-651-1520). Near Snow Hill, inns include Chanceford Hall (410-632-2231) and Snow Hill Inn (410-632-2102).

MAPS AND INFORMATION: Somerset and Wicomico Counties, Md. road maps. Princess Anne Visitor Center (410-651-2968).

MILES   DIRECTIONS & COMMENTS

0.0   **Right** from front of hotel on **SOMERSET AVENUE** (MD 675).

0.1   **Right** on **PRINCE WILLIAM STREET**.

0.2   Teackle Mansion. **Jog right** on **MD 363** (Deal Island Road). Cross under US 13.

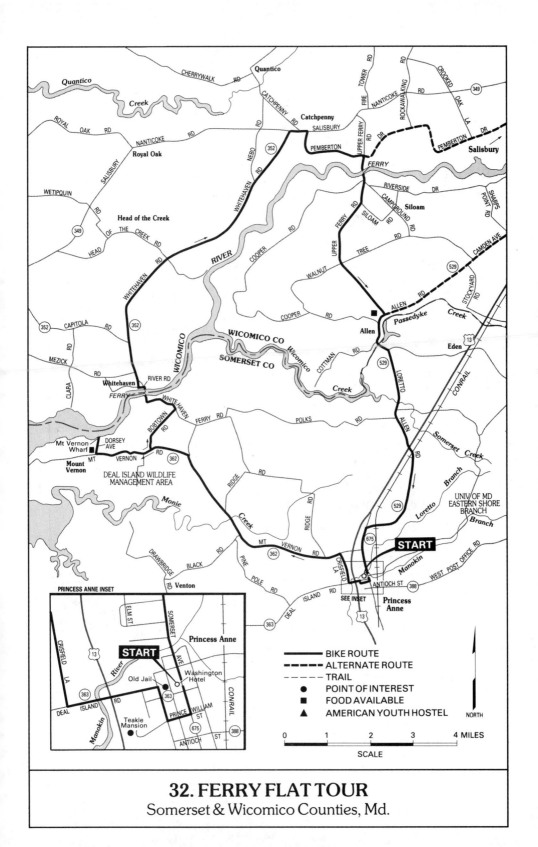

32. FERRY FLAT TOUR
Somerset & Wicomico Counties, Md.

0.6   **Right** on **CRISFIELD LANE.**

1.3   **Left** on **MOUNT VERNON ROAD** (MD 362) at T.

5.8   **Bear left** to stay on **MD 362.**

9.1   **Right** on **DORSEY AVENUE.**

9.4   Mount Vernon Wharf. Restaurant. **Reverse direction.**

9.6   **Left** on **MOUNT VERNON ROAD.**

12.0   **Left** on **BOBTOWN ROAD.**

13.1   **Left** on **WHITEHAVEN FERRY ROAD.**

14.0   Take **ferry** across Wicomico River into Wicomico County. After ferry, **left** on **RIVER ROAD**.

14.1   **Right** on **RIVER ROAD** at T. Becomes **WHITEHAVEN ROAD** (MD 352).

21.6   **Right** on **SALISBURY NANTICOKE ROAD** (MD 349).

22.0   **Right** on **PEMBERTON DRIVE.**

23.9   **Right** on **UPPER FERRY ROAD.** [Note: continue straight (east) on Pemberton Drive five miles into Salisbury for a wide selection of food and sights. Return south from Salisbury on Camden Avenue (MD 529), which becomes Allen Road. Pick up the cues at 28.2 miles. This change bypasses the Upper Ferry and adds approximately eight miles to the tour.]

24.2   Take **ferry** at Upper Ferry and ride back across Wicomico River.

28.2   **Right** on **ALLEN ROAD** at T in Allen. Store.

28.9   Cross county line back into Somerset County.

29.1   **Bear right** on **LORETTO ALLEN ROAD** (MD 529).

31.6   Cross US 13 and railroad tracks. *Caution: traffic.*

34.2   **Left** on **MD 675** (Somerset Avenue) at T in Princess Anne.

35.5   **Right** into **HOTEL.**

III. Old Dominion

33. SHENANDOAH VALLEY VENTURE

Traversing scenic farmland and picturesque small towns, this tour explores the Shenandoah River Valley. Highlights include the Burwell-Morgan Mill on Spout Run Creek. The 1782 stone and clapboard mill once ground grain into meal and flour and served as the commercial outlet for the wheat-growing region. Its wooden gears date to the mid-1700s, and the building remains a notable example of 18th century architecture and technology. Today, the Clarke County Historical Society maintains the mill, and meal and whole wheat flour are still ground and sold there.

Winchester, just west of the tour, was central to Civil War control of the fertile Shenandoah Valley. The town changed hands 72 times over the course of the war, including 13 times in one day. In 1862 Stonewall Jackson routed a much larger Union force commanded by Nathaniel Banks, alarming Federal officials who feared Jackson would wheel east to Washington. In 1864, Union forces under General Philip Sheridan were ordered into the Shenandoah to strip it so clean that "crows flying over it will have to carry their provender." Sheridan smashed Jubal Early's army at Winchester on September 19, driving the Confederate Army from the valley forever and ensuring Lincoln's reelection.

START: Cooley Elementary School at the intersection of BUS VA 7 and VA 636 in Berryville, Va. From the Capital Beltway, take VA 7 West and bear left onto BUS VA 7. Continue to Berryville; school is on the left at the far end of town. Berryville is 46 miles west of the Capital Beltway. **ALTERNATE START:** At 11.9 miles in Millwood. Park at mill. This allows a complete loop.

LENGTH: 45.7 miles. From **ALTERNATE START:** 33.8 miles, including northern loop.

TERRAIN: Rolling hills.

POINTS OF INTEREST: Carter Hall, headquarters of Project Hope, at 11.9 miles; and the Burwell-Morgan Mill (703-837-1799) at 33.9 miles, restored by the Clarke County Historical Society.

FOOD: Markets at 11.9, 24.5 and 33.4 miles. Burwell-Morgan Mill at 33.9 miles makes a good lunch stop.

LODGING: In Winchester, many choices including Travelodge (703-665-0685) at the junction of I-81 and US 17, and Holiday Inn East (703-667-3300) at the junction of US 50 and I-81. In Berryville, bed-and-breakfasts include the Battletown Inn, 102 West Main Street (703-955-4100). In Boyce, River House (703-837-1476). In White Post, L'Auberge Provincale (703-837-1375). In Paris, Ashby Inn (703-592-3900).

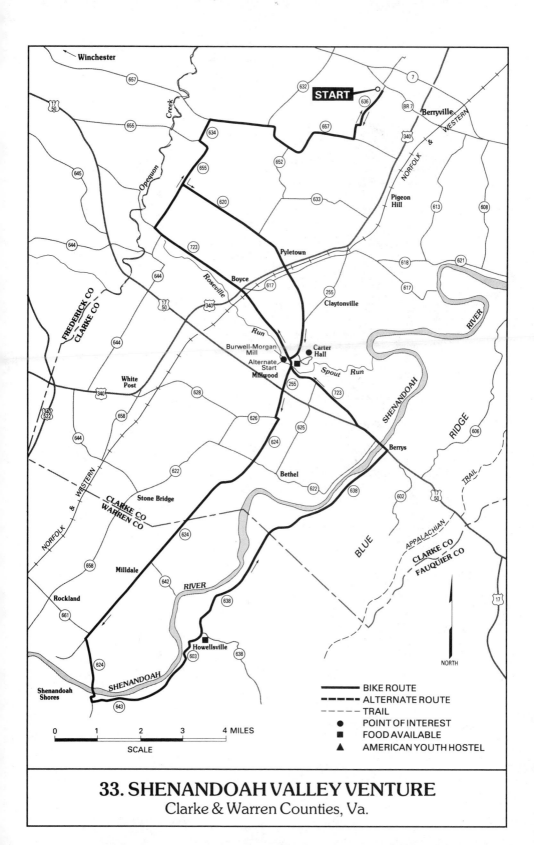

START

Winchester
657
17
50
632
636
BR 7
Berryville
7
655
634
652
NORFOLK & WESTERN
340
645
655
620
633
Pigeon Hill
613
608
644
723
Pyletown
618
621
644
Roseville
Boyce
617
255
Claytonville
617
RIVER
FREDERICK CO
CLARKE CO
644
17
50
340
Run
Burwell-Morgan Mill
Carter Hall
Spout Run
SHENANDOAH
RIDGE
White Post
Alternate Start
Millwood
255
723
606
340
628
522
658
626
625
Berrys
644
624
602
50
622
Bethel
638
TRAIL
CLARKE CO
WARREN CO
Stone Bridge
622
BLUE
APPALACHIAN
CLARKE CO
FAUQUIER CO
624
NORTH
658
Milldale
642
RIVER
638
17
Rockland
661
Shenandoah Shores
624
SHENANDOAH
603
Howellsville
638
643

0   1   2   3   4 MILES
SCALE

——— BIKE ROUTE
- - - ALTERNATE ROUTE
----- TRAIL
● POINT OF INTEREST
■ FOOD AVAILABLE
▲ AMERICAN YOUTH HOSTEL

33. SHENANDOAH VALLEY VENTURE
Clarke & Warren Counties, Va.

MAPS: Clarke and Warren Counties, Va. road maps.

MILES DIRECTIONS & COMMENTS

0.0 **Right** out of school parking lot to go south on **VA 636.**

1.4 **Right** on **VA 657** at T.

5.1 **Left** on **VA 634**.

5.6 **Bear left** on **VA 655.**

6.8 **Left** on **VA 620.**

9.7 Cross US 340. *Caution: traffic.*

11.0 **Bear right** on **VA 255.** *Caution: traffic.*

11.9 **Left** on **VA 723** in Millwood. Carter Hall and grocery store on left. ALTERNATE START begins here.

12.1 **Bear right** on **VA 255.**

12.6 **Straight** on **VA 624**, crossing US 17/50. *Caution: traffic.*

13.2 **Bear left** to stay on **VA 624.**

21.0 Cross Shenandoah River on low water bridge. *Caution: uneven joints.*

21.3 **Left** on **VA 643.**

22.3 **Straight** on **VA 603.**

24.5 **Left** on **VA 638** at T. General store on right.

30.5 **Left** on **US 17/50** at T. *Caution: heavy traffic.*

31.4 **Bear right** on **VA 723.**

33.4 **Bear right** to stay on **VA 723** in Millwood. Grocery store on right.

33.9 Burwell-Morgan Mill on left. Good lunch stop.

35.4 Cross US 340. *Caution: traffic.*

37.7 **Right** on **VA 655.**

40.1 **Bear right** on **VA 634.**

40.6 **Right** on **VA 657** at T.

44.4 **Left** on **VA 636.**

45.7 **Left** into **COOLEY SCHOOL.**

34. HARPERS FERRY 3-STATE TOUR

Leading you back in time, this tour accentuates the beauty and the history of Harpers Ferry, where Maryland, Virginia and West Virginia meet. Harpers Ferry grew from a sleepy 18th century mill town to the site of one of the nation's first gun factories, built at the urging of George Washington in 1796. The U.S. arsenal was captured in an 1859 raid by the notorious abolitionist, John Brown. The day after the raid, 90 marines led by Robert E. Lee and J.E.B. Stuart assaulted the armory and captured Brown. Brown's impassioned pleas in his defense won wide sympathy for his antislavery cause in the North, but he was hanged for treason nonetheless in nearby Charles Town, W.Va.

Harpers Ferry changed hands repeatedly during the Civil War, which destroyed its Potomac River bridge and much of its industry. Harpers Ferry was General Robert E. Lee's objective when his Confederate Army invaded the North, only to be turned away at Antietam (see Antietam Battlefield Loop, Tour 3).

The complete history of Harpers Ferry is explained at Harpers Ferry National Historical Park. From mid-June through Labor Day, National Park Service staff revive the 19th century atmosphere with period costumes, battle reenactments and interpretive displays.

This tour can be combined with Between the Hills to Harpers Ferry (Tour 55).

START: Harpers Ferry AYH-Hostel at 19123 Sandy Hook Road in Knoxville, Md. From the Capital Beltway, take I-270 North to Frederick and exit onto US 340 West (toward Charles Town, W.Va.). Continue 16 miles west on US 340 and turn left onto Keep Tryst Road (MD 180) at blinking yellow light. (If you cross over the bridge to Virginia, you have gone too far.) Continue 0.8 miles and turn right onto Sandy Hook Road. Hostel is first building on left. Sandy Hook is 75 miles north of Washington (across the Potomac River from Harpers Ferry, W.Va.). Knoxville is 48 miles northwest of the Capital Beltway.

LENGTH: 68.3 miles. **ALTERNATE ROUTE:** 23.3 miles.

TERRAIN: Rolling hills.

POINTS OF INTEREST: Town of Harpers Ferry at 3.2 miles; Harpers Ferry National Historical Park (304-535-6223) at 3.3 miles; and Burwell-Morgan Mill (703-837-1799) at 34.9 miles, restored by the Clarke County Historical Society.

FOOD: Markets at 3.2, 8.2, 13.2 (closed Sundays), 26.4, 39.9, 53.1 and 56.6 miles. Restaurants at 3.2 miles.

LODGING: Near Harpers Ferry, Harpers Ferry AYH-Hostel, 19123 Sandy Hook Road, Knoxville, Md. (301-834-7652); and Hilltop House (800-338-8319), on Ridge Street, 10 blocks from C&O Canal Towpath. At 59.9 miles, Frank's Campground (seasonal). In Charles Town, Carriage Inn (304-728-8003).

MAPS: Washington and Frederick Counties, Md., Jefferson County, W.Va., Clarke and Loudoun Counties, Va. road maps.

MILES   DIRECTIONS & COMMENTS

0.0 **Right** out of hostel driveway, then **first left** on **MD 180.**

0.5 **Right,** then **left** onto **US 340** at signal light. *Caution: traffic; use shoulder.* Walk bike across bridges. Cross Potomac River into Virginia, then cross Shenandoah River into West Virginia.

3.2 **Right** on **SHENANDOAH STREET.** Harpers Ferry National Historical Park is first right after crossing street.

4.0 **Left** on **HIGH STREET.** Climb hill. This becomes **WASHINGTON STREET.**

5.7 **Bear left,** then **right** on **US 340.**

6.4 **Left** on **BLOOMERY ROAD** (WV 27).

8.2 **Bear left** over railroad tracks in Millville, then **left** again. Grocery store.

12.3 **Right** on **WV 9.** ALTERNATE ROUTE begins here (see end of cues).

13.2 **Left** on **KABLETOWN ROAD** (WV 25). Grocery store (closed Sundays).

17.6 Myerstown. Stay on WV 25.

20.4 **Left** on **VA 608** (no sign) at white stucco house. Re-enter Virginia.

24.7 **Right** on **VA 7.**

25.7 **Left** on **BUS VA 7.**

26.4 **Left** on **VA 613,** then **left** to stay on **VA 613.** Grocery store.

29.9 **Right** on **VA 618.**

31.1 **Right** on **VA 617.**

32.0 **Left** on **VA 255.**

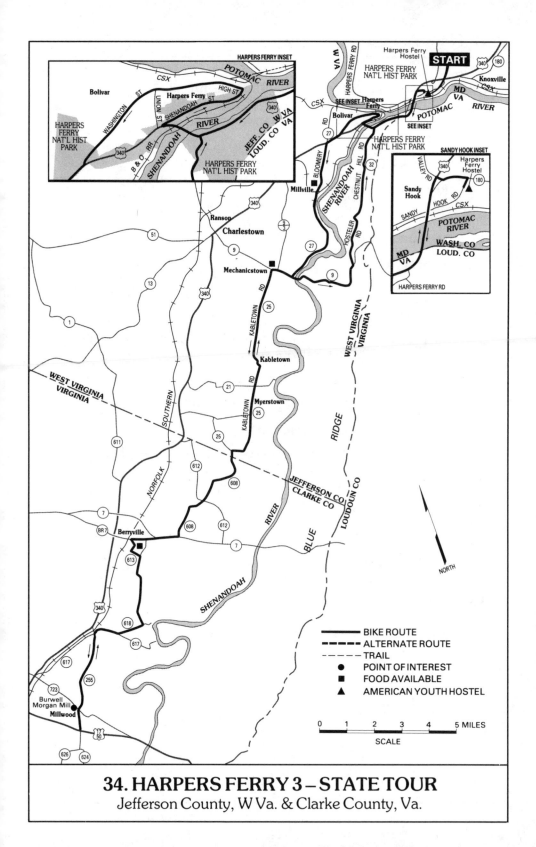

34. HARPERS FERRY 3 – STATE TOUR
Jefferson County, W Va. & Clarke County, Va.

34.9   Millwood. Burwell-Morgan Mill. **Reverse direction.**

37.8   **Right** on **VA 617.**

38.7   **Left** on **VA 618.**

39.9   **Left** on **VA 613. Right** to stay on **VA 613** in Berryville. Grocery store.

43.4   **Right** on **BUS VA 7.**

44.1   **Right** on **VA 7.**

45.1   **Left** on **VA 608.**

49.4   **Right** on **WV 25** (Kabletown Road) in West Virginia.

53.1   Grocery store.

56.6   **Right** on **WV 9.** Grocery.

57.5   Pass WV 27 on left. **Stay straight** on **WV 9.** Cross Shenandoah River and climb steep hill for 1.3 miles.

59.9   Frank's Campground.

60.6   **Left** on **HOSTELER ROAD.** *Caution: sharp, winding road.*

62.1   **Bear left** to stay on **HOSTELER ROAD.**

62.4   **Right** on **CHESTNUT HILL ROAD** (MD 32; no sign). Pass Blue Ridge Reserve on right.

66.3   **Right** on **US 340** at bottom of steep hill. Cross Potomac River. *Caution: traffic.* Walk bike on bridge.

67.9   **Right** on **MD 180** at signal light, then **right** on **SANDY HOOK ROAD**.

68.3   **Left** into **HOSTEL.**

ALTERNATE ROUTE

At 12.3 miles, turn **left** on **WV 9** and continue from 57.5-mile cue.

35. VINEYARD VISIT

Cycle through Virginia's rich wine region and view picture-postcard plantations in horse and hunt country. Enjoy a picnic lunch at Meredyth Vineyards and return to the historic town of Middleburg to see its beautiful homes and craft shops. Later, ride through The Plains, another quaint town of shops and antique stores. All of the roads have very little traffic.

Middleburg was acquired by Rawleigh Chinn in 1731 from the so-called Northern Neck Proprietary, a wilderness area. George Washington, Chinn's cousin, surveyed the area in 1787 and incorporated 50 acres as Middleburg. In 1863 Leven Powell purchased the town, divided it into lots and named all the streets after his Federalist friends. Middleburg soon became renowned for its bountiful hunting opportunities.

Meredyth Vineyards has grown hybrid grapes since 1970. Sip in moderation though -- one of the route's big hills awaits you upon your return to Middleburg!

START: Middleburg Elementary School on VA 626 in Middleburg, Va. From the Capital Beltway, take I-66 West for 33 miles to The Plains/Middleburg exit. Turn right onto VA 55 in The Plains and then take an immediate left onto VA 626. Continue 8.4 miles to Middleburg. Turn right onto US 50 then left onto VA 626 by the Red Fox Tavern. Continue for 0.2 miles; school is on right. Middleburg is 42 miles west of the Capital Beltway.

LENGTH: 36.4 miles.

TERRAIN: Rolling hills, except for two sizable climbs. Almost two miles of dirt road travelling to and from the vineyard.

POINTS OF INTEREST: Middleburg shops, buildings and Red Fox Tavern near start; The Plains at 22.8 miles; Meredyth Vineyards (703-687-6277) at 28.7 miles, which produces wine under its own label (open 10 a.m. to 4 p.m. daily, with free tours); and Piedmont Vineyards (a side trip) on VA 626, 1.7 miles past right turn on VA 679 (at 26.6 miles). Many notable horse farms along the route.

FOOD: Markets near start and at 9.2 miles (open till noon on Sundays). Restaurants near start, at 22.8 and 36.3 miles.

LODGING: In Middleburg, Red Fox Inn and Tavern (703-687-6301). Near Middleburg, Welbourne Inn (703-687-3201), on VA 743 one mile west of VA 611, a 1775 farm listed on the National Register of Historic Places.

MAPS: Loudoun and Fauquier Counties, Va. road maps.

MILES   DIRECTIONS & COMMENTS

0.0 **Right** out of school parking lot to go north on **VA 626** (Pot House Road).

4.7 **Left** on **VA 611** (New Ford Road) at stop sign.

8.5 **Right** on **US 50** at T. *Caution: heavy traffic.*

9.0 **First left** on **VA 713.**

9.2 **Bear left** to stay on **VA 713**. General store (open until noon on Sundays).

14.2 **Left** on **VA 710** at T.

15.3 **Left** on **VA 702.**

18.7 **Right** on **VA 709.**

19.9 **Left** on **VA 707.**

21.2 **Bear right** on **VA 704.**

21.8 **Left** on **VA 55** at T.

22.8 Enter The Plains. Railway Stop store on left. Last food before vineyard.

22.9 **Left** on **VA 626.** Some traffic.

26.6 **Right** on **VA 679** which immediately becomes **VA 628.** [To reach Piedmont Vineyards, continue instead on VA 626 for 1.7 miles.]

27.8 **Left** to stay on **VA 628** at Meredyth Vineyards sign. Dirt road.

28.1 **Left** into **STIRLING FARM.**

28.7 **Arrive** at Meredyth Vineyards. Picnicking and tours. **Reverse direction.**

29.3 **Right** on **VA 628** at farm gate.

29.7 **Left** on **VA 686** at stop sign.

31.9 **Bear left** on **VA 629.**

32.1 **Left** on **VA 776.**

36.3 **Straight** on **VA 626,** crossing US 50 at blinking light. Red Fox Tavern.

36.4 **Right** into **MIDDLEBURG ELEMENTARY SCHOOL.**

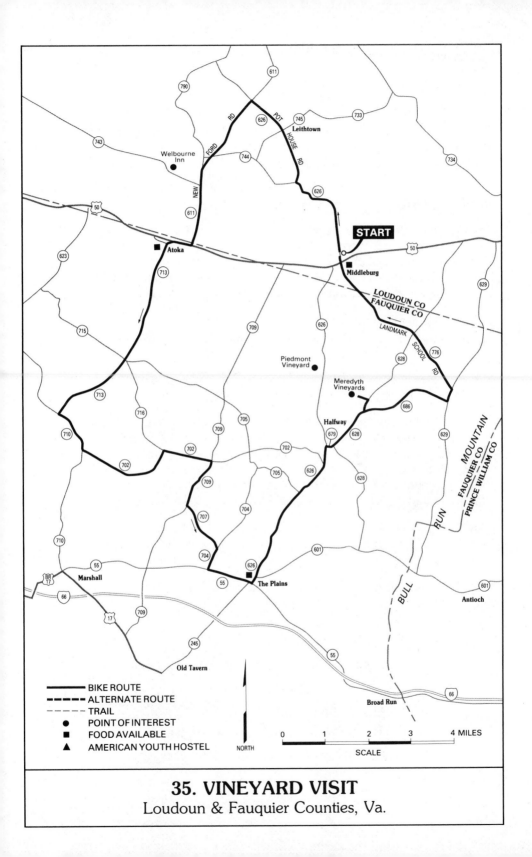

35. VINEYARD VISIT
Loudoun & Fauquier Counties, Va.

36. GREAT FALLS VIRGINIAN

Passing by posh homes, small parks and historical landmarks, this route takes you over lightly trafficked roads from Chain Bridge to Great Falls Park on the Virginia side of the Potomac River.

The alternate route avoids a high traffic segment of North Glebe Road but involves walking your bike up a short wooden staircase!

START: Chain Bridge (D.C. side), off Canal Road NW in Washington, D.C. Chain Bridge is the most northwestern of Washington's Potomac River bridges. Parking available just west of the bridge. Bridge is accessible from C&O Canal Towpath (Tour 65), but you have to walk your bike up stairs. [The starting point is within the Capital Beltway.] **ALTERNATE START:** Virginia side of Chain Bridge in Arlington at North Glebe Road and 41st Street North (see end of cues). **METRO START:** West Falls Church Metro station (Orange Line), 0.3 miles east of Idylwood Road and Leesburg Pike (VA 7), at 6.0 miles.

LENGTH: 36.5 miles.

TERRAIN: Hilly. Some narrow roads with fast-moving cars.

POINTS OF INTEREST: Kirby Park at 4.5 miles; Fairfax County Courthouse at 9.7 miles; Freedom Hill Fort Park at 10.0 miles; Wolf Trap Barns at 12.6 miles; Filene Center at 12.7 miles; Wolf Trap Performing Arts Center at 12.8 miles; Great Falls Park at 16.9 miles; W&OD Trail at 24.4 miles; Freeman House Museum at 26.3 miles; Fort Ethan Allen Civil War site and Gulf Branch Nature Center at 35.1 miles; and Chain Bridge at 35.4 miles.

FOOD: Frequent along the route. Markets at 30.9 and 32.6 miles. Fast food restaurants at 10.0 miles. Buy or bring food for a picnic at Great Falls Park or Freedom Hill Fort Park.

MAPS: *Bikeway Map* (Arlington County, Va.); Arlington and Fairfax Counties, Va. road maps.

MILES   DIRECTIONS & COMMENTS

0.0   Go **south** on **CHAIN BRIDGE** across Potomac River into Virginia.

0.4   **Bear left** on **NORTH GLEBE ROAD** at bridge end. *Caution: steep hill, traffic and no shoulder.* See ALTERNATE START at end of cues.

1.4   **Right** on **CHESTERBROOK ROAD** at traffic light.

2.7   **Left** on **KIRBY ROAD** (VA 695).

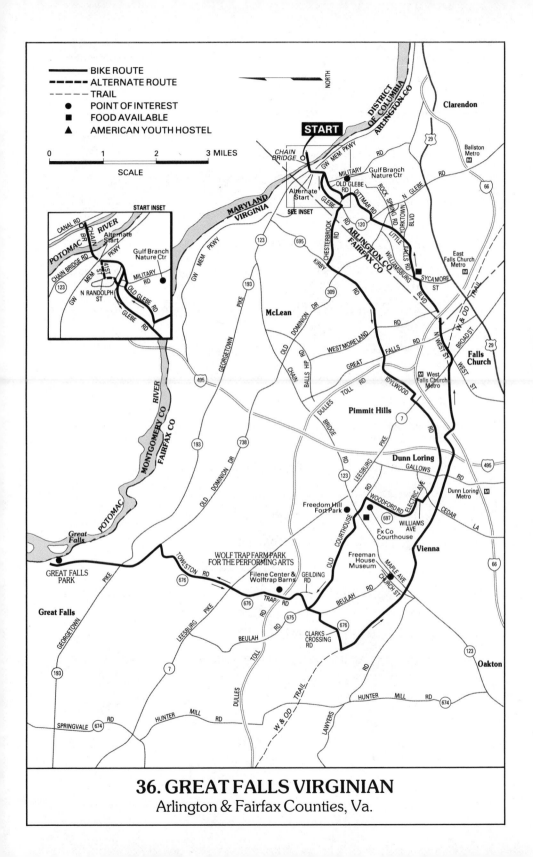

36. GREAT FALLS VIRGINIAN
Arlington & Fairfax Counties, Va.

4.2   Cross Westmoreland Road at traffic light. Pass Kirby Park at 4.5 miles.

4.9   **Straight** on **IDYLWOOD ROAD,** crossing Great Falls Road.

6.0   Cross Leesburg Pike (VA 7). To reach West Falls Church Metro station, go 0.3 miles east from this corner.

8.2   **Right** on **WILLIAMS AVENUE** (VA 896). Development area.

8.4   **Left** on **VA 697** (Electric Avenue). This road follows an old trolley route to Vienna.

8.7   **Right** on **WOODFORD ROAD** (VA 697).

9.7   **Left** on **OLD COURTHOUSE ROAD** at T. Pass Fairfax County Courthouse.

10.0   Cross Chain Bridge Road (VA 123). Fast food, traffic. Buy food here for a picnic in one of the parks.

10.1   **First left** to stay on **OLD COURTHOUSE ROAD.**

10.2   Freedom Hill Fort Park on left. Picnic areas.

12.3   **Right** on **TRAP ROAD** (VA 676).

12.6   Follow Trap Road around to left. Pass Wolf Trap Barns, then Filene Center and Wolf Trap Performing Arts Center, on right.

13.6   **Straight** on **TOWLSTON ROAD.** Road markings unclear.

14.0   Cross Leesburg Pike (VA 7). Beautiful homes.

16.0   **Left** on **OLD DOMINION DRIVE** at T.

16.9   Cross Georgetown Pike (VA 193) into Great Falls Park.

17.9   Parking and picnic area. **Reverse direction.**

18.9   Cross Georgetown Pike (VA 193), staying on **OLD DOMINION DRIVE.**

20.1   **Right** on **TOWLSTON ROAD.**

21.9   **Straight** on **TRAP ROAD**. Pass theaters. **Right** to stay on **TRAP ROAD** and avoid Geilding Road.

23.3   **Straight** on **BEULAH ROAD** (VA 675), crossing Old Courthouse Road.

23.5   **Right** on **CLARKS CROSSING ROAD,** passing horse farm. Follow to end of road.

24.4   **Left** (east) on **W&OD TRAIL.**

26.3   Town of Vienna. Freeman House Museum on left, between Church Street and Maple Avenue (VA 123).

30.9   City of Falls Church. **Right** on **WEST BROAD STREET** (VA 7), pass row of shops and McDonald's on right. **Left** at first traffic light on **WEST STREET.** Follow West Street as it **bears right, then left,** becoming **NORTH WEST STREET.** [Note: future site of a W&OD Trail bicycle overpass over West Broad Street. If the bridge is complete, cross over it and turn left immediately on North West Street.]

31.6   **Bear left** on **WILLIAMSBURG BOULEVARD,** before I-66 overpass.

32.6   **Left** at People's Drug Store (food available on Sycamore Street). **Bear right** on **LITTLE FALLS ROAD,** following signed bike route.

32.9   **Bear right** to stay on **LITTLE FALLS ROAD** at Yorktown Boulevard.

33.4   Cross Yorktown Boulevard, leaving bike route, to stay on **LITTLE FALLS ROAD.**

33.7   **Bear left** to stay on **LITTLE FALLS ROAD** at Rock Spring Road.

34.2   **Straight** on **DITTMAR ROAD** crossing North Glebe Road.

35.1   **Right** on **OLD GLEBE ROAD.** Pass Fort Ethan Allen Civil War site and Gulf Branch Nature Center, both on right.

35.6   **Right** on **MILITARY ROAD** at stop sign, toward Chain Bridge.

35.4   **Left** on **CHAIN BRIDGE RAMP.** Becomes **NORTH GLEBE ROAD.**

36.5   **Arrive** at D.C. side of **CHAIN BRIDGE.**

ALTERNATE START

From Virginia end of Chain Bridge, **bear left** on **NORTH GLEBE ROAD,** then:

0.4   **Immediate right** on **41ST STREET NORTH.** Climb hill.

0.5   **Bear left** toward railroad tie **STAIRCASE.** Carry or walk bike up stairs.

0.6   **Left** on **NORTH RANDOLPH STREET** after leaving path.

0.7   **Right** on **OLD GLEBE ROAD. Bear left** over bridge.

1.1   **Left** on **NORTH GLEBE ROAD** at stop sign.

1.2   **Right** on **CHESTERBROOK ROAD** at traffic light. Pick up main route at 1.4 miles.

37. ARLINGTON HISTORY RIDE

Some of Arlington's best and least-known bicycle paths form the spine of this urban tour, which traces the county's rich history and takes you by interesting historic spots.

A pamphlet available at the Arlington Historical Museum provides a map with historical background for each stop. Historical markers at the sites also furnish general information.

[Note: This route takes you through Fort Myer, an active military base. Identification (such as a driver's license) is required for entry. Fort Myer also may restrict civilian bicycle access without notice. Call the Fort Myer Welcome Center (703-696-3025) for current regulations.]

START: Arlington Historical Museum at 1805 South Arlington Ridge Road in Arlington, Va. From the Pentagon, take Washington Boulevard and exit onto South Joyce Street, going south. Turn right onto 20th Street South. Continue to South Arlington Ridge Road and turn right. Museum is on right. Arlington is located across the Potomac River from Washington. [Arlington is within the Capital Beltway.] **METRO STARTS:** Ballston Metro station (Orange Line) is one block west of route at 6.4 miles; Pentagon City Metro station (Blue and Yellow Lines) is near the start; Arlington Cemetery Metro station (Blue Line) is near the route at 2.5 miles.

LENGTH: 22.8 miles.

TERRAIN: Level with a few steep but short hills. Some gravel on the bike paths.

POINTS OF INTEREST: Arlington Historical Museum (703-892-4204) at start (open Fridays and Saturdays from 11 a.m. to 3 p.m. and Sundays from 2 p.m. to 5 p.m.); Arlington National Cemetery with Tomb of the Unknown Soldier, John Fitzgerald Kennedy and Robert Kennedy memorial grounds and U.S.S. Maine memorial at 2.5 miles; Arlington House at 2.8 miles, home of the Custis family and Robert E. Lee; the Glebe House at 7.2 miles, a colonial parson's farmhouse; Maple Shade Mansion at 9.5 miles; original western cornerstone of the District of Columbia at 11.6 miles; Bon Air Park Rose Garden at 14.6 miles; Ball-Sellers house at 16.5 miles, an early working-class settler's home; George Washington's survey marker at 17.2 miles; and Prospect Hill overlook at 22.4 miles.

FOOD: Frequent along the route. Picnic area at 14.6 miles.

MAPS: *Bikeway Map* (Arlington County, Va.).

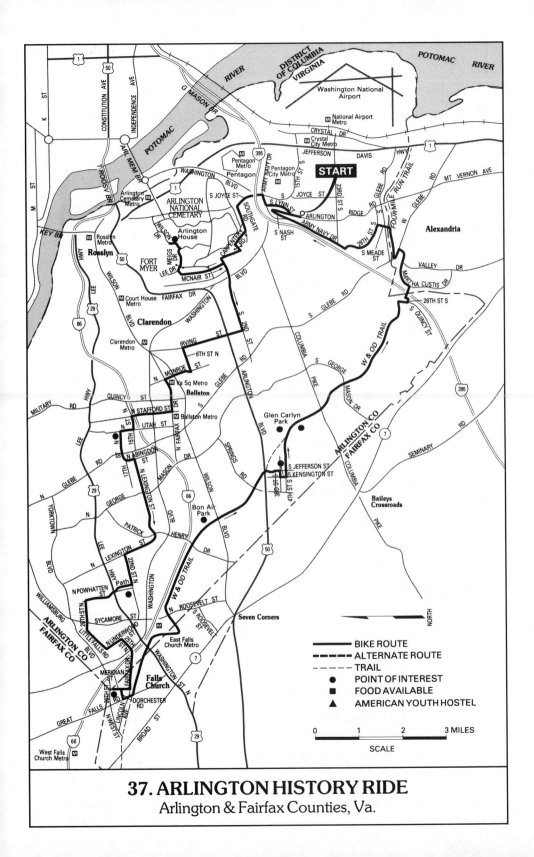

37. ARLINGTON HISTORY RIDE
Arlington & Fairfax Counties, Va.

MILES   DIRECTIONS & COMMENTS

0.0   **Right** out of museum to go north on **SOUTH ARLINGTON RIDGE ROAD.**

0.2   **First right** on **SOUTH LYNN STREET.**

0.6   **First right** on **ARMY-NAVY DRIVE.**

0.7   **First left** on **SOUTH JOYCE STREET,** under I-395. To reach Pentagon City Metro station, go straight on Army-Navy Drive and right on South Hayes Street.

1.0   **Straight** on **SOUTHGATE ROAD.**

1.3   **Bear right** through **HENDERSON HALL GATE.**

1.6   **Right** through **PEDESTRIAN GATE** into Fort Myer. **Straight** on **CARPENTER ROAD,** along red stone wall.

2.0   **Right** on **McNAIR ROAD.**

2.5   **Right** on **LEE DRIVE,** through Arlington Cemetery gate. Becomes **MEIGS DRIVE.**

2.8   **Arrive** at **ARLINGTON HOUSE** on Wilson Drive. **Reverse direction.**

3.1   **Left** on **McNAIR ROAD.**

3.7   **Right** on **CARPENTER ROAD.**

4.6   **Right** on **IRVING STREET.**

5.3   **Left** on **6TH STREET NORTH.**

5.6   **Right** on **NORTH MONROE STREET.**

6.0   **Left** on **NORTH FAIRFAX DRIVE.**

6.4   **Right** on **NORTH STAFFORD STREET.** Ballston historic marker on left. Ballston Metro station ahead on left. To reach Ballston Common Shopping Center with restaurants and fast food, turn left on North Stafford Street.

6.9   **Left** on **15TH STREET NORTH.**

7.0   **Right** on **NORTH UTAH STREET.**

7.2   **Left** on **17TH STREET NORTH.** Pass the Glebe House on right, at 4727 North Glebe Road. Cross North Glebe Road.

7.6   **Left** on **NORTH ABINGDON STREET** at T.

7.7 **Second right** on **16TH STREET NORTH.** *Caution: heavy traffic.*

8.5 **Bear right** on **NORTH LEXINGTON STREET.**

9.1 **Left** on **22ND STREET NORTH.**

9.5 **Right** on **PATH** at 6125 22nd Street North. Maple Shade Mansion on left, at 2230 North Powhatan Street. **Straight** on **NORTH POWHATAN STREET.**

10.0 **Left** on **28TH STREET NORTH.** Cross North Sycamore Street. Becomes **LITTLE FALLS ROAD.**

10.7 **Left** on **NORTH UNDERWOOD STREET.**

10.9 **Right** on **25TH STREET NORTH,** which becomes **NORTH FAIRFAX DRIVE,** crossing I-66. Victorian houses on left.

11.6 **Right** on **MERIDIAN STREET.** Western Boundary Stone on left at 11.8 miles. **Reverse direction.**

11.9 **Right** on **DORCHESTER ROAD.**

12.0 **Left** on **GREAT FALLS ROAD.**

12.1 **Left** on **W&OD TRAIL.** Water at 14.3 miles.

14.6 Pass Bon Air Park Rose Garden and picnic area to left.

16.3 Pass under Arlington Boulevard (US 50) bridge high overhead, and **immediate right** on **GRAVEL PATH** up hill.

16.5 **Left** on **SOUTH JEFFERSON STREET. Right** on **3RD STREET SOUTH.** Ball-Sellers house on left at 5620 3rd Street South.

16.6 **Left** on **SOUTH KENSINGTON STREET. Left** on **4TH STREET SOUTH** into Glencarlyn Park. Hill.

17.2 Pass bridge. **Right** on **W&OD TRAIL.** George Washington's survey marker on right.

19.6 **Right** on **SOUTH QUINCY STREET. First left** on **28TH STREET SOUTH.** Bike shop and food in Shirlington Village. Follow bike route signs to ramp and pedestrian crossway over I-395.

19.9 **Left** on **MARTHA CUSTIS DRIVE** at bottom of ramp.

20.5 **Left** on **WEST GLEBE ROAD** at T.

20.7 **Right** on **FOUR MILE RUN BIKE PATH** at traffic light (South Glebe Road in Arlington).

21.1 **Left** on **SOUTH MEADE STREET.** [Bike path continues to National Airport and Mount Vernon Trail (Tour 62).]

21.2 **First left** on **28TH STREET SOUTH.**

21.7 **Right** on **ARMY-NAVY DRIVE** at T.

22.1 **Straight** on **SOUTH NASH STREET** where Army-Navy Drive curves left.

22.4 **Follow U-turn** on **SOUTH ARLINGTON RIDGE ROAD** at Prospect Hill, a hairpin turn. View Washington skyline.

22.8 **Left** into **ARLINGTON HISTORICAL MUSEUM.**

38. WARRENTON WANDERER

Escape to the Fauquier County countryside on this tour, dotted with farmlands, historic houses and an occasional barking dog. The loop route takes you on low-traffic roads through the charming town of Warrenton. It can be combined with portions of Pedaling the Piedmont (Tour 47) and Warrenton Wanderlust (Tour 50), which both start in Warrenton.

START: Intersection of VA 28 and VA 603 in Calverton, Va. (11 miles southwest of Manassas). From the Capital Beltway, take I-66 West and exit onto VA 28 South (toward Manassas). Continue south to intersection with VA 603 on right. Calverton is 25 miles southwest of the Capital Beltway.

LENGTH: 21.0 miles.

TERRAIN: Rolling hills.

POINTS OF INTEREST: Warrenton at 12.0 miles; and 18th-century Neavil's Mill at 5.3 miles. Historic clapboard houses along the route.

FOOD: Markets at start and 12.0 miles. Restaurants at 12.0 miles.

MAPS: Fauquier County, Va. road map.

MILES   DIRECTIONS & COMMENTS

0.0   Go **north** on **VA 603** (a right turn from Manassas).

3.1   **Left** on **VA 667.**

5.3   **Bear left** to stay on **VA 667.** Pass Neavil's Mill on left.

5.8   **Left** on **VA 602** over bridge, then **right** on **VA 670** at T.

9.8   **Right** on **VA 674** (unmarked; it is 0.3 miles past power plant on left).

10.4   **Left** on **VA 672** (East Street). Pass old and new houses.

11.5   **Right** on **VA 643**, then **right** on **FALMOUTH STREET** at T. Follow it as it turns **left** and becomes **MAIN STREET** in Warrenton.

12.0   **Reverse direction** at Warrenton town center, at BUS VA 211. Many food stops; try lunch at Fergi's (2nd Street, just off Main Street).

12.5   **Bear left** on **VA 643** (Meetze Road).

17.0   **Left** on **VA 616.**

18.2   **Bear right** to stay on **VA 616** before railroad tracks.

20.9   **Left** on **VA 28** at T.

21.0   **Arrive** at **VA 603** intersection.

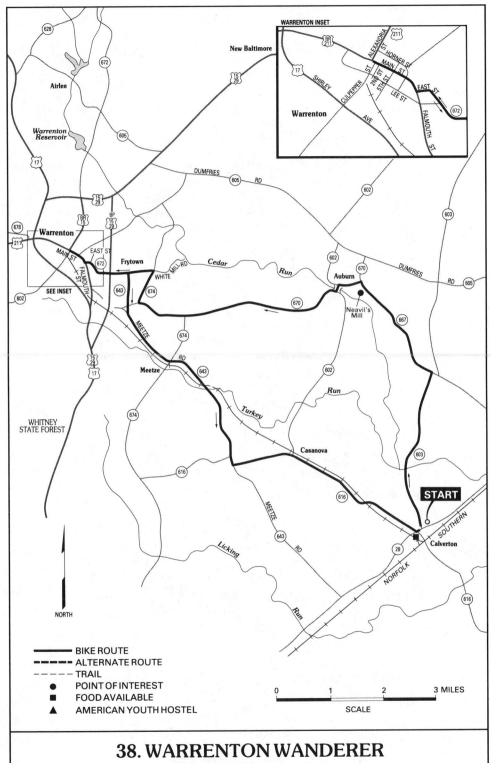

WARRENTON INSET

New Baltimore

Warrenton

Airlee

Warrenton
Reservoir

Frytown

Cedar   Run   Auburn

Neavil's
Mill

DUMFRIES   RD

Meetze

Turkey   Run

Casanova

WHITNEY
STATE FOREST

Licking

START

Calverton

NORFOLK   SOUTHERN

NORTH

——————— BIKE ROUTE
- - - - - - - ALTERNATE ROUTE
– – – – – TRAIL
● POINT OF INTEREST
■ FOOD AVAILABLE
▲ AMERICAN YOUTH HOSTEL

0   1   2   3 MILES

SCALE

38. WARRENTON WANDERER
Fauquier County, Va.

39. HILL HATERS HALF HUNDRED KILOMETERS

Boasting easy hills, aromatic evergreen forests, scenic views of the distant Blue Ridge Mountains and low-traffic roads, this tour offers an ideal route for novice cyclists. Parks and country stores along the way provide rest stops for eating, dawdling or napping. For even lighter traffic, try the alternate route.

START: Brentsville District High School in Nokesville, Va. From the Capital Beltway, take I-66 West for 11 miles and exit onto VA 28 South. Continue south for 14 miles and turn left onto VA 652 (Fitzwater Drive). Continue one mile; school is at end of road. Nokesville is 26 miles southwest of the Capital Beltway.

LENGTH: 32.3 miles. **ALTERNATE ROUTE:** 12.7 miles.

TERRAIN: Easy rolling hills, well maintained surfaces.

POINTS OF INTEREST: Quantico Marine Base with National Cemetery and Marine Corps Museum at 5.5 miles; George Hellwig Memorial Park at 12.5 miles; Brentsville Recreational Area at 17.4 miles, with fitness par course, creek and rope swings; Brentsville Historic Area also at 17.4 miles, with historic marker, jail and courthouse (c.1822) and county parks information center; and Bristow Manor at 19.9 miles, a beautifully preserved old mansion. Dairy farms, hardwood and evergreen forests along the route.

FOOD: Markets (open Sundays) at 5.5, 12.0, 17.4 and 25.1 miles.

MAPS: Prince William County, Va. road map.

MILES   DIRECTIONS & COMMENTS

0.0   Go **right** out of high school on **ADEN ROAD** (VA 646).

0.7   **Right** on **COLVIN LANE** (VA 671).

2.6   **Right** on **VALLEY VIEW DRIVE** (VA 611). Pass cemetery on right.

3.6   **Right** on **PARKGATE DRIVE** (VA 653).

3.8   **First left** on **FLEETWOOD DRIVE** (VA 611).

5.5   **Left** on **ADEN ROAD** (VA 646). General store at Aden Crossroads. Traffic. Pass Quantico Marine Base with cemetery and museum on right. ALTERNATE ROUTE begins here (see end of cues).

11.7   **Left** on **JOPLIN ROAD** (VA 619).

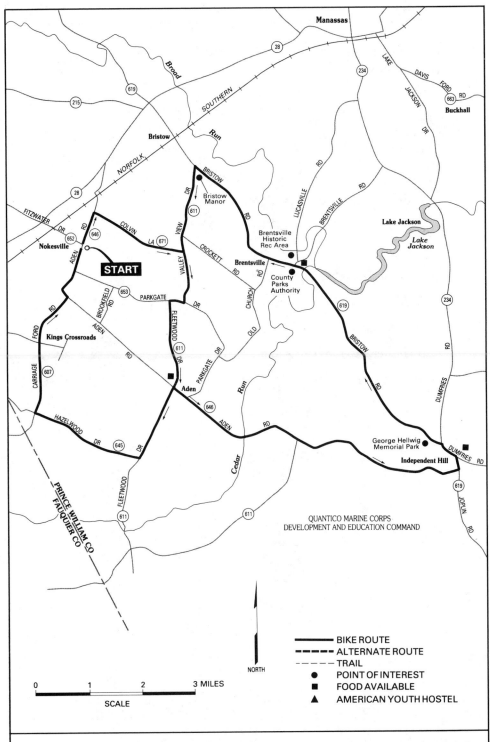

39. HILL HATERS HALF HUNDRED KILOMETERS
Prince William County, Va.

12.0   **Left** on **DUMFRIES ROAD** (VA 234) in Independent Hill. *Caution: busy intersection.* General store, park office, old courthouse.

12.4   **Bear left** on **BRISTOW ROAD** (VA 619). George Hellwig Memorial Park (with toilets) on left. Shaded road through forest.

17.4   Brentsville Recreational Area on right. General store and Brentsville Historic Area.

19.9   **Left** on **VALLEY VIEW DRIVE** (VA 611). Bristow Manor on left.

22.5   **Right** on **PARKGATE ROAD** (VA 653).

23.4   **Left** on **FLEETWOOD DRIVE** (VA 611).

25.1   Aden Road intersection. General store.

25.9   **Right** on **HAZELWOOD DRIVE** (VA 645).

28.0   **Right** on **CARRIAGE FORD ROAD** (VA 607) at T.

30.0   **Left** on **ADEN ROAD** (VA 646) at T. Victory Baptist Church on left.

32.3   **Right** into **SCHOOL PARKING LOT.**

ALTERNATE ROUTE

This alternate route eliminates the more-trafficked first loop of the tour. Simply skip over the first few cues and begin at 5.5 miles, following next cue at 26.6 miles.

40. MANASSAS MAULER

The Manassas National Battlefield Park is the centerpiece of this enjoyable tour.

The 1861 Manassas engagement marked the first major battle of the Civil War. Confederate forces under Generals Pierre Beauregard and Stonewall Jackson held off a larger Union army at Bull Run. The Federal troops fled with the arrival of Confederate reinforcements under General Joseph Johnston.

Thirteen months later, in August 1862, Stonewall Jackson's Confederate forces decimated General John Pope's Union army in the Second Battle of Manassas, on virtually the same spot. More than 25,000 lives were lost, five times the previous engagement.

As the Confederate victory did not result in much-sought intervention by European nations, General Robert E. Lee set his eyes on the Union arsenal at Harpers Ferry. He crossed the Potomac River to the Maryland village of Sharpsburg for the fateful battle of Antietam (see Antietam Battlefield Loop, Tour 3).

The Third Battle of Manassas was fought from 1988 to 1989, when historic preservationists successfully persuaded the U.S. Congress to claim land adjacent to the National Battlefield to protect the historic park from encroachment by commercial development.

START: Burke Town Plaza Shopping Center at the intersection of Old Keene Mill Road, Lee Chapel Road and Burke Center Parkway in Burke, Va. From the Capital Beltway, take I-95 South and exit onto Old Keene Mill Road (VA 644), the first exit to Springfield. Continue west for five miles; shopping center is on the right. Burke is six miles southwest of the Capital Beltway.

LENGTH: 42.2 miles.

TERRAIN: Hilly. Bent Tree Lane and part of Signal Hill Road are unpaved for one mile, and may be unsuitable for narrow tires.

POINTS OF INTEREST: Burke Lake County Park at 4.4 miles, with camping, bike trail, boating; picturesque town of Clifton at 7.6 miles; Manassas National Battlefield Park (703-754-7107) at 19.8 miles; Manassas Museum (703-368-1873) at 25.6 miles (open Tuesday-Sunday, 10 a.m. to 5 p.m.); Bull Run Regional Park at 31.1 miles; and Fountainhead Regional Park at approximately 34.0 miles. A bike shop and old Victorian homes are also located along the route.

FOOD: Markets at start, 4.4, 7.6, 13.6 and 26.5 miles. Fast food at 7.6 and tea house at 17.8 miles.

LODGING: Camping at Burke Lake County Park.

MAPS: Fairfax and Prince William Counties, Va. road maps.

MILES   DIRECTIONS & COMMENTS

0.0   **Right** out of shopping center, to go west on **OLD KEENE MILL ROAD** (VA 644).

0.2   **Right** on **SPRING LAKE DRIVE.**

0.9   **Left** on **BURKE LAKE ROAD** (VA 645). *Caution: road is narrow.* Burke Lake County Park and general store at 4.4 miles. Large homes.

7.6   Enter Clifton. **Left** on **SCHOOL STREET,** then **right** on **MAIN STREET.** Tea house and general store. Historic houses and hotel.

8.0   **Left** to stay on **CLIFTON ROAD** (VA 645).

8.7   **Left** on **COMPTON ROAD** (VA 658). *Caution: narrow road.*

9.8   Cross one-lane bridge over stream.

10.5 **Left** to stay on **COMPTON ROAD.** *Use caution at intersection.*

12.5 **Left** on **ORDWAY ROAD.**

13.6 Convenience store and Mexican market.

14.3 **Right** on **YORKSHIRE LANE.**

15.1 **Left** on **AMHERST DRIVE.**

15.7 **Right** on **LOMOND DRIVE.**

16.1 **Right** to stay on **LOMOND DRIVE** at T.

17.8 **Right** on **SUDLEY ROAD** (VA 234). Fast food at intersection. *Caution: road is heavily travelled.* [Note: if you wish to skip the trip into the Battlefield, turn left onto Sudley Road and continue on to Stonewall Road, resuming cues at 24.5 miles.]

19.8 **Right** into driveway of **MANASSAS NATIONAL BATTLEFIELD PARK,** to Visitors Center. **Reverse direction** after tour. **Left** out of driveway for return along **SUDLEY ROAD.**

24.5 **Right** on **STONEWALL ROAD,** quick **left** on **PEABODY STREET.**

25.6 **Left** on **CENTER STREET.** Manassas Museum.

26.3 **Right** on **FAIRVIEW AVENUE.**

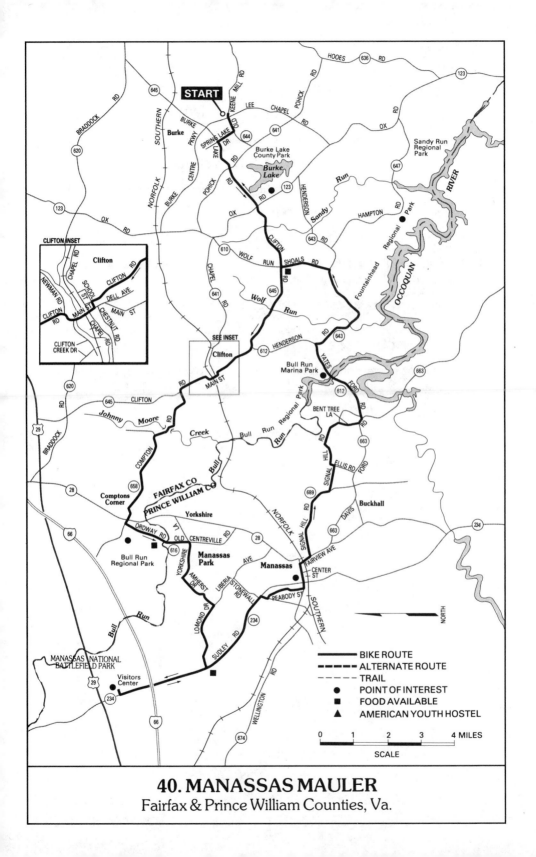

40. MANASSAS MAULER
Fairfax & Prince William Counties, Va.

26.5 **Left** on **SIGNAL HILL ROAD** (VA 689). Fairview Grocery on left.

27.8 **Right** to stay on **SIGNAL HILL ROAD** (VA 689).

28.9 **Left** to stay on **SIGNAL HILL ROAD.**

29.5 **Right** to stay on **SIGNAL HILL ROAD** on dirt road downhill.

30.2 **Right** on **BENT TREE LANE** (VA 664) on unpaved secluded downhill.

30.5 **Left** on **DAVIS FORD ROAD** (VA 663). *Caution: traffic.*

31.1 **Left** on **YATES FORD ROAD** (VA 612). Pass Bull Run Regional Park.

33.3 **Right** on **HENDERSON ROAD** (VA 643). Fountainhead Regional Park on right at approximately 34.0 miles.

35.9 **Left** on **WOLF RUN SHOALS ROAD** (VA 610) as Henderson Road goes to right.

37.1 **Right** on **CLIFTON ROAD** (VA 645). Suburban palaces.

38.7 **Straight** to stay on **CLIFTON ROAD** (VA 645), crossing Ox Road. After Ox Road, Clifton Road becomes **BURKE LAKE ROAD.**

41.4 **Right** on **SPRING LAKE DRIVE.**

41.8 **Left** on **OLD KEENE MILL ROAD** (VA 644).

42.2 **Left** into **SHOPPING CENTER.**

41. GUNSTON HALL TOUR

This tour takes you along forested roads from Burke Lake County Park through wildlife refuges and recreational areas to historic Gunston Hall.

Gunston Hall was built in 1755 by George Mason, the American statesman who wrote the Virginia Declaration of Rights and the first Constitution of Virginia. The Virginia Constitution provided the model for the American Declaration of Independence and the French Declaration of the Rights of Man. Mason ultimately refused to sign the U.S. Constitution because of the absence of a Bill of Rights. The first ten amendments later were crafted using Mason's suggestions.

Described as "a cottage on the outside, a palace inside," Gunston Hall was meticulously constructed in the 16th century Palladian style by an Englishman named William Buckland. The Hall's interior woodwork is considered unsurpassed in the colonial era.

START: Burke Lake County Park on Ox Road (VA 123) in Burke, Va. From the Capital Beltway, take I-95 South and exit onto Keene Mill Road (VA 644). Continue west for six miles and turn right onto Pohick Road (VA 641). At Burke Lake Road (VA 645) turn left. Continue until Ox Road (VA 123) and turn left. Park entrance is on left. Burke is six miles southwest of the Capital Beltway.

LENGTH: 31.3 miles.

TERRAIN: Rolling hills. Narrow, one-lane roads, but light traffic for this area.

POINTS OF INTEREST: Burke Lake County Park at start, with camping, bike trail, boating; Occoquan Reservoir; Fountainhead Regional Park at 4.0 miles; Gunston Hall (703-550-9220) at 17.8 miles; Mason Neck State Park, Mason Neck National Wildlife Refuge and Potomac Shoreline Regional Park at 18.0 miles; and Pohick Bay Regional Park at 18.2 miles.

FOOD: Markets at 7.5 miles (open Sundays) and 14.9 miles. Snack bar at 19.0 miles.

LODGING: At Burke Lake County Park, public campgrounds.

MAPS: Fairfax County, Va. road map.

MILES   DIRECTIONS & COMMENTS

0.0   Exit Burke Lake County Park, then turn **left** onto **OX ROAD** (VA 123).

0.8   **Right** on **HENDERSON ROAD** (VA 643).

2.9   **Left** on **HAMPTON ROAD** (VA 647).

4.0   Fountainhead Regional Park on right. Picnic areas, nature trail, boating, soda machine.

7.5   **Right** on **OX ROAD** (VA 123) at T. Market on Ox Road. *Caution: traffic.*

8.8   **Left** on **FURNACE ROAD** (VA 611).

9.7   **Bear left** on **LORTON ROAD** (VA 642).

9.8   **Bear right,** back to **FURNACE ROAD** (VA 611).

12.6   Cross US 1 (Richmond Highway).

13.0   **Left** on **OLD COLCHESTER ROAD** (still VA 611).

14.9   **Right** on **GUNSTON ROAD** (VA 242). Small grocery.

17.8   **Left** into **GUNSTON HALL. Tour** of house and gardens. Allow one hour. Exit grounds and turn **right** on **GUNSTON ROAD.** [Note: To reach Mason Neck State Park, Mason Neck National Wildlife Refuge and Potomac Shoreline Regional Park, turn left on Gunston Road for 0.2 miles, then right into the parks.]

18.2   **Right** into **POHICK BAY REGIONAL PARK.**

19.0   **Arrive** at park facilities. Snack bar, boat launching ramp, picnic area, sailboat and pedal boat rentals, observation deck, frisbee golf and miniature golf, bridle paths, camping, swimming pool, restrooms.

19.8   **Right** on **GUNSTON ROAD** (VA 242).

23.5   **Straight** on **GUNSTON COVE ROAD** (VA 600), crossing US 1 (Richmond Highway). Winding road; one-lane wooden bridge over railroad tracks at 23.9 miles.

24.7   **Left** on **LORTON ROAD** (VA 642). Pass I-95 interchange.

24.9   **Right** on **SILVERBROOK ROAD** (VA 600).

28.9   **Bear right** on **OX ROAD** (VA 123).

31.3   **Right** into **BURKE LAKE COUNTY PARK.**

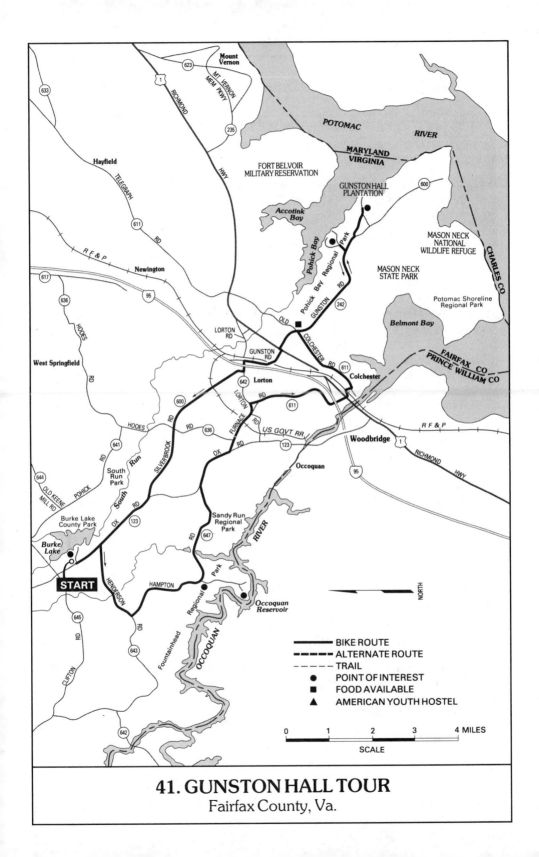

41. GUNSTON HALL TOUR
Fairfax County, Va.

42. PRINCE WILLIAM PARK

Featuring the roads and trails of Prince William Forest Park, this ride will give the outdoor enthusiast ample opportunity to view white-tailed deer, wild turkey and beaver.

Prince William Forest Park is located on land formerly farmed by Scottish settlers. After years of soil depletion and extensive erosion, the land was reclaimed by the Civilian Conservation Corps in the 1930s. The National Park Service now operates a park and nature center, where rangers and volunteers explain the delicate ecological balance.

Surprisingly close to Washington, the park offers picnic grounds, fishing, hiking trails, and the chance for cyclists to pedal without traffic.

START: Headquarters of Prince William Park on Fuller Road in Prince William County, Va. From the Capital Beltway, take I-95 South approximately 20 miles and exit onto VA 619 West (Fuller Road). Turn right and continue 0.5 miles to park entrance; bear right to headquarters. The starting point is 21 miles southwest of the Capital Beltway.

LENGTH: 13.5 miles.

TERRAIN: Rolling hills and well-maintained roads. No shoulders.

POINTS OF INTEREST: Prince William Park (703-221-7181) with hiking trails and wildlife; and Prince William Nature Center at 9.7 miles.

FOOD: None in the park. Bring lunch or purchase food in historic Dumfries, just east of the park.

LODGING: Regular and primitive campsites available (a written permit is required for the latter).

MAPS AND INFORMATION: *Prince William Forest Park* guide, available at Park Headquarters.

MILES   DIRECTIONS & COMMENTS

0.0   Leave Park Headquarters on **PARK ROAD, bearing right** past entrance road.

2.2   **Bear right** on **SCENIC DRIVE.**

9.3   **Left** to **NATURE CENTER.**

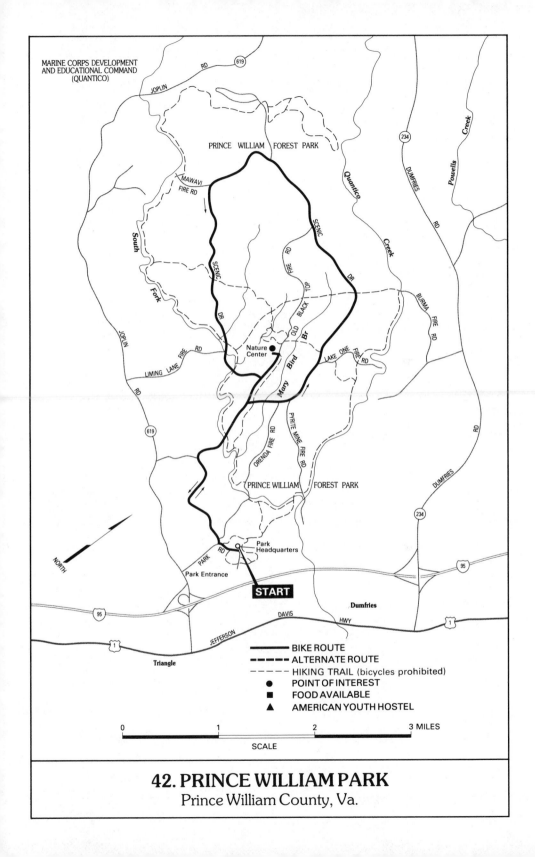

MARINE CORPS DEVELOPMENT
AND EDUCATIONAL COMMAND
(QUANTICO)

PRINCE WILLIAM FOREST PARK

MAWAVI FIRE RD

South Fork

JOPLIN RD

LIMING LANE FIRE RD

SCENIC DR

Nature Center

619

ORENDA FIRE RD

Mary Bird Br

OLD BLACK TOP

FIRE RD

SCENIC DR

Quantico Creek

234

DUMFRIES RD

Powells Creek

BURMA FIRE RD

LAKE ONE FIRE RD

PYRITE MINE FIRE RD

PRINCE WILLIAM FOREST PARK

DUMFRIES RD

234

NORTH

Park Headquarters

PARK RD

Park Entrance

START

95

Dumfries

95

DAVIS HWY

JEFFERSON

1

Triangle

1

BIKE ROUTE
ALTERNATE ROUTE
HIKING TRAIL (bicycles prohibited)
● POINT OF INTEREST
■ FOOD AVAILABLE
▲ AMERICAN YOUTH HOSTEL

0   1   2   3 MILES

SCALE

42. PRINCE WILLIAM PARK
Prince William County, Va.

9.7   Nature Center to your left. **Reverse direction.** Continue past Scenic Drive loop.

13.0   Straight past park entrance.

13.5   **Arrive** at **PARK HEADQUARTERS.**

43. BLUE RIDGE BREAKAWAY

A challenge for the ambitious cyclist, this tour runs through almost mountainous terrain north of Charlottesville. Take time to enjoy the many scenic vistas, with the Blue Ridge Mountains looming majestically in the distance.

For a full two-day ride, include the steeply ascending side trip to Skyline Drive and the Shenandoah Mountains. Lodging is available at Rockfish Gap.

START: Rotunda of the University of Virginia in Charlottesville, Va. From the Capital Beltway, take I-66 West and exit onto US 29 South (toward Charlottesville). In Charlottesville, BUS US 250 leads to the university. The Rotunda also is the endpoint of the Charlottesville Chaser (Tour 60). Charlottesville is 120 miles southwest of the Capital Beltway.

LENGTH: 51.3 miles. **SIDE TRIP** to Skyline Drive adds another 34 miles, mostly up steep hills (see end of cues).

TERRAIN: Hilly. No shoulders, but good country roads.

POINTS OF INTEREST: University of Virginia at start and finish; bike shop near start; and Rivanna Reservoir at 4.9 miles. Scenic views of the Blue Ridge Mountains along the route.

FOOD: Markets at start, 4.2, 11.8, 12.4 and 37.8 miles. Restaurant at start.

LODGING: See Charlottesville Chaser (Tour 60) for accommodations in town. Holiday Inn at Rockfish Gap (side trip).

MAPS AND INFORMATION: Charlottesville, Va. and Albemarle County, Va. maps, available in city stores and from Chamber of Commerce (open weekdays, 804-295-3141).

MILES   DIRECTIONS & COMMENTS

0.0   Go **north** on **RUGBY ROAD.**

0.8   **Left** on **RUGBY ROAD** at traffic light.

1.0   **Bear right** to stay on **RUGBY ROAD** (no sign).

1.4   **Bear right** to stay on **RUGBY ROAD.**

1.9   **Straight** on **HYDRAULIC ROAD** (VA 743), crossing US 250.

2.4   Cross US 29 (Emmet Street). *Caution: traffic.*

4.2   **Left** to stay on **VA 743.** Convenience store.

4.9   **Left** on **VA 676** just before bridge. Rivanna Reservoir on right.

7.4   **Right** on **VA 660.**

11.8 **Left** on **VA 743** at stop sign. Grocery store.

12.4 **Bear left** on **VA 663.** Earlysville General Store on right.

13.8 **Straight** on **VA 664,** where VA 663 bears right.

14.2 **Straight** on **VA 665,** where VA 664 bears right.

18.8 **Bear right** on **VA 601** in Free Union.

25.7 **Left** on **VA 810** at T.

31.5 **Left** to stay on **VA 810** at T.

37.8 **Left** on **VA 614/810**. White Hall. Garrison's Grocery on right.

37.9 **Straight** to stay on **VA 614.** Gas station on left. For **SIDE TRIP** to Skyline Drive, turn right on VA 810 and see cues below.

43.1 **Bear left** on **VA 676** (Garth Road).

47.0 **Right** on **VA 601** before steep incline.

49.0 **Straight** on **OLD IVY ROAD** (VA 754), crossing over US 29. *Caution: traffic.*

49.8 **Bear left** on **IVY ROAD** (US 250) at stop sign. Enter Charlottesville.

50.0 **Right** on **ALDERMAN ROAD** at traffic light.

50.6 **Left** on **McCORMICK ROAD** at traffic light. Enter university campus.

51.3 **Right** into **ROTUNDA.**

SIDE TRIP TO SKYLINE DRIVE

37.9 **Right** on **VA 810** (no sign) in White Hall.

42.4 **Straight** on **VA 240** in Crozet.

42.6 **Right** on **VA 691** (Jarmon Gap Road).

46.6 **Right** on **VA 690.** Begin steep incline.

50.1 **Right** on **VA 796** at T.

50.5 **Right** on **US 250** at T.

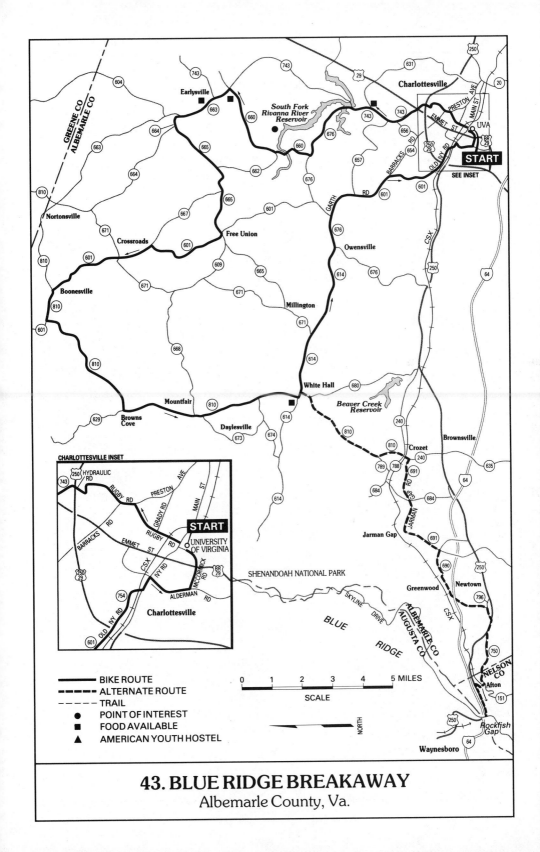

43. BLUE RIDGE BREAKAWAY
Albemarle County, Va.

51.1 **Left** on **VA 750.** Steep inclines.

53.0 **Right** on **VA 151.** Keep climbing.

53.6 **Left** on **US 250.** *Caution: fast traffic.*

54.8 **Arrive** at **ROCKFISH GAP.** Skyline Drive to north, Blue Ridge Parkway to south. Motels. Appalachian Trail. **Reverse direction** for return to main route.

44. JAMESTOWN LOOP

Explore a segment of the famed "Colonial Triangle" and an important part of early American history on this loop between Williamsburg and Jamestown Island. Considered the first permanent English settlement in the United States, little remains of Jamestown today except for the Old Church Tower (1639). The island features a variety of historical displays and a network of short nature loops open to bicycles. The Visitors Center provides information, water and restrooms.

Jamestown Festival Park lies just west of Jamestown Island and features a reconstructed fort, three ships and other attractions. (There are entrance fees to the island and park.)

The Williamsburg Information Center offers a brochure of bicycle tours in the Colonial Triangle (Williamsburg, Yorktown, Jamestown). Also see Charlottesville Chaser (Tour 60) and Yorktown Yonder (Tour 61). In addition, a 20-minute ferry (15 cents for bicycles) takes you from Jamestown to Scotland on the south bank of the James River -- a nice place for a picnic.

START: Williamsburg Information Center on VA 132Y in Williamsburg, Va. From the Capital Beltway, take I-95 South (to Richmond) and exit onto I-295 East (to Norfolk). Then take I-64 East and exit onto VA 132 (to Williamsburg). VA 132Y is a spur of VA 132. Williamsburg is 160 miles south of the Capital Beltway. For a bike route to Williamsburg, see Yorktown Yonder (Tour 61).

LENGTH: 23.2 miles (does not include a 5.2-mile loop on Jamestown Island).

TERRAIN: Rolling hills. Cobblestone surface on the Colonial Parkway makes for slow going. Bike lanes on some roads.

POINTS OF INTEREST: Williamsburg at start; James River Ferry at 13.9 miles; Jamestown Island (804-229-1733) at 14.1 miles, with nature loops, information center and Glasshouse (c.1608), Old Church Tower, craft exhibits; and College of William and Mary (1693) at 22.1 miles, the second oldest college in the country with Sir Christopher Wren building and Sunken Garden. Jamestown Festival Park (804-229-1607) lies west of Jamestown Island.

FOOD: Markets in Williamsburg and Jamestown, and at 6.6 miles. Picnic areas along the Colonial Parkway with scenic views of the James River.

LODGING: In Jamestown, Jamestown Beach Campsites (804-229-8366). Williamsburg Chamber of Commerce (804-229-1000) publishes a brochure describing campgrounds, and Colonial Williamsburg Foundation (804-229-2141) has hotel information.

MAPS AND INFORMATION: *Bike Map: Historic Triangle* available from Williamsburg Information Center or Virginia Department of Transportation (804-786-2964).

MILES   DIRECTIONS & COMMENTS

0.0   Go **right** out of Information Center, and **right** on **VA 132** (Henry Street).

0.4   **Left** on **US 60.** Bikeway on south side of road.

1.6   **Right** on **BUS US 60.** *Caution: heavy traffic.*

1.9   **Left** on **IRONBOUND ROAD** (VA 615), then immediate **right** on **LONGHILL ROAD** (VA 612). Pleasant, shady road.

6.6   **Left** on **VA 614.** Grocery.

11.7   **Right** on **VA 5** (John Taylor Highway).

11.8   **Left** on **VA 614.**

13.9   **Straight** on **VA 359.** (Right on VA 31 to Jamestown-Scotland Ferry.)

14.1   **Right** on **COLONIAL PARKWAY** to Jamestown Island. [Note: the cue sheet and mileage do not include exploring Jamestown Island, which should not be missed!] **Reverse direction** and take **left** on **COLONIAL PARKWAY** for return.

21.8   **Right** on **RAMP,** following signed bike route.

21.9   **Right** on **NEWPORT AVENUE.**

22.1   **Right** on **HENRY STREET.** College of William and Mary.

23.0   **Right** on **VA 132Y.**

23.2   **Left** at **WILLIAMSBURG INFORMATION CENTER.**

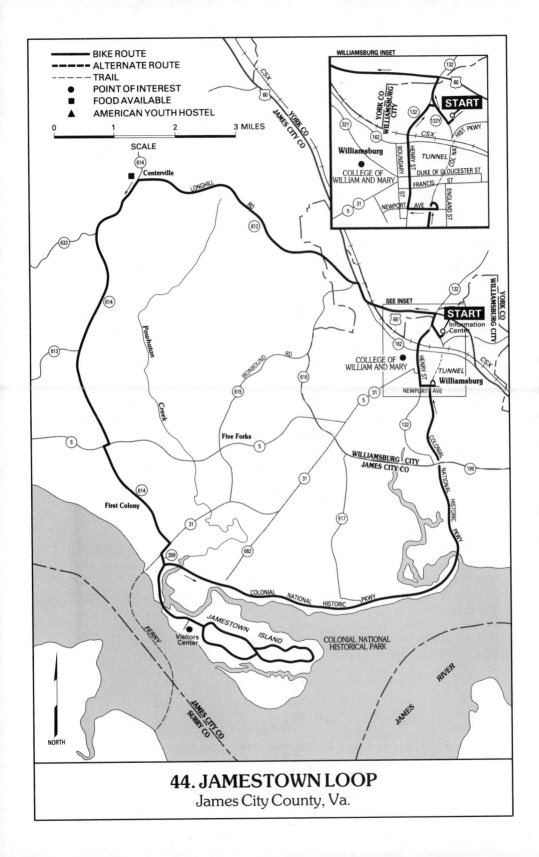

44. JAMESTOWN LOOP
James City County, Va.

45. ZAP THE GAP

Offering beautiful views of the Blue Ridge Mountains, this challenging route travels round-trip from Marshall to Front Royal, Va. You will pass the Oasis Vineyard and the hilltop home of Chief Justice John Marshall.

The strenuous three-mile climb over Chester Gap is more than rewarded by a four-mile descent into Front Royal! During the long descent keep your eyes open for giraffes, wildebeest and other exotic animals at the Smithsonian Conservation and Research Center. The flea market in Front Royal, at the intersection of VA 522 and VA 55, offers another diversion.

Front Royal has two notable Civil War museums located next door to each other. The Belle Boyd Cottage at 101 Chester Street (703-636-1446), a former tavern, now houses a museum dedicated to the career of the "Siren of the South." When Union officers turned Boyd's house into a military headquarters during the Shenandoah campaigns of 1862, she spied on the officers and passed the information to Confederate leaders. Next door at 95 Chester Street is the Warren Rifles Confederate Museum (703-636-6982), operated by the United Daughters of the Confederacy.

START: Marshall Auditorium on BUS US 17 in Marshall, Va. From the Capital Beltway, take I-66 West for 36 miles and exit onto US 17 (toward Marshall/Warrenton). Continue north for 0.7 miles on BUS US 17 into Marshall. Continue straight beyond the city limits for 0.1 miles; auditorium parking lot is on the right. Marshall is 37 miles west of the Capital Beltway.

LENGTH: 56.3 miles.

TERRAIN: Hilly.

POINTS OF INTEREST: Home of Chief Justice Marshall at approximately 9.0 miles; Oasis Vineyard at 18.6 miles, on VA 635 just west of Hume; Smithsonian Conservation and Research Center at approximately 30.0 miles; and flea market on Commerce Street at 32.0 miles. In Front Royal, the Shenandoah National Park and Skyline Drive.

FOOD: Markets at 10.0, 18.6 (closed Sundays), 27.4 miles (closed Sundays); 32.0 and 40.7 miles.

MAPS: Fauquier and Warren Counties, Va. road maps.

MILES   DIRECTIONS & COMMENTS

  0.0   **Right** out of parking lot onto **VA 710.**

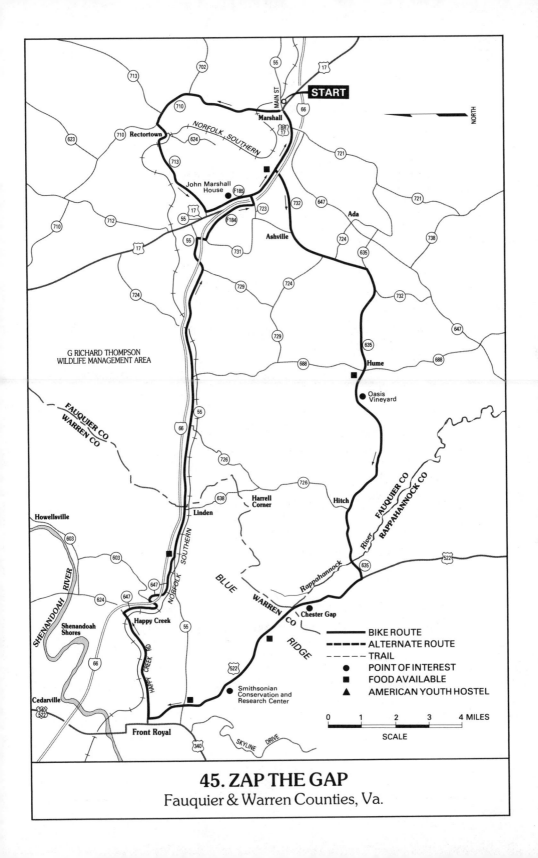

45. ZAP THE GAP
Fauquier & Warren Counties, Va.

4.4   **Left** on **VA 713** in Rectortown.

4.8   **Straight** at fork to stay on **VA 713.**

5.3   Cross railroad tracks.

8.0   **Left** on **VA F-185.** DO NOT proceed one block to intersection of VA 55/17 and VA 713. Chief Justice Marshall home at approximately 9.0 miles.

10.0   General store.

10.6   **Right** on **VA 732.**

15.3   **Right** on **VA 635.**

18.6   **Straight** to stay on **VA 635** in Hume, crossing VA 688. General store on right.

26.2   **Right** on **US 522** at T. *Caution: heavy traffic.* Begin 3-mile climb over Chester Gap.

27.4   Store. Smithsonian Conservation and Research Center at approximately 30.0 miles.

32.0   High's Dairy Store at intersection of VA 55 and US 522, where US 522 becomes **COMMERCE AVENUE** in Front Royal.

33.9   **Right** on **HAPPY CREEK ROAD.** This becomes **VA 624.**

37.5   **Right** on **VA 647.**

40.7   **Left** on **VA 55.** High's Dairy Store at intersection.

50.7   **Right** on **VA 731** at T. (VA 55 continues left.)

50.8   **Left** on **VA F-184,** immediately after crossing under I-66.

52.8   **Left** on **VA 723.**

52.9   **Right** on **VA F-185.** This becomes **MAIN STREET** in Marshall.

56.3   **Right** into **MARSHALL AUDITORIUM PARKING LOT.**

46. VIRGINIA HUNT COUNTRY

This ride tours the heart of Virginia Hunt County and takes you through several small towns to the north and west of Middleburg. More challenging than the Middleburg Meander (Tour 48), this hilly ride offers beautiful views of the Blue Ridge Mountains and a glimpse of many expansive country estates.

START: Middleburg Elementary School on VA 626 in Middleburg, Va. From the Capital Beltway, take I-66 West for 33 miles to The Plains/Middleburg exit. Turn right onto VA 55 in The Plains and then take an immediate left onto VA 626. Continue 8.4 miles to Middleburg. Turn right onto US 50 then left onto VA 626 by the Red Fox Tavern. Continue for 0.2 miles; school is on right. Middleburg is 42 miles west of the Capital Beltway.

LENGTH: 43.1 miles.

TERRAIN: Hilly.

POINTS OF INTEREST: Middleburg shops, buildings and Red Fox Tavern near start; and The Plains at 31.3 miles.

FOOD: Markets near start, at 17.7 and 31.3 miles. Restaurants near start and at 31.3 miles (open Sundays).

LODGING: In Middleburg, Red Fox Inn and Tavern (703-687-6301). Near Middleburg, Welbourne Inn (703-687-3201), on VA 743 one mile west of VA 611, a 1775 farm listed on the National Register of Historic Places.

MAPS: Loudoun and Fauquier Counties, Va. road map.

MILES   DIRECTIONS & COMMENTS

0.0	**Left** on **VA 626** from school parking lot.
0.1	**Left** on **US 50.**
0.9	**Left** on **VA 748.**
4.3	**Left** on **VA 734** at stop sign.
9.5	**Left** on **VA 611.**
17.0	**Right** on **VA 50** at stop sign.
17.5	**Left** on **VA 713.**
17.7	**Left** to stay on **VA 713** at Rectors Store. Food available.
22.7	**Left** on **VA 710** at stop sign in Rectortown.

23.8   **Left** on **VA 702.**

27.2   **Right** on **VA 709** at stop sign.

28.4   **Left** on **VA 707.**

29.7   **Bear right** on **VA 704.**

30.3   **Left** on **VA 55** at stop sign.

31.3   The Plains. Try the Rail Stop for lunch.

31.4   **Left** on **VA 626.**

35.2   **Right** on **VA 679.** Become **VA 628/686.**

38.6   **Bear left** on **VA 629.**

38.8   **Left** on **VA 776.**

42.9   Cross US 50. Pick up **VA 626** to **right.**

43.1   **Arrive** at **MIDDLEBURG ELEMENTARY SCHOOL.**

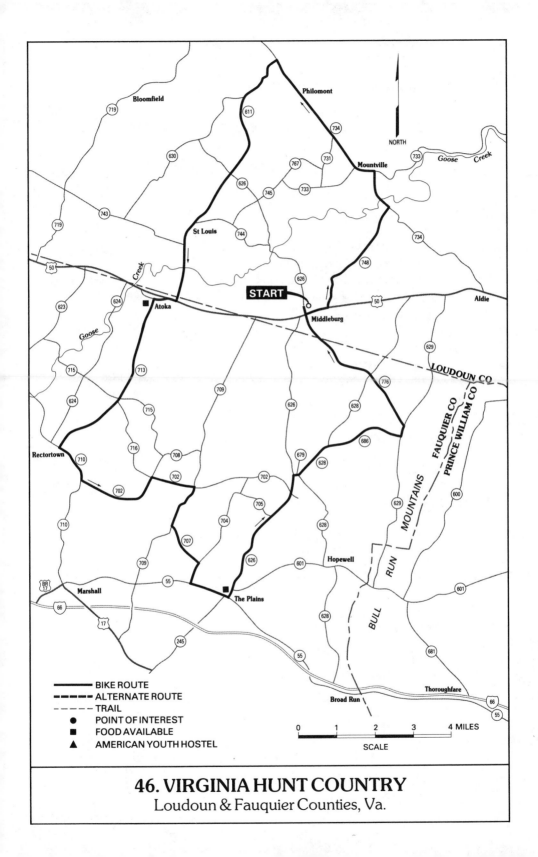

Bloomfield

Philomont

719

611

734

NORTH

630

731

733

Goose   Creek

767

Mountville

626

745

733

743

St Louis

744

734

719

748

50

Creek

626

START

50

Aldie

623

624

Atoka

Middleburg

Goose

629

LOUDOUN CO

715

713

776

624

709

626

628

715

716

708

679

686

Rectortown

710

702

628

702

702

629

600

705

704

628

710

707

MOUNTAINS

626

601

Hopewell

FAUQUIER CO

PRINCE WILLIAM CO

BR
17

709

55

628

601

Marshall

66

The Plains

RUN

17

628

245

BULL

681

55

Thoroughfare

Broad Run

66

55

——— BIKE ROUTE
– – – ALTERNATE ROUTE
– – TRAIL
● POINT OF INTEREST
■ FOOD AVAILABLE
▲ AMERICAN YOUTH HOSTEL

0   1   2   3   4 MILES

SCALE

46. VIRGINIA HUNT COUNTRY
Loudoun & Fauquier Counties, Va.

47. PEDALING THE PIEDMONT

The Virginia Piedmont offers you rolling meadows, rural countryside and an occasional steep hill -- a visual treat and physical challenge to the well-trained cyclist. Eighteenth and nineteenth century farmhouses dot the landscape, along with open fields and Blue Ridge Mountain vistas. Naked Mountain Vineyard is located on VA 688, just north of Markham.

START: Parking lot on Ashby Street in Warrenton, Va. From the Capital Beltway, take I-66 West for 22 miles and exit onto US 29 South at Gainesville. Continue on US 29/211 for 12 miles and bear right onto BUS US 29/15. At first traffic light, turn left onto Culpeper Street and continue one mile. Turn right onto Main Street and then turn left onto Ashby Street. Continue on Ashby Street to the parking lot. Warrenton is 36 miles west of the Capital Beltway.

LENGTH: 65.2 miles.

TERRAIN: Rolling hills to moderately hilly.

POINTS OF INTEREST: Naked Mountain Vineyard and Sky Meadows State Park at 24.7 miles. Views of Blue Ridge Mountains and farmhouses along the route.

FOOD: Markets at 12.8, 19.1, 37.6 and 48.4 miles.

MAPS: Fauquier County, Va. road map.

MILES   DIRECTIONS & COMMENTS

  0.0   **Left** out of parking lot on **LEE STREET.**

  0.2   **Right** on **CHESTNUT STREET.**

  0.3   **Left** on **WATERLOO STREET** (BUS US 211).

  0.8   Cross US 29.

  0.9   **Right** on **RAPPAHANNOCK STREET.**

  1.0   **Left** on **WATERLOO ROAD** (VA 678).

  5.0   **Left** on **VA 691.**

  7.2   **Right** on **VA 688** in Waterloo.

 12.8   Pass through Orlean. General store.

 19.1   Pass through Hume. General store.

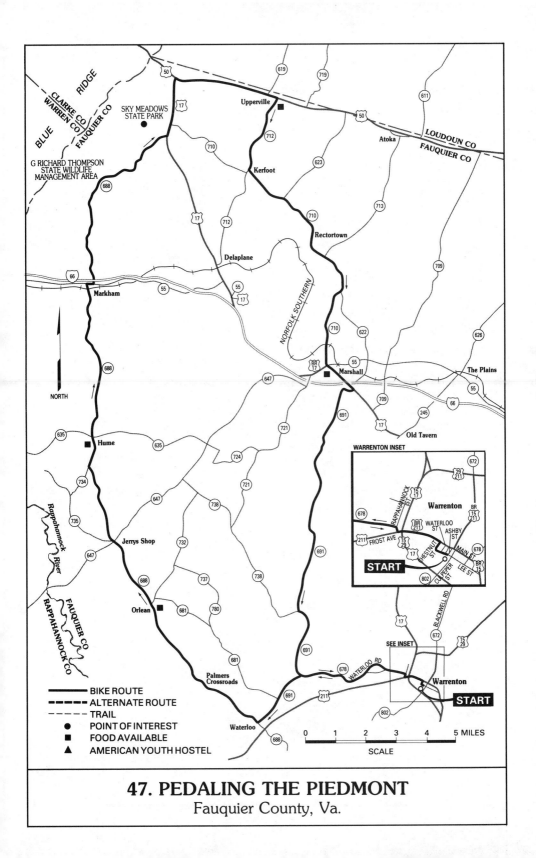

CLARKE CO
WARREN CO

BLUE RIDGE

FAUQUIER CO

SKY MEADOWS
STATE PARK

G RICHARD THOMPSON
STATE WILDLIFE
MANAGEMENT AREA

50

619

719

611

Upperville

712

50

Atoka

LOUDOUN CO
FAUQUIER CO

17

710

623

713

Kerfoot

17

712

710

Rectortown

709

Delaplane

66

55

55

Markham

17

NORFOLK SOUTHERN

626

NORTH

688

710

622

BR
17

55

Marshall

The Plains

647

691

709

55

721

245

17

Old Tavern

66

635

Hume

635

724

721

734

738

Rappahannock River

735

647

732

738

691

Jerrys Shop

647

688

737

FAUQUIER CO
RAPPAHANNOCK CO

Orlean

681

780

691

681

691

678

Waterloo RD

Palmers
Crossroads

691

211

Waterloo

688

WARRENTON INSET

672

29
211

RAPPAHANNOCK ST

15
17

678

Warrenton

BR
15
211

BR
211

WATERLOO
ST

ASHBY
ST

211

FROST AVE

15
29

17

CHESTNUT ST

MAIN ST

678

BR
15

LEE ST

START

802

CULPEPER ST

17

BLACKWELL RD

SEE INSET

672

15
29

Warrenton

START

802

BIKE ROUTE
ALTERNATE ROUTE
TRAIL
● POINT OF INTEREST
■ FOOD AVAILABLE
▲ AMERICAN YOUTH HOSTEL

0   1   2   3   4   5 MILES

SCALE

47. PEDALING THE PIEDMONT
Fauquier County, Va.

24.7   **Jog right** on **VA 55** then **left** to continue on **VA 688** under I-66. Pass Naked Mountain Vineyard. Sky Meadows State Park on left.

31.6   **Left** on **US 17.** *Caution: traffic.*

33.6   **Right** on **US 50.**

37.6   **Right** on **VA 712.** Town of Upperville. General store. Water at firehouse on right.

40.2   **Left** on **VA 710.**

48.4   Cross VA 55. Marshall. 7-Eleven.

49.4   **Right** on **VA 691** after crossing I-66.

57.7   **Left** to stay on **VA 691.**

60.2   **Straight** on **VA 678.**

64.2   **Right** on **RAPPAHANNOCK STREET.**

64.3   **Left** on **FROST AVENUE** (VA 211).

64.4   Cross VA 29 (becomes Waterloo Street).

64.9   **Right** on **CHESTNUT STREET.**

65.0   **Left** on **LEE STREET.**

65.2   **Right** into **PARKING LOT.**

48. MIDDLEBURG MEANDER

A quiet respite from the bustle of urban life, this pleasant ride through Virginia Hunt Country offers you smooth cycling on country roads. Views of the Blue Ridge Mountains serve as a backdrop to the many elegant country estates, expansive farmland and grazing horses.

START: Middleburg Elementary School on VA 626 in Middleburg, Va. From the Capital Beltway, take I-66 West for 33 miles to The Plains/Middleburg exit. Turn right onto VA 55 in The Plains and then take an immediate left onto VA 626. Continue 8.4 miles to Middleburg. Turn right onto US 50 then left onto VA 626 by the Red Fox Tavern. Continue for 0.2 miles; school is on right. Middleburg is 42 miles west of the Capital Beltway.

LENGTH: 44.8 miles.

TERRAIN: Rolling hills to moderately hilly.

POINTS OF INTEREST: Middleburg shops, buildings and Red Fox Tavern near start; and The Plains at 31.8 miles. Views of the Blue Ridge Mountains and country estates and horse farms along the route.

FOOD: Markets near start and at 10.0, 19.3 and 31.8 miles. Restaurants near start and at 31.8 miles.

LODGING: In Middleburg, Red Fox Inn and Tavern (703-687-6301). Near Middleburg, Welbourne Inn (703-687-3201), on VA 743 one mile west of VA 611, a 1775 farm listed on the National Register of Historic Places.

MAPS: Fauquier County, Va. road map.

MILES DIRECTIONS & COMMENTS

0.0 **Left** out of parking lot onto **VA 626** (Madison Street).

0.1 **Right** on **US 50** (Washington Street). *Caution: traffic.*

1.4 **Left** on **VA 709.**

6.5 **Right** on **VA 702.** Sign is obscure; look for it on left side of stop sign.

10.0 **Right** on **VA 710** at T. General store.

13.7 **Right** on **VA 623** (no sign).

17.3 **Right** on **US 50.** *Caution: high speed traffic.*

18.9 **Right** on **VA 828.**

19.3   **Right** on **VA 713.** General store.

24.3   **Left** on **VA 710** at T.

25.3   **Left** on **VA 702.**

28.8   **Right** on **VA 709.**

30.0   **Left** on **VA 707.**

31.3   **Bear right** on **VA 704.**

31.8   **Left** on **VA 55.** *Caution: traffic.* Enter The Plains. Restaurants and markets.

32.8   **Left** on **VA 626.**

36.7   **Right** on **VA 679.** Becomes **VA 628/686.**

36.9   **Bear left** on **VA 628.** Becomes **VA 686.**

40.2   **Bear left** on **VA 629.**

40.4   **Left** on **VA 776.** This becomes **SOUTH MADISON STREET** in Middleburg.

44.7   **Straight** on **SOUTH MADISON STREET** (VA 626). Cross US 50.

44.8   **Right** into **MIDDLEBURG ELEMENTARY SCHOOL.**

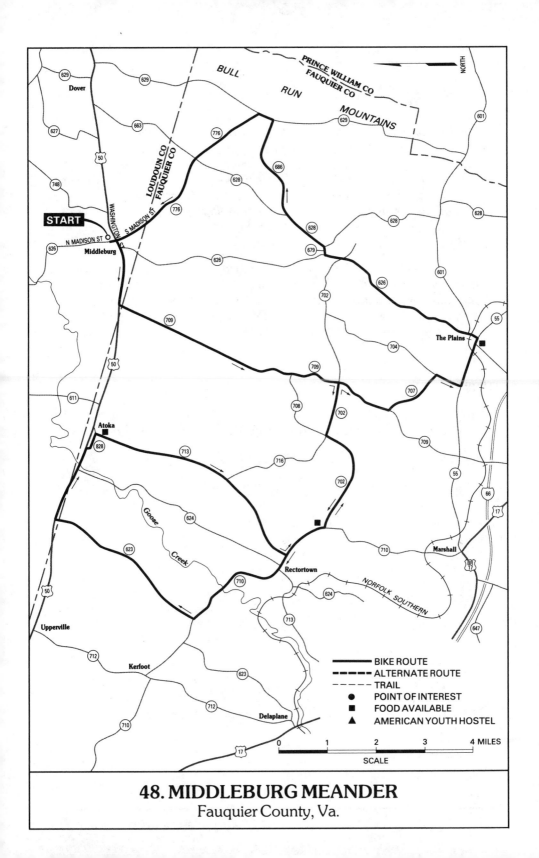

START

NORTH

BULL RUN MOUNTAINS

PRINCE WILLIAM CO
FAUQUIER CO

LOUDOUN CO
FAUQUIER CO

629   Dover
629
627
663
776
629
628
686
628
601
50
748
776
628   628
628
WASHINGTON   S MADISON ST
START
N MADISON ST
626   Middleburg
626
679
626
601
702
709
704   The Plains
709
611
708   702
707
Atoka
828   713   716   702   709
55
624
66
623   17
Goose   702
Creek
710   Marshall
Rectortown
710
624
NORFOLK SOUTHERN
Upperville   713
712
647
Kerfoot
623
712
710   Delaplane
17

BIKE ROUTE
ALTERNATE ROUTE
TRAIL
● POINT OF INTEREST
■ FOOD AVAILABLE
▲ AMERICAN YOUTH HOSTEL

0   1   2   3   4 MILES

SCALE

48. MIDDLEBURG MEANDER
Fauquier County, Va.

49. THE RESPLENDENT RAPPAHANNOCK

Traversing the foothills of the Blue Ridge Mountains, this challenging ride boasts spectacular views of the Upper Rappahannock River Valley, an important watershed for the Virginia Piedmont. The route passes through several small villages with quaint stone houses and hunt country estates surrounded by elegant stone fences. You will cross the Rappahannock River and its tributaries several times, offering cool relief in summer and views of colorful foliage in autumn. Oasis Vineyard is located just west of Hume on VA 635.

START: Marshall Auditorium on BUS US 17 in Marshall, Va. From the Capital Beltway, take I-66 West for 36 miles and exit onto US 17 (toward Marshall/Warrenton). Continue north for 0.7 miles on BUS US 17 into Marshall. Continue straight beyond the city limits for 0.1 miles; auditorium parking lot is on the right. Marshall is 37 miles west of the Capital Beltway.

LENGTH: 55.0 miles.

TERRAIN: Hilly.

POINTS OF INTEREST: Oasis Vineyard at 9.8 miles; and Rappahannock River at 17.0 miles. Views of the Blue Ridge Mountains along the route.

FOOD: Markets at 9.8, 25.0 and 35.0 miles.

MAPS: Fauquier and Rappahannock Counties, Va. road maps.

MILES   DIRECTIONS & COMMENTS

0.0   From Marshall Auditorium, turn **left** onto **VA 710.**

0.1   **Right** on **US 17.** *Caution: traffic.*

0.8   **Left** on **VA 647.**

1.1   **Right** to stay on **VA 647.** Turn is just past I-66 bridge.

5.6   **Right** on **VA 635.**

9.8   **Straight** on **VA 635.** Hume. Oasis Vineyard. Food stores. *Caution: big hills and narrow curves follow.*

17.0   **Left** on **US 522.** Cross the Rappahannock River. Arrive at the Blue Ridge! *Caution: traffic.*

20.0   **Right** on **VA 630.**

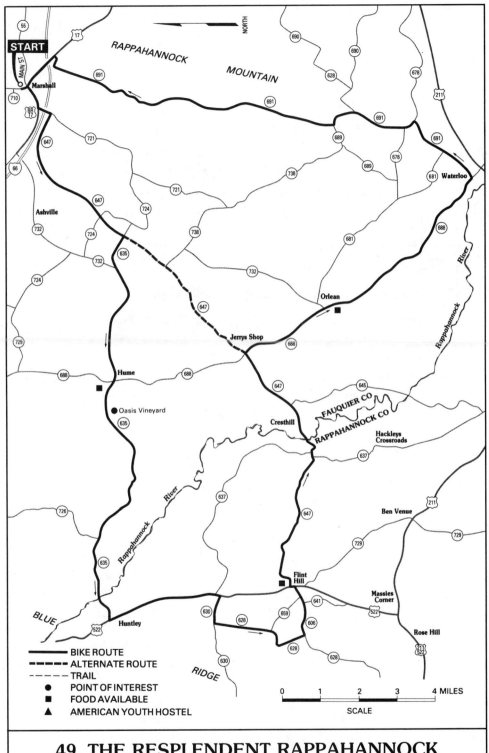

49. THE RESPLENDENT RAPPAHANNOCK
Fauquier & Rappahannock Counties, Va.

20.8   **Left** on **VA 628.** Climb, climb, climb!

23.5   **Left** on **VA 606.**

24.7   **Left** on **US 522.** Rest stop at Flint Hill.

25.0   **Right** on **VA 647.** Food stores. More hills follow.

32.6   **Right** on **VA 688.** [Note: for an alternate short-cut back to Marshall, do not turn here, and instead go straight on VA 647.]

35.0   **Straight** to stay on **VA 688.** Rest stop and food in Orlean.

40.5   **Left** on **VA 691** in Waterloo.

42.6   **Left** approaching Rappahannock Mountain.

44.4   **Bear left** to stay on **VA 691.**

45.0   **Right** to stay on **VA 691.** Do not miss this turn!

53.3   **Left** on **US 17.** *Caution: traffic.* Arrive in Marshall. **Right** on **VA 710** to **AUDITORIUM.**

50. WARRENTON WANDERLUST

The three counties of Fauquier, Rappahannock and Culpeper set the scene for this tour. Passing through serene, wooded countryside over lightly travelled roads, you also will experience a taste of history. Farmsteads and small villages throughout the valley remain virtually unchanged since Civil War days. Views to the west afford excellent panoramas of the Blue Ridge Mountains.

The tour takes you through Brandy Station, location of the largest cavalry engagement in U.S. history. In June 1863 Union cavalry under Alfred Pleasonton clashed with J.E.B. Stuart's Confederate raiders. More than 21,000 mounted troops battled to a standoff.

START: Fauquier County High School on VA 678 in Warrenton, Va. From the Capital Beltway, take I-66 West for 22 miles and exit onto US 29 South at Gainesville. Continue on US 29/211 for 12 miles and bear right onto BUS US 29/15 (toward Warrenton/Winchester). Continue for 0.8 miles and turn right onto US 211. Take first right onto Rappahannock Street, then immediately left onto VA 678. Continue for 0.5 miles; the high school is on the right. Warrenton is 36 miles west of the Capital Beltway.

LENGTH: 78.3 miles.

TERRAIN: Rolling hills to moderately hilly.

POINTS OF INTEREST: Rappahannock River at 16.7 miles; Brandy Station at 50.2 miles; and Victorian homes in Warrenton at 77.2 miles.

FOOD: Markets at 11.4, 21.5, 25.4, 57.5 and 77.2 miles.

MAPS: Fauquier, Rappahannock and Culpeper Counties, Va. road maps.

MILES   DIRECTIONS & COMMENTS

0.0   Leave Fauquier County High School by turning **right** on **VA 678.**

3.7   **Left** on **VA 691.**

5.8   **Right** on **VA 688** in Waterloo.

11.4   **Straight** to stay on **VA 688.** General stores in Orlean.

13.8   **Left** on **VA 647.**

16.7   **Straight** to stay on **VA 647.** Cross Rappahannock River into Rappahannock County.

21.5   **Left** on **US 522.** General store in Flint Hill.

21.9   **Left** on **VA 729.**

25.4   Cross US 211. General store.

30.9   **Left** to stay on **VA 729.**

31.9   **Bear right** to stay on **VA 729.** [Note: VA 640 comes in from the left twice!]

34.6   **Left** to stay on **VA 729.** Enter Culpeper County.

35.1   **Bear right** to stay **VA 729.**

43.5   **Bear left** on **VA 685.**

44.7   Cross VA 229. Catalpa. Continue on VA 685.

46.0   **Right** to stay on **VA 685.**

50.2   Cross VA 663 at Brandy Station (left across US 29).

52.3   Cross US 29. **Left** on **VA 678.**

52.7   **Straight** on **VA 674.** Elkwood.

54.4   **Left** on **VA 673.**

56.8   **Right** on **BUS US 29.** Cross Rappahannock River.

57.5   **Left** on **VA 651.** General store in Remington.

58.0   Cross US 29.

58.1   **Right** on **VA 658.**

60.4   **Right** on **VA 786.**

62.1   **Left** on **VA 661.**

65.1   **Right** on **VA 651.**

67.0   **Left** on **VA 687.**

70.4   **Right** on **VA 802.** Fauquier White Sulphur Springs.

76.8   Cross US 29, onto **CULPEPER STREET.**

77.2   **Left** on **BUS VA 15.** Downtown Warrenton. General stores.

78.0   Cross US 29. **Right** on **VA 678.**

78.3   **Right** into **FAUQUIER COUNTY HIGH SCHOOL.**

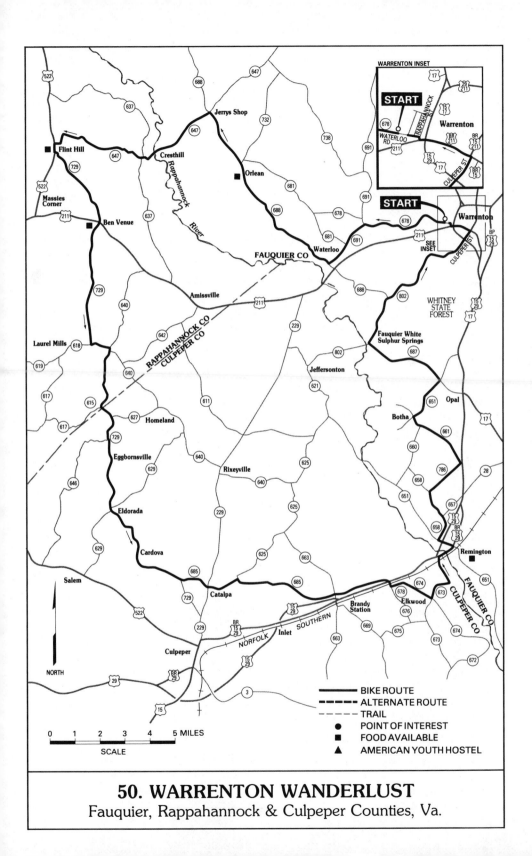

50. WARRENTON WANDERLUST
Fauquier, Rappahannock & Culpeper Counties, Va.

IV. Tour Network

51. WASHINGTON TO HARPERS FERRY HOSTEL

From its start in downtown Washington, D.C., this scenic tour takes you through prime Montgomery County biking territory (including Seneca, Beallsville and Point of Rocks) and delivers you to the Harpers Ferry AYH-Hostel in Knoxville, Md., just across the Potomac River from Harpers Ferry.

The Harpers Ferry hostel is on the Appalachian Trail, a hiking trail that extends from Maine to Georgia. The hostel also serves as a terminus for tours to the Antietam Battlefield (Tour 3), Harpers Ferry National Historical Park (Tour 34), and Bear's Den AYH-Hostel (Tour 55), as well as a waypoint on the C&O Canal Towpath (Tour 65).

The tour offers sweeping views of the Potomac River and rolling farmland. Allow time for the long, steep hills on MD 464, just west of Point of Rocks. An alternate route swings through Brunswick, adding a popular restaurant and some small-town scenery.

START: Washington Circle at Pennsylvania Avenue NW and 23rd Street NW in Washington, D.C. [The starting point is within the Capital Beltway.]
METRO START: From the Foggy Bottom Metro station (Blue and Orange Lines), go north one block on 23rd Street NW to Pennsylvania Avenue NW.

LENGTH: 60.3 miles.

TERRAIN: Hilly.

POINTS OF INTEREST: Montrose Park at 0.8 miles; Dumbarton Oaks at 0.8 miles, site of the drafting of the United Nations Charter (1944); Glover Archibald Park at 1.7 miles; Dalecarlia Reservoir at 2.8 miles; Bonfield's Texaco station (1927), 6124 MacArthur Boulevard, at 4.5 miles; Glen Echo Park at 6.8 miles; Cabin John Bridge at 9.0 miles; Monocacy Aqueduct (1833) at 37.5 miles; and C&O Canal and Point of Rocks at 43.5 miles, with restored 19th century railroad station.

FOOD: Markets near start and at 8.2, 13.3, 22.4, 35.3 and 43.5 miles. Restaurants near start, at 13.3 miles, at end (Cindy Dee's has good pies), and on alternate route at 52.3 miles.

LODGING: Near Harpers Ferry, Harpers Ferry AYH-Hostel, 19123 Sandy Hook Road, Knoxville, Md. (301-834-7652); and Hilltop House (800-338-8319), on Ridge Street, 10 blocks from C&O Canal Towpath.

MAPS: *ADC's Washington Area Bike Map;* Montgomery, Frederick and Washington Counties, Md. road maps.

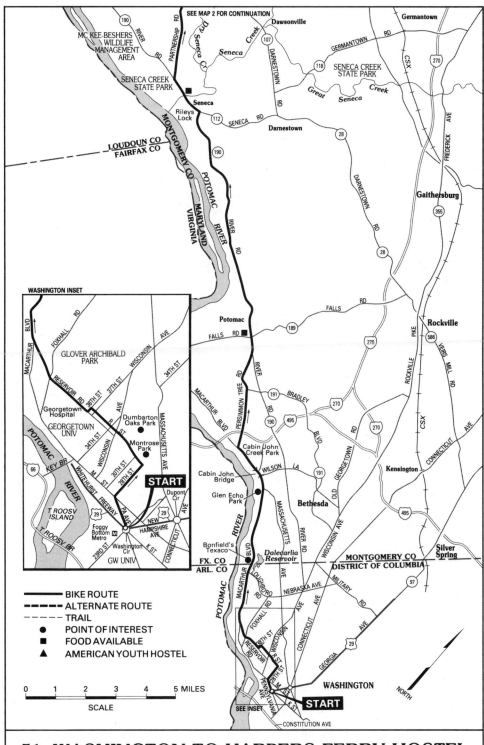

51. WASHINGTON TO HARPERS FERRY HOSTEL
Dist. of Col. & Montgomery County, Md.   Map 1 of 2

MILES DIRECTIONS & COMMENTS

0.0 Go **west** on **PENNSYLVANIA AVENUE NW** toward Georgetown.

0.3 **Right** on **28TH STREET NW,** just before Pennsylvania Avenue NW merges with M Street NW.

0.8 **Left** on **R STREET NW** at T. Pass Montrose Park and Dumbarton Oaks on right.

1.3 Cross Wisconsin Avenue NW.

1.7 **Left** on **38TH STREET NW** at T, then **first right** on **RESERVOIR ROAD NW** at T. Georgetown Hospital on left. Pass through Glover Archibald Park.

2.3 **Bear right** to stay on **RESERVOIR ROAD NW.** Cross Foxhall Road NW.

2.8 **Bear right** to stay on **MACARTHUR BOULEVARD NW.** Pass Dalecarlia Reservoir and enter Montgomery County. [Note: the proposed Capital Crescent Trail right-of-way from D.C. to Silver Spring passes here.] A poorly maintained bicycle trail begins on left. Pass Bonfield's Texaco (4.5 miles) and Glen Echo Park (6.8 miles).

8.2 Bethesda Food Co-op. Pass through Cabin John Park, over one-lane Cabin John Bridge, the world's largest stone arch when built (220 feet).

9.4 **Right** on **PERSIMMON TREE ROAD.**

10.0 **Straight** to stay on **PERSIMMON TREE ROAD.**

11.4 Cross Bradley Boulevard to remain on **PERSIMMON TREE ROAD.**

13.0 **Left** on **RIVER ROAD** (MD 190). *Caution: traffic.*

13.3 Cross Falls Road (MD 189) in Potomac. Restaurants, fast food and general stores.

21.7 **Left** to stay on **RIVER ROAD.** Turns into **MD 112** in Seneca at T.

22.4 Cross Great Seneca Creek. Riley's Lock one mile to left on C&O Canal. Poole's General Store on right.

23.1 **Right** on **PARTNERSHIP ROAD.** [End of Map 1 instructions.]

27.0 **Bear left** on **MD 107.**

29.5 **Right** on **BEALLSVILLE ROAD** (MD 109) in Poolesville.

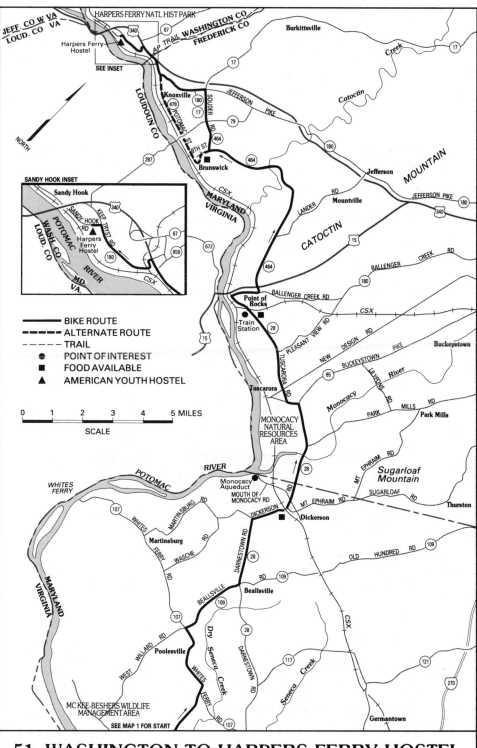

SANDY HOOK INSET

- BIKE ROUTE
- - - ALTERNATE ROUTE
- - - TRAIL
● POINT OF INTEREST
■ FOOD AVAILABLE
▲ AMERICAN YOUTH HOSTEL

0 1 2 3 4 5 MILES

SCALE

51. WASHINGTON TO HARPERS FERRY HOSTEL
Montgomery & Frederick Counties, Md.   Map 2 of 2

32.0   **Left** on **MD 28** (Darnestown Road) in Beallsville.

35.3   Enter Dickerson. MD 28 becomes **DICKERSON ROAD.** Store. Pass under railroad tracks. Mount Ephraim Road to right leads to Sugarloaf Mountain. At 35.7 miles, Mouth of Monocacy Road to left leads to Monocacy Aqueduct. Stay on **DICKERSON ROAD** (MD 28).

39.1   **Left** to stay on **MD 28** (Tuscarora Road) at fork. MD 85 (Buckeystown Pike) goes right. *Caution: MD 28 seems to go down to right.*

43.5   Enter Point of Rocks. Food, train station, C&O Canal Towpath.

43.9   **Right** on **BALLENGER CREEK ROAD.** *Caution: fast traffic.*

44.9   **Left** on **MD 464.** Very hilly.

45.0   Cross US 15.

52.1   **Right** on **SOUDER ROAD** (MD 464) at traffic light. ALTERNATE ROUTE stays straight (see end of cues).

53.1   **Straight** on **MD 17.**

54.2   **Left** on **MD 180.**

55.9   Enter Knoxville, a hilltop at intersection of MD 478, on left.

58.2   **Bear left** to merge onto **US 340.** *Caution: heavy traffic.*

59.9   **Left** on **KEEP TRYST ROAD** uphill.

60.1   **Right** on **SANDY HOOK ROAD/HARPERS FERRY ROAD.**

60.3   **Left** into **HOSTEL.**

ALTERNATE ROUTE

At 52.1 miles, go **straight** on **SOUDER ROAD** (MD 464) at traffic light. This route passes through Brunswick; its quaintness may compensate for the added traffic. This alternate adds less than one mile to the main route.

52.1   **Straight** on **9TH STREET** into Brunswick.

52.3   Berlin Cafe. Good food here.

53.3   **Left** on **MD 478** at blinking light. Follow as it bends sharply back to right and descends to **POTOMAC STREET.**

54.5   Pass under bridge over Potomac River. Stay on **MD 478.**

56.6   **Left** on **MD 180** in Knoxville. Pick up main route at 55.9 miles.

52. WASHINGTON TO BALTIMORE

With the vibrant city of Baltimore as its destination, this tour provides a circuitous but relatively low-traffic route from downtown Washington, D.C. Baltimore boasts a nationally acclaimed aquarium, a beautifully renovated harbor, the nation's largest railroad museum, the birthplace of Babe Ruth and an interesting historic district.

Starting from Washington's Union Station, the trip is also ideal for out-of-town tourists who want to experience both cities. The tour ends at the Baltimore International AYH-Hostel, conveniently located a few blocks from the Baltimore Inner Harbor and the Camden Yards baseball stadium. A few hilly stretches lie along the way, but the novice bicyclist should be able to complete the ride in one day.

START: Union Station bike racks on the west side of Union Station at the corner of Massachusetts Avenue and First Street NE in Washington, D.C. [The starting point is within the Capital Beltway.] **ALTERNATE START:** Silver Spring Metro station (Red Line) at Colesville Road, two blocks northeast of 16th Street and the District line (see end of cues). **METRO STARTS:** Union Station Metro station (Red Line) is at start; Silver Spring Metro station (Red Line) is at alternate start; Rhode Island Metro station (Red Line) is on the route at 1.3 miles.

LENGTH: 42.7 miles. From **ALTERNATE START:** 42.0 miles.

TERRAIN: Relatively level, with some hilly stretches. Demands some skills with traffic. [Note: the proposed Metropolitan Branch Trail right-of-way will run from Union Station to Takoma Park/Silver Spring with a connecting trail to Prince Georges County and, when built, may substitute for the on-street route.]

POINTS OF INTEREST: National Shrine of the Immaculate Conception (202-526-8300) at 2.5 miles; bike shops in Riverdale at 7.2 miles and at alternate start; Northwest Branch and Northeast Branch parks, starting at 5.5 miles; College Park Airport with museum at 9.4 miles, the nation's oldest continuously operating general aviation facility; National Agricultural Research Station at 14.1 miles; Van Horn Tavern marker at 15.0 miles; old Richmond-to-Philadelphia stage coach route at 18.8 miles; Carroll Park at 40.2 miles, home of signer of Declaration of Independence. In Baltimore at end: Harborplace (410-332-4191) with U.S.S. Constellation (410-539-1797), built in 1797; National Aquarium (410-576-3800); B&O Railroad Museum (410-752-2490); Lexington Market; Babe Ruth birthplace; Pratt Library; and scenic old Baltimore neighborhoods.

FOOD: Frequent along the route.

LODGING: In Baltimore, Baltimore International AYH-Hostel, 17 West Mulberry Street (410-576-8880). Inns include: Admiral Fell, 888 South Broadway (410-522-7377); Celie's Waterfront Bed and Breakfast, 1714 Thames Street (410-522-2323); Shirley Madison Inn, 205 West Madison Street (410-728-6550); Society Hill Hotel, 58 West Biddle Street (410-837-3630); Governor's House, 1125 North Calvert Street (410-752-7722); and Hopkins Inn, 3404 St. Paul Street (410-235-8600).

MAPS: *ADC's Washington Area Bike Map; Baltimore Area Bike Map.*

MILES DIRECTIONS & COMMENTS

0.0 **Right** on **1ST STREET NE** (downhill on bikepath). **Follow BIKEROUTE U.** Pass Trailways/Greyhound Station. For ALTERNATE START from Silver Spring Metro station, see end of cues.

0.8 **Jog right** at end of road at **FLORIDA AVENUE NE** to **ECKINGTON PLACE NE.**

1.0 **Right** at end of road, onto **R STREET NE.**

1.1 **Left** on **3RD STREET NE.**

1.3 **Right** on **T STREET NE,** then **left** on **4TH STREET NE.** Cross Rhode Island Avenue NE (US 1). Rhode Island Avenue Metro station on right. Proposed Metropolitan Branch Trail right-of-way is west of railroad tracks.

2.5 **Right** on **MICHIGAN AVENUE NE** at National Shrine of the Immaculate Conception. *Caution: traffic.* **Follow BIKEROUTE M.** Cross over Metro tracks.

3.7 Cross South Dakota Avenue NE (use bikepath on right). **Bear right** on **VARNUM STREET NE** at traffic light (use roadway).

4.2 **Left** at end of road onto **22ND STREET NE.** Cross Eastern Avenue (end Bikeroute M) and enter Maryland. Go **straight** on **ARUNDEL ROAD.**

4.9 **Right** on **34TH STREET** at traffic light, then **left** on **WINDOM STREET.**

5.3 **Left** on **38TH STREET** (no sign). Cross Northwest Branch.

5.5 **Right** on **BIKEPATH** in park. *Caution: poor pavement.*

5.7 **Left** on **BIKEPATH** (on leg of T). Pass through Magruder Park.

6.0 **Straight** on **40TH AVENUE,** then **bear right** to stay on 40th Avenue.

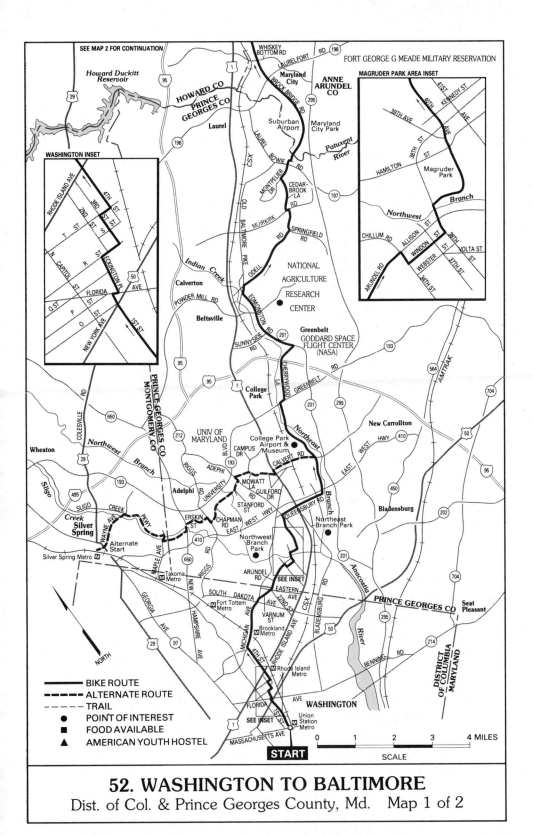

SEE MAP 2 FOR CONTINUATION

FORT GEORGE G MEADE MILITARY RESERVATION

MAGRUDER PARK AREA INSET

WASHINGTON INSET

52. WASHINGTON TO BALTIMORE
Dist. of Col. & Prince Georges County, Md.   Map 1 of 2

BIKE ROUTE
ALTERNATE ROUTE
TRAIL
● POINT OF INTEREST
■ FOOD AVAILABLE
▲ AMERICAN YOUTH HOSTEL

0   1   2   3   4 MILES

SCALE

START

6.5   Pass store, then continue **straight** on **41ST AVENUE.**

6.7   **Right** on **QUEENSBURY ROAD.** Pass Leland Hospital at 7.1 miles.

7.2   Cross Baltimore Pike (US 1). Riverdale. All services, including bike shop. Cross railroad tracks.

7.7   **Straight** at "No Outlet" sign at Taylor Street.

7.8   **Straight** at end of road and follow **DIRT PATH** across bridge.

7.9   **Left** on paved **BIKEPATH.** Northeast Branch becomes Indian Creek. Cross over East-West Highway.

9.0   (ALTERNATE START joins here; see end of cues.) Cross under Calvert Street.

9.4   College Park Airport with museum.

9.7   **Jog right** across creek.

10.9 **Right** on **GREENBELT ROAD SIDEWALK.**

11.0 **Left** on **CHERRYWOOD LANE** (use roadway). Cross over Capital Beltway at 12.0 miles.

12.6 **Left** at end of road onto **EDMONSTON ROAD** (MD 201). At 13.5 miles pass Sunnyside Avenue. National Agriculture Research Station on right at 14.1 miles. Pass traffic light at Powder Mill Road.

14.7 **Right** on **OLD BALTIMORE ROAD.** *Caution: steep uphill.*

15.0 **Right** on **ODELL ROAD.** *Caution: narrow, poor pavement.* Site of Van Horn Tavern marker.

16.2 **Bear right** to stay on **ODELL ROAD** at Ellington Road by electrical substation. Pass through wooded portion of Research Station. Pass Springfield Road.

17.4 **Sharp left** at end of road onto **MUIRKIRK ROAD,** then **right** on **CEDARBROOK LANE.** Pass through development area. Pass recreation center with swimming pool.

18.3 **Right** at end of road onto **MONTPELIER DRIVE.** Cross Laurel Bowie Road (MD 197) at traffic light at 18.7 miles.

18.8 **Left** at end of road onto **BROCK BRIDGE ROAD** (this is the old Richmond-to-Philadelphia stage coach route). Cross Brock Bridge (county line) at 19.0 miles.

19.3 **Jog right** onto **BIKEPATH** in Maryland City Park. Airport at 19.7 miles.

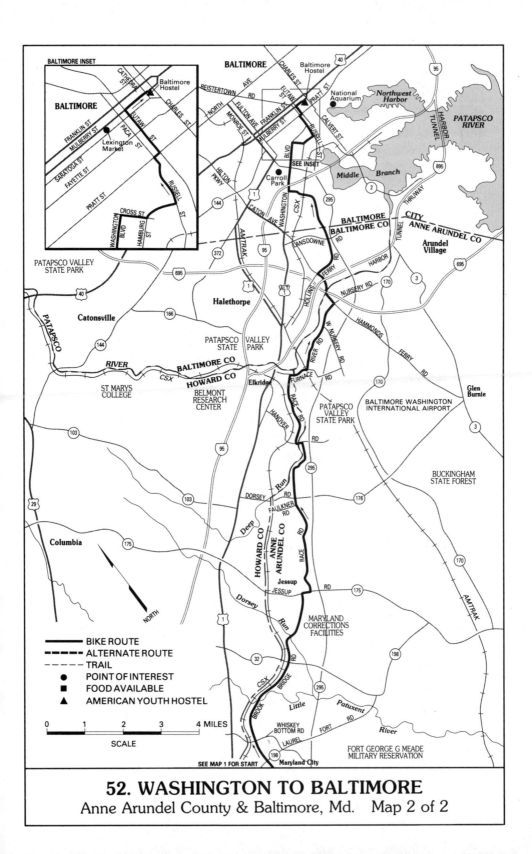

52. WASHINGTON TO BALTIMORE
Anne Arundel County & Baltimore, Md.   Map 2 of 2

20.6 **Straight** at end of bikepath to rejoin roadway. Pass store. [End of Map 1 instructions.]

21.4 Cross Laurel Fort Road (MD 198) at traffic light. Stores. Pass Laurel Raceway Stables. Cross Whiskey Bottom Road at 22.0 miles and Little Patuxent River at 23.2 miles. Cross under highway at 24.0 miles. Cross railroad tracks, traffic light at MD 32 at 24.6 miles.

24.6 **Left** on **SERVICE ROADWAY,** then **right** onto **BROCK BRIDGE ROAD** (before railroad). Pass Maryland Surplus Property store. Cross Dorsey Run at 25.5 miles. Pass prison at 25.9 miles.

26.7 **Right** on **JESSUP ROAD** (MD 175).

26.9 **Left** on **RACE ROAD** (before MD 295). Hilly.

27.2 **Bear right** to stay on **RACE ROAD.**

29.5 **Bear right** to stay on **RACE ROAD** at Faulkner Road. Cross Dorsey Road (MD 176) at traffic light.

31.3 **Left** at end of road onto **HANOVER ROAD,** then **right** on **RACE ROAD.**

33.4 **Right** at end of road onto **FURNACE ROAD.** Note Elkridge Furnace Inn. Cross Deep Run.

33.5 **Left** on **FURNACE ROAD.** Uphill. Cross Stony Run, then cross under railroad tracks and I-195.

33.9 **Left** on **FURNACE ROAD.** Becomes **RIVER ROAD.**

34.2 **Bear left** to stay on **RIVER ROAD.**

35.1 **Left** at end of road onto **WEST NURSERY ROAD.**

35.7 **Left** on **HAMMONDS FERRY ROAD** at traffic light. Stores. Cross under I-695 (Baltimore Beltway) at 36.1 miles. Cross Patapsco River. Cross under I-895 (Tunnel Thruway) at 36.4 miles.

36.7 **Right** on **HOLLINS FERRY ROAD** at traffic light. Cross traffic light at Lansdowne Road at 37.7 miles. Enter Baltimore at 38.2 miles. Cross many railroad tracks, including tracks at **bad angle** at 39.6 miles.

39.7 **Right** at end of road onto **WASHINGTON BOULEVARD.** Cross under I-95, then cross river and railroad tracks. Pass Carroll Park on left at 40.2 miles.

40.9 **Right** on **CROSS STREET** at traffic light at bend.

41.1 **Left** onto **HAMBURG STREET** at traffic light.

41.4   **Left** at end of street onto **RUSSELL STREET**. Turns into **PACA STREET**. *Caution: traffic; avoid ramps to King Drive and I-95.*

41.8   **Right** on **PRATT STREET** for one block, then **left** on **EUTAW STREET**. [Note: B&O Railroad Museum is one-half mile left on Pratt Street, on left.]

42.4   **Right** on **MULBERRY STREET**.

42.7   **Arrive** at **HOSTEL,** 17 West Mulberry Street, on right.

ALTERNATE START

0.0   From Silver Spring Metro station Metrobus area, go **right** (uphill) on **WAYNE AVENUE**. Cross Georgia Avenue (MD 97), staying on **WAYNE AVENUE**.

1.2   **Right** on **SLIGO CREEK PARKWAY**. Sligo Creek Trail starts on left, to Wheaton Regional Park. **Jog right** on **MAPLE STREET** to stay on Sligo Creek Parkway, and **left** at next intersection to continue on **SLIGO CREEK PARKWAY.**

3.9   **Left** on **NEW HAMPSHIRE AVENUE** (MD 650) at T. *Caution: traffic.* **First right** on **ERSKINE STREET.**

4.9   **Right** on **RIGGS ROAD** at T. Use far sidewalk if traffic is heavy.

5.1   **First left** on **CHAPMAN ROAD** (awkward turn).

5.9   **Straight** on **NORTHWEST BRANCH PARK TRAIL.** Pass tennis court and parking lot, then **left** over **FOOTBRIDGE.**

6.1   **Left** on **STANFORD STREET** at corner of Wells Boulevard. Climb hill.

6.4   **Left** on **ADELPHI ROAD.** *Caution: busy street.* **First right** on **CAMPUS DRIVE** at traffic light. Enter University of Maryland campus.

6.7   **Right** on **MOWATT LANE,** near parking toll booth. Follow this to **left** as it becomes **GUILFORD DRIVE,** a divided road.

7.5   **Left** on **US 1** at traffic light. **First right** on **CALVERT ROAD.**

8.3   **Pick up** Northeast Branch Park Trail, just past Linson Pool-Wells Ice Rink, on right. **Enter trail** from pool parking lot, then **follow to left,** passing under Calvert Road. Joins with main route at cue 9.0.

53. QUEENSTOWN TO YE LANTERN INN

For a delightful investigation into the history and charm of the Eastern Shore, try this route from historic Queenstown in northern Kent County, Md. to the waterfront town of Betterton, Md. on the Chesapeake Bay.

Kent County was settled in 1642. Chestertown, the county seat, was founded in 1706. Washington College, founded in Chestertown in 1782, is the tenth oldest liberal arts college in the United States. The town's notable colonial architecture is further explained in the Rock Hall Ramble (Tour 28).

Betterton sits in the northern corner of Maryland's Eastern Shore. Ye Lantern Inn AYH-Hostel, built in 1905 as part of a large Victorian-era resort, remains the only inn out of the 16 originally constructed in the area. It operates as both a bed-and-breakfast and hostel. A public beach is a three-minute walk from the inn.

START: Parking lot on Main Street (across from Post Office) in Queenstown, Md. From the Capital Beltway, take US 50 East over the Chesapeake Bay Bridge. Continue for nine miles past the bridge and exit onto MD 18 North. Continue one mile to Queenstown. Queenstown is 52 miles west of the Capital Beltway.

LENGTH: 36.2 miles.

TERRAIN: Level.

POINTS OF INTEREST: Penn Dutch Farmers Market and birth site of Charles Wilson Peale near start; historic Centreville at 6.4 miles; Washington College at 22.6 miles; and Betterton at 35.9 miles, with public beach and tennis courts.

FOOD: Markets at 6.4 and 22.6 miles; closest grocery to Ye Lantern Inn is three miles away. Restaurants at 6.4 and 22.6 miles.

LODGING: In Betterton, Ye Lantern Inn AYH-Hostel (410-348-5809). In Queen Annes County, Tuckahoe State Park (410-634-2810) public campgrounds. Near Chestertown, Duck Neck campgrounds (410-778-3070). In Chestertown, inns include The Imperial (410-778-5000), Mitchell House (410-778-6500) and White Swan Tavern (410-778-2300).

MAPS: Queen Annes and Kent Counties, Md. road maps.

MILES   DIRECTIONS & COMMENTS

0.0   **Bear left** on **MAIN STREET.** Pass fire station in Queenstown.

0.8   **Bear left** on **MD 18** at fork, moving away from US 50/301.

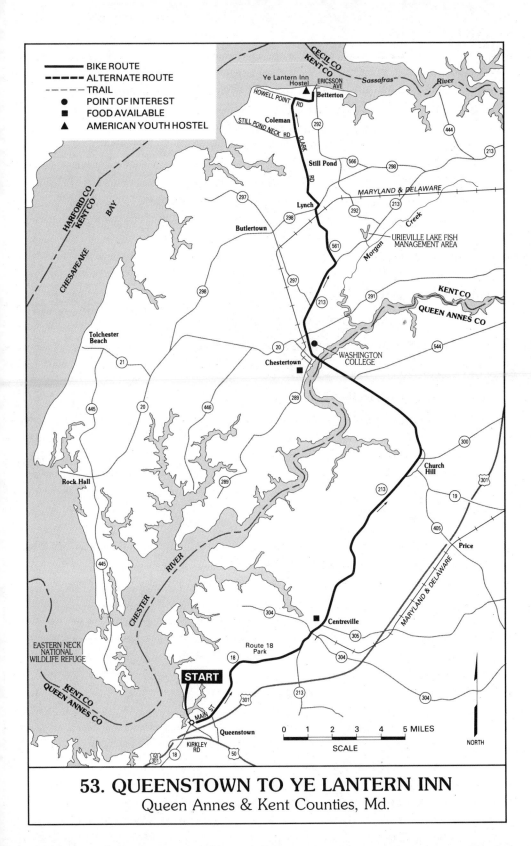

BIKE ROUTE
ALTERNATE ROUTE
TRAIL
● POINT OF INTEREST
■ FOOD AVAILABLE
▲ AMERICAN YOUTH HOSTEL

CECIL CO
KENT CO

Sassafras River

Ye Lantern Inn Hostel
ERICSSON AVE
Betterton
HOWELL POINT RD
Coleman
STILL POND NECK RD
CLARK RD
292
444
213
Still Pond
566
298
MARYLAND & DELAWARE
Lynch
297
298
292
213
Creek
Butlertown
561
Morgan
URIEVILLE LAKE FISH MANAGEMENT AREA
297
213
291
KENT CO
QUEEN ANNES CO
Tolchester Beach
20
544
21
Chestertown
WASHINGTON COLLEGE
445
20
446
289
300
Rock Hall
289
Church Hill
301
19
405
Price
445
CHESTER RIVER
MARYLAND & DELAWARE
EASTERN NECK NATIONAL WILDLIFE REFUGE
304
Centreville
305
KENT CO
QUEEN ANNES CO
213
304
START
Route 18 Park
18
MAIN ST
301
213
304
Queenstown
KIRKLEY RD
50
50
301
18

0 1 2 3 4 5 MILES
SCALE

NORTH

53. QUEENSTOWN TO YE LANTERN INN
Queen Annes & Kent Counties, Md.

3.8   4-H Campground on left (no public sites).

6.4   **Left** on **MD 213.** Enter Centreville. Grocery store, restaurants, historic homes and courthouse.

7.7   Pass MD 305.

16.4   Cross MD 300.

22.6   Cross Chester River into Chestertown. General store, restaurants, Washington College. **Continue** on **MD 213.**

24.0   Pass MD 291.

27.5   **Left** on **MD 561.**

30.0   **Right** on **MD 298** at T.

30.3   **Left** on **CLARK ROAD** (no sign), toward Coleman.

33.5   Cross Still Pond Neck Road at stop sign.

35.1   **Right** on **HOWELL POINT ROAD.**

35.9   **Left** on **ERICSSON AVENUE** in Betterton.

36.2   **Left** into **YE LANTERN INN AYH-HOSTEL.**

54. VIRGINIA CREEPER TO BEAR'S DEN

Taking you from the terminus of the Washington and Old Dominion (W&OD) Trail in Purcellville, Va., this short but challenging trip explores the rural communities of Round Hill and Bluemont and ends at the Bear's Den AYH-Hostel. The tour can be combined with the W&OD Trail (Tour 64) for an excellent two-day trip. An exciting trip on its own, this route also can be extended by adding portions of the W&OD Trail.

The W&OD Trail takes its name from the railroad that ran along the right-of-way from 1859 to 1968. When train service was abandoned, the corridor was converted into a trail, connecting parks and recreational facilities along its 45-mile length. For additional historical information and the trail route from Washington to Purcellville, see W&OD Trail (Tour 64).

Bluemont, originally called Indian Thoroughfare, was renamed Snickersville after an early settler. When the railroad arrived, the present name was adopted to attract tourists, who rented carriages to the Bear's Den picnic grounds. Bluemont now hosts a popular fall fair.

Bear's Den AYH-Hostel is a mountaintop mansion built in the 1930s by Wagnerian diva Francesca Caspar Lawson. It offers a sweeping view of the Shenandoah Valley and serves as a hiking and bicycling stopover on the way to Front Royal and Shenandoah National Park.

For a trip to Harpers Ferry, combine this tour with Between the Hills to Harpers Ferry (Tour 55).

START: Intersection of the W&OD Trail and VA 690 (21st Street North) in Purcellville, Va. From the Capital Beltway, take VA 7 West (Leesburg Pike) to Purcellville (VA 7 is called Main Street in Purcellville). Turn right onto 21st Street North; trail is on the right. The route also can be started at the intersection of VA 7 and VA 690. Purcellville is 39 miles west of the Capital Beltway.

LENGTH: 8.8 miles.

TERRAIN: Level, with extended and steep uphill climb to the hostel.

POINTS OF INTEREST: W&OD Trail at start; Purcellville at 0.1 miles; Round Hill at 2.9 miles, elevation 548 feet; Hill High Orchards at 4.1 miles; Bluemont at 6.7 miles, with fall fair and picnic grounds; Bear's Den at end, with scenic overlook.

FOOD: Markets at start, 2.9, 4.1 and 6.8 miles (open Sundays). Restaurants at start, 2.9 miles. Picnic area at 4.1 miles.

LODGING: In Purcellville, Purcellville Inn (703-338-2850) on Main Street (VA 7). Near Bluemont, Bear's Den AYH-Hostel (703-554-8708) on Blue Ridge Mountain Road (VA 601).

MAPS AND INFORMATION: *W&OD Railroad Regional Park Trail Guide,* a detailed book of strip maps and information available for $4 postpaid from Northern Virginia Regional Park Authority, 5400 Ox Road, Fairfax Station, VA 22039 (703-352-5900); Loudoun County, Va. road map.

MILES   DIRECTIONS & COMMENTS

0.0   **Left** from W&OD Trail to go south on **VA 690** (21st Street North).

0.1   **Right** on **MAIN STREET** (Bus VA 7). Purcellville. Markets, fast food, restaurants, inn. Pass 7-Eleven at 0.5 miles.

2.9   Round Hill, elevation 548 feet. Diner and two general stores (closer one has hand-dipped ice cream) to right, on VA 719.

4.1   Hill High Orchards. Food and picnic areas with duck pond.

6.5   **Left** on **VA 760** toward Bluemont. Spectacular view to left (east) of valley and Sugarloaf Mountain.

6.8   **Right** on **VA 734** at T in Bluemont. General store with ice cream and food. Climb hill.

7.3   **Left** on **VA 7.**

8.0   **Left** on **VA 601** at Snickers Gap, on crest of Blue Ridge.

8.4   **Right** on **GRAVEL DRIVEWAY.**

8.8   **Arrive** at **BEAR'S DEN AYH-HOSTEL**, elevation 1,300 feet.

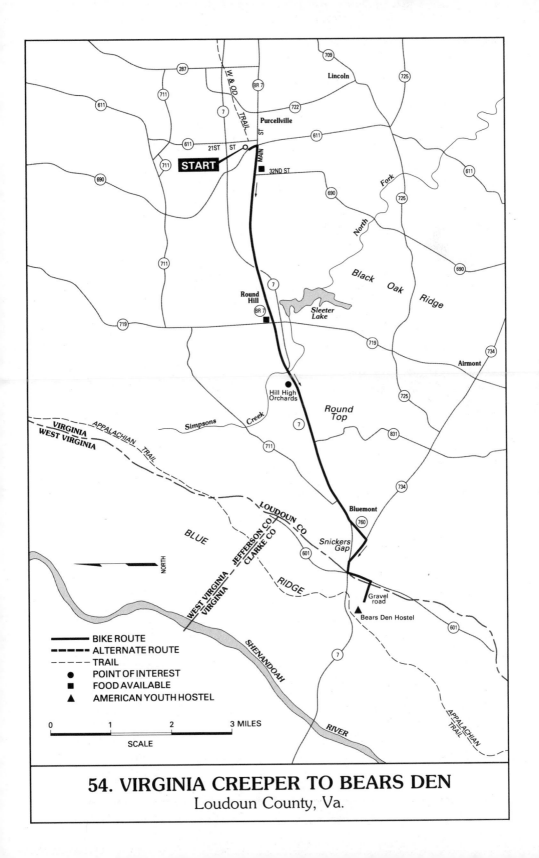

287
711
709
Lincoln
725
611
711
W & OD TRAIL
BR 7
722
7
Purcellville
611
611
611
21ST ST
MAIN ST
START
32ND ST
725
711
690
North Fork
611
890
Black Oak Ridge
690
711
7
Round Hill
BR 7
Sleeter Lake
719
719
Airmont
734
Hill High Orchards
Round Top
725
Simpsons Creek
831
VIRGINIA
WEST VIRGINIA
APPALACHIAN TRAIL
711
7
Bluemont
734
LOUDOUN CO
760
BLUE
JEFFERSON CO
CLARKE CO
Snickers Gap
601
WEST VIRGINIA
VIRGINIA
RIDGE
NORTH
Gravel road
Bears Den Hostel
601
SHENANDOAH
7
APPALACHIAN TRAIL

——— BIKE ROUTE
- - - ALTERNATE ROUTE
- - - TRAIL
● POINT OF INTEREST
■ FOOD AVAILABLE
▲ AMERICAN YOUTH HOSTEL

RIVER

0   1   2   3 MILES
SCALE

54. VIRGINIA CREEPER TO BEARS DEN
Loudoun County, Va.

55. BETWEEN THE HILLS TO HARPERS FERRY

Presenting you with a view of the Blue Ridge Mountains on the left and Short Hill on the right, this tour runs through an area of hilly farms and abundant wildlife. If you succeeded in climbing to Bear's Den AYH-Hostel (Tour 54), you are rewarded with downhill wheeling to the Harpers Ferry AYH-Hostel in Knoxville, Md., across the river from Harpers Ferry.

While in Harpers Ferry, take a side trip to Harpers Ferry National Historical Park, off US 340 in West Virginia. The park surrounds the town, which was captured in September 1862 by Confederate forces under Stonewall Jackson. Over 2,700 Union troops surrendered in the battle, the largest mass surrender in U.S. military history until World War II. The park also memorializes John Brown's famous 1859 raid on Harpers Ferry's arsenals.

The route in western Loudoun County uses fairly low-traffic roads, but they are narrow, without shoulders, and hedged with foliage. The tour is recommended for bicyclists with experience on narrow roads.

For a direct route back to Washington, D.C., see Washington to Harpers Ferry Hostel (Tour 51) or the C&O Canal Towpath (Tour 65).

START: Bear's Den AYH-Hostel on VA 601 (Blue Ridge Mountain Road) near Bluemont, Va. From the Capital Beltway, take VA 7 West through Leesburg and turn left onto VA 601. Continue 0.5 miles; hostel is on the right. Bluemont is 48 miles west of the Capital Beltway.

LENGTH: 21.4 miles.

TERRAIN: Level or downhill. Narrow roads.

POINTS OF INTEREST: Bluemont at 0.5 miles, with fall fair and picnic grounds; Round Hill at 5.3 miles; Potts Mill at 9.4 miles, built in 1842 and partly destroyed during the Civil War; Hillsboro at 11.1 miles, an early 1800s mill village; Old St. Paul's Church at 12.8 miles; Mechanicsville also at 12.8 miles, named after the blacksmith and wheelwright who repaired wagons that broke down on the badly rutted roads; and Harpers Ferry National Historical Park (304-535-6223) at end.

FOOD: Markets at 1.3 (open Sundays), 3.9. 5.3 (open Sundays), 11.1, 12.8 and 19.4 miles. Restaurant at 20.9 miles.

LODGING: Near Bluemont, Bear's Den AYH-Hostel (703-554-8708) on Blue Ridge Mountain Road (VA 601). Near Harpers Ferry, Harpers Ferry AYH-Hostel, 19123 Sandy Hook Road, Knoxville, Md. (301-834-7652); and Hilltop House (800-338-8319), on Ridge Street, 10 blocks from C&O Canal Towpath.

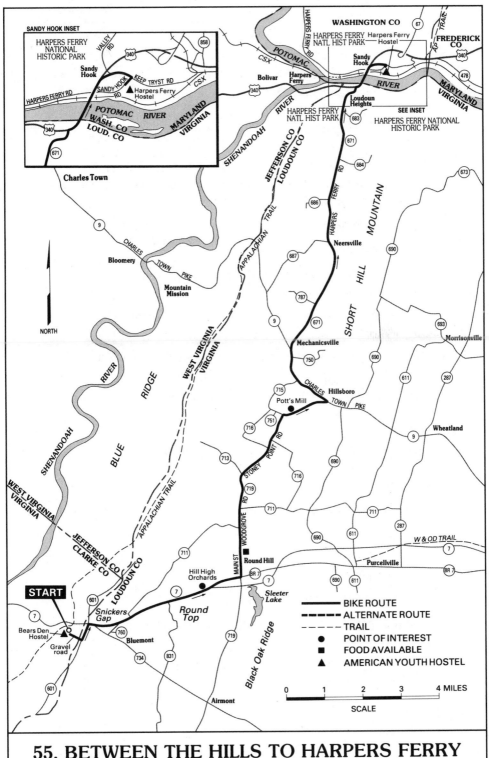

55. BETWEEN THE HILLS TO HARPERS FERRY
Loudoun County, Va.

MAPS: Loudoun County, Va. road map.

MILES   DIRECTIONS & COMMENTS

0.0   Leave Bear's Den AYH-Hostel by **GRAVEL ROAD.**

0.4   **Left** on **VA 601** at T.

0.8   **Right** on **VA 7,** and descend mountain. (Right on VA 734 for 0.5-mile side trip to Bluemont, with general store and historical buildings. Return by going north on VA 760 to VA 7.)

3.9   Hill High Orchards on left where VA 7 becomes a two-lane road.

4.0   **Left** on **BUS VA 7.**

5.3   **Left** on **VA 719** (Main Street) in Round Hill, at diner. Two general stores in town.

8.0   **Bear right** to stay on **VA 719** (Woodgrove Road), where gravel VA 713 goes straight.

9.9   **Right** to stay on **VA 719** (Stoney Point Road) at T. Pass Pott's Mill on left.

11.1   **Sharp left** on **VA 9** (Charles Town Pike) at Hillsboro line. Turn right to town center for markets, churches and restored homes. *Caution: fast traffic.*

12.8   **Bear right** on **VA 671** (Harpers Ferry Road) in Mechanicsville. Lineberry's Store (closed Sundays). Pass Old St. Paul's Church on left at 16.5 miles.

19.4   Butts Grocery on left, as downhill to Potomac River begins.

20.1   **Right** on **US 340** at T. Cross bridge over Potomac River on walkway.

20.9   **Bear right** on **MD 180** (Keep Tryst Road). Pass Cindy Dee Diner on left (good pie).

21.2   **Right** on **SANDY HOOK ROAD.**

21.4   **First left** up hill to **HARPERS FERRY AYH-HOSTEL** parking lot.

56. FIT FOR A PRINCE

Fredericksburg, Va., with its multitude of historic sites and antique shops, is the destination of this classic tour. On quiet roads well-suited for bicycling, the trip can be completed in one day by strong cyclists. Picnic and exploration stops along the way add other delightful attractions to the day's cycling.

Fredericksburg is the destination of the tour and offers enough historical sites to occupy the industrious tourist for a week. A bare-bones visit should include stops at Mary Washington's house; Kenmore House (1752), the Georgian home of Washington's sister Betty; Hugh Mercer's Apothecary Shop; and the James Monroe Museum and Library. The city also deserves recognition for its many excellent antique shops and The Great Outdoors Shop, a valuable resource for bicyclists. The route ends at the Fredericksburg Visitor Center, a source of free maps of the city and its historic sites.

Just southwest of the city limits is the Fredericksburg and Spotsylvania National Military Park (Fredericksburg Battlefield). Following his defeat at the Battle of Antietam in Sharpsburg, Md. (see Antietam Battlefield Loop, Tour 3), General Robert E. Lee's Confederate Army retreated here. In December 1862, he was engaged by Union General Ambrose Burnside. Lee emerged victorious. Over 12,000 Union soldiers fell, while the South lost about 5,000 men, mostly desertions for Christmas. Some of the heaviest fighting took place at Mayre's Heights, now Mary Washington College (1908) in the center of town.

START: Prince William County Recreation Center on Davis Ford Road (VA 642) in Prince William County, Va. From the Capital Beltway, take I-95 South and exit onto Horner Road. Turn left onto Davis Ford Road and continue to the Recreation Center. Starting point is approximately 10 miles southwest of the Capital Beltway.

LENGTH: 46.5 miles.

TERRAIN: Rolling hills.

POINTS OF INTEREST: Prince William County Recreation Center (703-590-9292) at start; Ashbury Church at 15.5 miles; Curtis Lake at 32.2 miles; picnic area at 32.5 miles; and Fredericksburg at 46.5 miles, with many historic sites, antique shops and Visitor Center. Fredericksburg and Spotsylvania National Military Park (Fredericksburg Battlefield), with Battlefield Visitors Center and Stonewall Jackson shrine, on BUS US 1 (Lafayette Boulevard), is less than one mile southwest of Fredericksburg Visitor Center.

FOOD: Markets at 5.4, 7.3, 14.3 and 35.5 miles, and at end. Restaurants at end.

LODGING: In Fredericksburg, budget motels include Colonial Motel, 1914 Princess Anne Street (703-373-5539) and Payne's Motel, 1902 Princess Anne Street (703-373-6435); inns include Kenmore Inn (703-371-7622), Richard Johnston Inn (703-899-7606), McGrath House (703-371-4363) and Fredericksburg Colonial Inn (703-371-5666); campgrounds include Fredericksburg KOA, 4100 Guinea Station Road (703-898-7252). North of Fredericksburg, Aquia Pines Campgrounds (703-659-3447), near Stafford.

MAPS AND INFORMATION: Maps of Fredericksburg available at the Fredericksburg Visitor Center (open 9 a.m. to 5 p.m.); Prince William and Stafford Counties, Va. road map.

MILES DIRECTIONS & COMMENTS

0.0 **Right** out of **PRINCE WILLIAM RECREATION CENTER,** then first **left** on **HOADLY ROAD** (VA 642). Horse farm on right of Hoadly Road.

5.4 **Left** on **DUMFRIES ROAD** (VA 234). Convenience store on right.

7.3 **Right** on **JOPLIN ROAD** (VA 619 East). General store on left. Buy food here for picnic at Curtis Lake.

7.5 **Right** on **ADEN ROAD** (VA 646). Cows and estates hoof by roof.

14.3 **Left** on **FLEETWOOD DRIVE** (VA 611; U.S. Bikecentennial Route 1) at Aden Grocery. Historic Ashbury Church at 15.5 miles.

18.0 Cross stream on one-lane bridge.

18.2 **Right** on **U.S. BIKE ROUTE 1** (unmarked). Woods and houses.

25.8 **Right** to stay on **VA 612** where sign says VA 610 and 612.

29.2 **Left** on **POPLAR ROAD** (VA 616). Rolling hills and meadows. Curtis Lake, at 32.5 miles, is a good picnic stop.

35.5 General store.

36.4 **Left** on **TRUSLOW ROAD** (VA 652).

41.4 **Right** to stay on **TRUSLOW ROAD.**

44.2 **Right** on **US 1.**

45.0 **Left** on **BUS US 1** (Princess Anne Street), after crossing the Rappahannock River into Fredericksburg.

46.5 **Left** on **CHARLOTTE STREET. Left** into **FREDERICKSBURG VISITOR CENTER.**

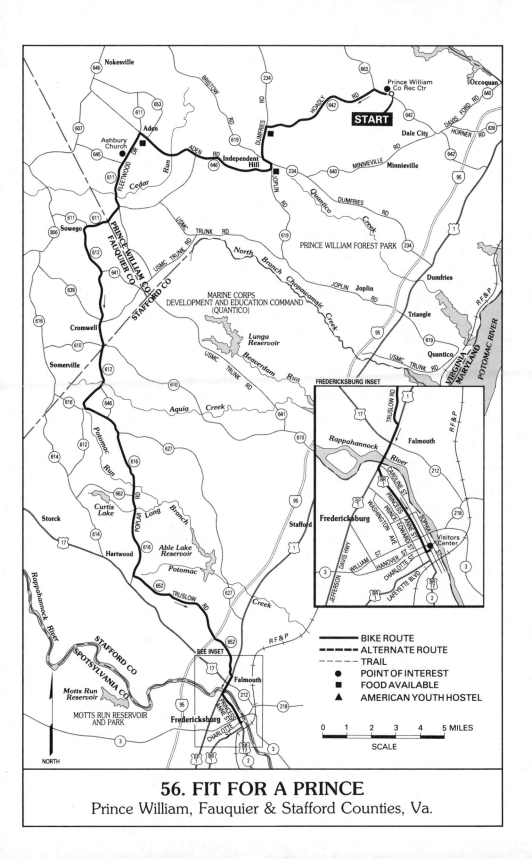

56. FIT FOR A PRINCE
Prince William, Fauquier & Stafford Counties, Va.

57. FREDERICKSBURG TO SANGRAAL HOSTEL

You will enjoy pristine forests, large plantations and various historic sites on your way from Fredericksburg through Southern flatland to the Sangraal-by-the-Sea AYH-Hostel in Urbanna, Va. Leave time for a side trip by ferry to Tangier Island.

Cyclists of average ability can make this trip in two days by spending one night at a campground or motel halfway along the route. From Urbanna, you can continue to Williamsburg and onward to Virginia's historic Colonial Triangle.

CAUTION: Traffic moves quickly on many roads along this route. If you are unskilled in bicycling with traffic, you should choose alternate, less-travelled routes. Use detailed ADC maps to identify alternate side-roads.

START: Fredericksburg Visitor Center, on the corner of Charlotte and Caroline Streets in Fredericksburg, Va. From the Capital Beltway, take I-95 South to Fredericksburg. Exit onto Germanna Highway (VA 3) East; this becomes William Street. Turn right onto Princess Anne Street (VA 2) and left onto Charlotte Street. Visitor Center is one block on right. Fredericksburg is 43 miles southwest of the Capital Beltway.

LENGTH: 114.4 miles.

TERRAIN: Hilly to rolling hills.

POINTS OF INTEREST: Fredericksburg Area Museum (703-371-5668) near start at 904 Princess Anne Street; Ingleside Plantation and Winery at 33.6 miles, with tours; side trip to Washington Birthplace National Monument at 35.5 miles; Westmoreland State Park at 39.5 miles, with boating and swimming; Stratford Hall (804-493-8038) at 44.3 miles, a working plantation and birthplace of Robert E. Lee; and Tangier Island ferry at 83.3 miles.

FOOD: Markets near start and at 20.7, 35.5, 44.3, 45.2, 70.5 and 88.7 miles. Restaurants near start.

LODGING: In Urbanna, Sangraal-by-the-Sea AYH-Hostel (804-776-6500). At Westmoreland State Park (804-493-8821), campgrounds at 39.5 miles. In Montrose, Callao, Wicomico Church, and at 108.4 miles, various motels.

MAPS: Virginia state highway map.

MILES   DIRECTIONS & COMMENTS

0.0   **Left** out of Visitor Center to go north on **CAROLINE STREET.**

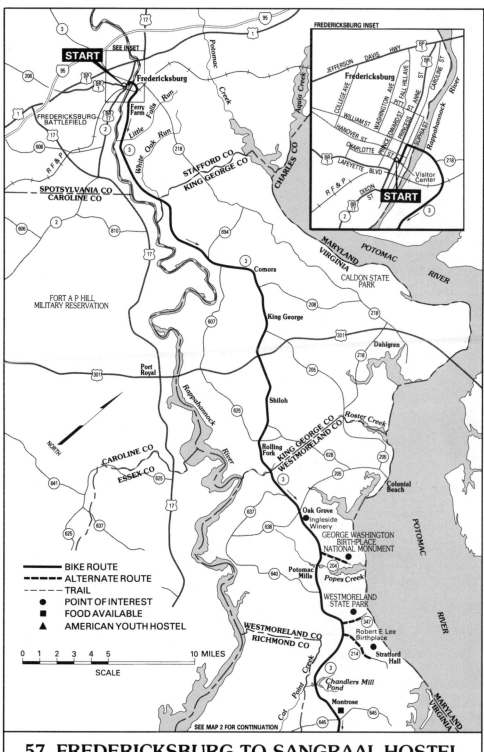

57. FREDERICKSBURG TO SANGRAAL HOSTEL
Stafford, King George & Westmoreland Counties, Va.   Map 1 of 2

0.2 **Right** on **VA 3.** Cross Rappahannock River.

20.7 General store.

33.6 Pass Ingleside Plantation and Winery on left. Tours given.

35.5 **SIDE TRIP** to Washington Birthplace National Monument: Left on VA 204 for one mile. Monument on left, on Popes Creek. Reverse direction to VA 3. General store on left.

39.5 Westmoreland State Park on left. Camping.

44.3 **SIDE TRIP** to Lee's home, Stratford Hall: Left on VA 214 for 1.2 miles. Home and general store on left. Reverse direction to VA 3.

45.2 Enter Montross. Motel, restaurants, markets. [End of Map 1 instructions.]

49.6 **Left** on **VA 202.**

67.8 Enter Callao. Motel. **Straight** on **US 360.**

75.1 Enter Heathsville. Junction of VA 201. Stay **straight** on **US 360.**

83.3 **Right** on **VA 200. SIDE TRIP:** Stay straight on US 360 then right on VA 646, following signs to Tangier Island ferry. Reverse direction to VA 200. Distance is five miles. Bed-and-breakfast lodging on Tangier Island: Hilda Crockets Chesapeake House (804-891-2331).

88.7 Enter Wicomico Church. Markets and historic buildings.

96.2 Enter Kilmarnock. **Continue south** on **VA 200.**

100.7 **Bear left** to stay on **VA 200.**

101.9 **Right** on **VA 3** in White Stone.

102.4 **Cross RAPPAHANNOCK RIVER BRIDGE.** Two miles long, bicycles permitted; no pedestrians allowed. Hummel Airport on right.

108.4 **Left** on **VA 3 AND 33,** where they merge. Motels.

110.6 **Left** on **VA 626,** at sign for Sangraal-by-the-Sea.

112.1 **Right** at Sangraal sign, staying on **VA 626.**

113.5 **Left** to stay on **VA 626** at post office.

114.4 **Left** into **HOSTEL.**

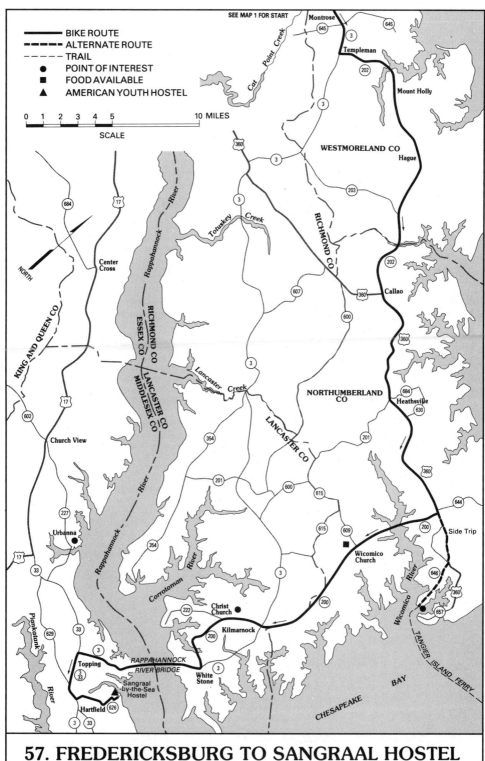

SEE MAP 1 FOR START

BIKE ROUTE
ALTERNATE ROUTE
TRAIL
● POINT OF INTEREST
■ FOOD AVAILABLE
▲ AMERICAN YOUTH HOSTEL

0 1 2 3 4 5   10 MILES
SCALE

Montrose
Templeman
Mount Holly

WESTMORELAND CO
Hague

RICHMOND CO

Center Cross

Totuskey Creek

Callao

King and Queen Co

Church View

607
600

NORTHUMBERLAND CO
Heathsville

LANCASTER CO

Lancaster Creek

Urbanna

Wicomico Church

Side Trip

Christ Church

Kilmarnock

Corrotoman River

Pianketank

Topping

RAPPAHANNOCK RIVER BRIDGE

White Stone

Sangraal by-the-Sea Hostel

Hartfield

TANGIER ISLAND FERRY

CHESAPEAKE BAY

Rappahannock River

Essex Co
Middlesex Co

57. FREDERICKSBURG TO SANGRAAL HOSTEL
Westmoreland, Northumberland & Lancaster Counties, Va.   Map 2 of 2

58. SANGRAAL HOSTEL TO YORKTOWN

Using generally low traffic roads from the Sangraal-by-the-Sea AYH-Hostel, this tour provides you with an excellent route to Virginia's Colonial Triangle. Average cyclists can complete this trip in one day, although you should be prepared for heavy traffic on US 17.

START: Sangraal-by-the-Sea AYH-Hostel on VA 626 in Urbanna, Va. From the Capital Beltway, take I-95 South through Fredericksburg and exit onto US 17 South (toward Norfolk). Go 69 miles and exit onto VA 602 into Urbanna. Urbanna is 118 miles south of the Capital Beltway.

LENGTH: 40.8 miles.

TERRAIN: Level.

POINTS OF INTEREST: Gloucester at 17.7 miles, a wonderfully quaint town; Walter Reed birthplace at 18.7 miles; and Colonial Battlefield at 38.5 miles. For Yorktown attractions, see Yorktown Yonder (Tour 61).

FOOD: Markets (locations are approximate) at 5.5, 20.7, 24.9 and 28.5 miles. Fast food at 33.3 miles.

LODGING: In Urbanna, Sangraal-by-the-Sea AYH-Hostel (804-776-6500). See also Yorktown Yonder (Tour 61).

MAPS AND INFORMATION: Middlesex, Mathews, Gloucester and York Counties, Va. road maps; Virginia state highway map. For information on Yorktown, call the Visitor Center (804-898-3400).

MILES   DIRECTIONS & COMMENTS

  0.0   **Right** out of hostel to go south on **VA 626.**

  0.9   **Right** to stay on **VA 626** at T. Post office opposite.

  2.3   **Bear left** to stay on **VA 626.**

  2.8   **Left** on **VA 3/33** at T.

  3.3   **Bear right** on **VA 3.**

  6.5   Cross Piankatank River into Mathews County.

  8.0   **Right** to stay on **VA 3** (VA 198) at T.

  9.5   **Left** to stay on **VA 3.**

 11.6   **Right** on **VA 3/14** and cross North River.

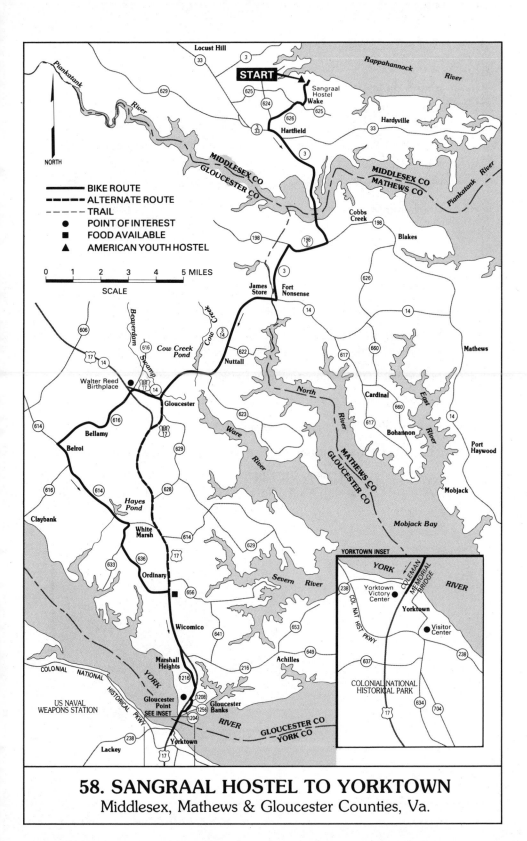

58. SANGRAAL HOSTEL TO YORKTOWN
Middlesex, Mathews & Gloucester Counties, Va.

15.6   **Bear right** to stay on **VA 3/14.**

17.7   **Right** on **VA 14** at T, through Gloucester. ALTERNATE ROUTE: turn left on BUS US 17 (turns into US 17) and follow it to junction with VA 636. Then, staying on US 17, pick up main route cues at 33.3 miles.

18.7   **Bear left** on **VA 616.** Birthplace of Walter Reed.

20.7   Food, laundromat.

25.5   **Left** on **VA 614** at T.

29.8   **Right** on **VA 633.**

30.7   **Bear left** on **VA 636,** just past church on right.

33.3   **Right** on **US 17** at T. Fast food.

35.3   **Bear right** on **VA 1216** (only to avoid traffic; otherwise continue on US 17 for shortest route to Yorktown). Alternate route rejoins here.

38.5   **Merge** onto **US 17.** Pass Colonial Battlefield on right.

38.8   **Bear left** on **VA 1208** (to avoid traffic).

39.6   **Right** on **VA 1204,** and **first left** on **US 17.**

39.8   Cross Coleman Memorial Bridge over York River. *Caution: traffic.*

40.8   **Right** into **YORKTOWN VICTORY CENTER.** [For a 12-mile trip to Williamsburg, continue 0.5 miles on US 17, turning right on Colonial Parkway.]

59. RICHMOND RESPITE

Originating in Nokesville, Va., this route explores rural Virginia on lightly travelled back roads. Extend your cycling holiday by continuing west to Charlottesville (Tour 60) and east to Williamsburg and Yorktown (Tour 61).

This region is steeped in Civil War history, and the route passes through the sites of several major battles. For example, Chancellorsville National Battlefield preserves the two-day battle in May 1863, where General Robert E. Lee's 60,000 rebels battled Joseph Hooker's 115,000 Federal troops. Lee's victory was brilliant but costly: more than 30,000 soldiers died in the battle. Lee also lost his most trusted and competent general, Stonewall Jackson. Wounded by friendly fire, Jackson succumbed to complications resulting from a battlefield amputation of his left arm.

The one-way route ends at Capitol Square, a 12-acre historic park in downtown Richmond. The state capital building was designed by Thomas Jefferson. Other notable attractions include the Valentine Museum, the Museum of the Confederacy and many restored Colonial homes.

START: Brentsville District High School in Nokesville, Va. From the Capital Beltway, take I-66 West for 11 miles and exit onto VA 28 South. Continue south for 14 miles and turn left onto VA 652 (Fitzwater Drive). Continue one mile; school is at end of road. Nokesville is 26 miles southwest of the Capital Beltway.

LENGTH: 111.7 miles.

TERRAIN: Rolling hills to Chancellorsville; easy hills into Richmond.

POINTS OF INTEREST: Kellys Ford at 20.2 miles; Chancellorsville National Battlefield at 39.0 miles; Fredericksburg and Spotsylvania National Military Park (703-371-0802) at 46.5 miles, with Stonewall Jackson shrine; and side trip to Scotchtown home of Patrick Henry at 82.6 miles. In Richmond: Monument Avenue; Museum of the Confederacy, 1201 East Clay Street (804-649-1861); Valentine Museum; Science Museum of Virginia, 2500 West Broad Street (804-367-1081); and Capitol Square.

FOOD: Markets at 3.7, 14.6, 44.6, 50.0, 60.0 and 78.5 miles. Restaurants at 50.0 miles. Many food options after 98.5 miles.

LODGING: In Richmond, many choices include the Catlin-Abbott House, 2304 East Broad Street (804-780-3746), and Mr. Patrick Henry's Inn, 2300 East Broad Street (804-644-1322). For bed-and-breakfast information call 804-648-7560.

MAPS: Champion Map of Metropolitan Richmond; Prince William, Fauquier, Culpeper, Spotsylvania, Caroline, Hanover and Henrico Counties, Va. road maps; Virginia state highway map.

MILES DIRECTIONS & COMMENTS

0.0 **Left** out of high school on **ADEN ROAD** (VA 646).

3.7 **Right** on **FLEETWOOD DRIVE** (VA 611) at Aden General store.

7.2 **Right** to stay on **VA 611.**

9.0 **Left** on **VA 612.**

9.9 **Right** on **VA 609.**

11.7 **Left** on **VA 806.**

14.6 Cross US 17 in Morrisville. General store on left. **Straight** on **VA 634.**

18.0 **Right** on **VA 651.**

20.2 **Left** on **VA 620.** Cross Kellys Ford Bridge and enter Culpeper County.

20.6 **Left** to stay on **VA 620.**

26.1 **Left** on **VA 610.** Charlottesville Chaser (Tour 60) begins here by turning right on VA 610.

39.0 Chancellorsville National Battlefield.

40.2 Cross VA 3. General store in Chancellorsville.

42.0 **Right** on **VA 612.**

44.6 **Left** on **VA 624.** General store at intersection.

46.5 **Left** on **VA 613.** Pass through Spotsylvania National Military Park.

50.0 **Straight** to stay on **VA 208** in Spotsylvania. Grocery store and restaurant.

54.0 **Straight** on **VA 738** in Snell.

56.1 **Left** on **VA 647** in Blades Corner. [End of Map 1 instructions.]

60.0 **Right** on **VA 605** in Marye. General store.

61.4 **Left** on **VA 604.**

64.0 **Right** on **VA 603** in Blanton. Cross North Anna River at Londora Bridge.

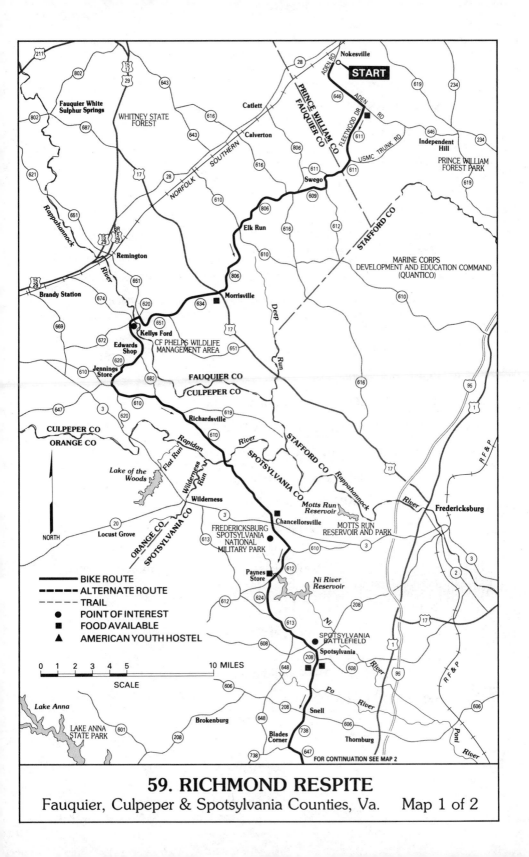

59. RICHMOND RESPITE
Fauquier, Culpeper & Spotsylvania Counties, Va.   Map 1 of 2

68.1   **Bear right** to stay on **VA 603.**

68.2   **Bear left** to stay on **VA 603.**

73.8   **Left** on **VA 684** at T.

74.5   **Right** on **VA 601.**

78.0   **Right** on **VA 738** in Coatesville.

78.5   **Left** on **VA 671.** General store on left.

82.6   **Right** to stay on **VA 671** at T. **SIDE TRIP:** Left on VA 685 to Scotchtown home of Patrick Henry.

82.8   Cross VA 54. *Caution: traffic.* Fire lookout tower 0.25 miles to left.

85.2   **Left** on **VA 657.** Cross two creeks and the South Anna River.

91.2   **Right** on **VA 666** in Lanes Corner.

92.0   **Left** on **VA 623** at T.

93.6   **Right** on **VA 648.**

94.5   **Right** on **VA 660** at T. Winn's Baptist Church at corner.

94.6   **Left** on **GREENWOOD ROAD** (VA 625).

98.5   **Right** on **WOODMAN ROAD.** Cross I-295.

102.7 **Straight** on **HERMITAGE ROAD.** Cross Hilliard Road.

103.9 **Left** on **DUMBARTON AVENUE.**

104.1 **Right** on **LAKESIDE AVENUE** (VA 161). This becomes **HERMITAGE ROAD.** Pass Joseph Bryan Park and enter Richmond.

106.2 **Bear right** on **BOULEVARD.** Pass under I-95, then **immediate left** on **ROBIN HOOD ROAD.**

106.4 **Right** on **HERMITAGE ROAD.**

107.7 **Bear right** on **MEADOW STREET**, crossing Broad Street.

108.2 **Left** on **MONUMENT AVENUE.** Beautiful homes, statues of Confederate heros. This becomes **FRANKLIN STREET.**

111.7 **Arrive** at **CAPITOL SQUARE.**

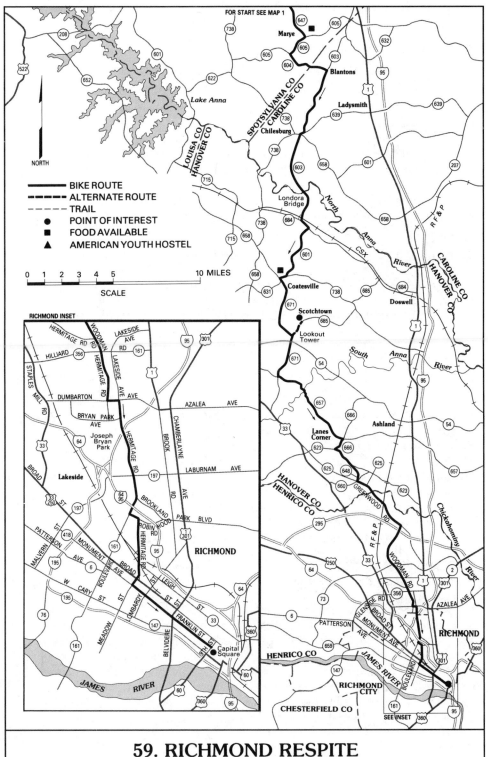

59. RICHMOND RESPITE
Caroline, Hanover & Henrico Counties, Va.   Map 2 of 2

60. CHARLOTTESVILLE CHASER

Traversing Virginia countryside and ending in historic Charlottesville, this route rewards the well-trained cyclist with a Jeffersonian treat. The terminus of the tour is the University of Virginia, founded by President Thomas Jefferson in 1825. The university Rotunda was designed by Jefferson as an exact half-size replica of the Roman Pantheon. Adjacent to the Rotunda lie the Lawn and the Pavilions, two rows of living quarters in the Greco-Roman tradition. The famous Serpentine Wall borders the Pavilions and formal gardens. In designing the walls, Jefferson adapted the undulating French design to strengthen construction. Free tours of the university begin hourly at the Rotunda during the summer months.

This route is also a branch of the Richmond Respite (Tour 59).

START: Brentsville District High School in Nokesville, Va. From the Capital Beltway, take I-66 West for 11 miles and exit onto VA 28. Continue south for 14 miles and turn left onto VA 652 (Fitzwater Drive). Continue one mile to school at end of road. Nokesville is 26 miles southwest of the Capital Beltway.

LENGTH: 84.5 miles.

TERRAIN: Hilly.

POINTS OF INTEREST: Kelly's Ford at 20.2 miles. In Charlottesville: George Rogers Clark Museum at 80.1 miles, a refurbished 1740 house named for the Revolutionary War hero; Albemarle County Courthouse at 83.3 miles, an 1803 colonial-style courthouse approved by Thomas Jefferson; and Court Square at 83.4 miles, which is in the oldest part of town and houses the county historical society museum and library at 220 Court Square. Near Charlottesville: Michie Tavern, a restored 18th century inn; Monticello (804-295-8181), Jefferson's 35-room home; and Ash Lawn (804-293-9539; admission charged), home of President James Monroe (designed by Jefferson in 1799).

FOOD: Markets at 3.7, 14.6 and 46.7 miles. Restaurants at 53.6, 56.4 and 66.5 miles. Many food options in Charlottesville area.

LODGING: At Lake Reynovia campgrounds (804-296-1910): from Charlottesville go two miles south on VA 20, then one mile west on VA 742 and take Avon Street exit. In Orange, President Madison Inn, 120 Caroline Street (703-672-2321). In Charlottesville, Howard Johnson Motor Lodge (804-296-8121) on University Avenue; EconoLodge Motel, 400 Emmet Street (804-296-2104), opposite University Hall; Silver Thatch Inn north of town (804-978-4686); High Meadows Vineyard Inn (804-286-2218); and Inn at the Crossroads (804-979-6452). For bed-and-breakfast information, call 804-979-7264.

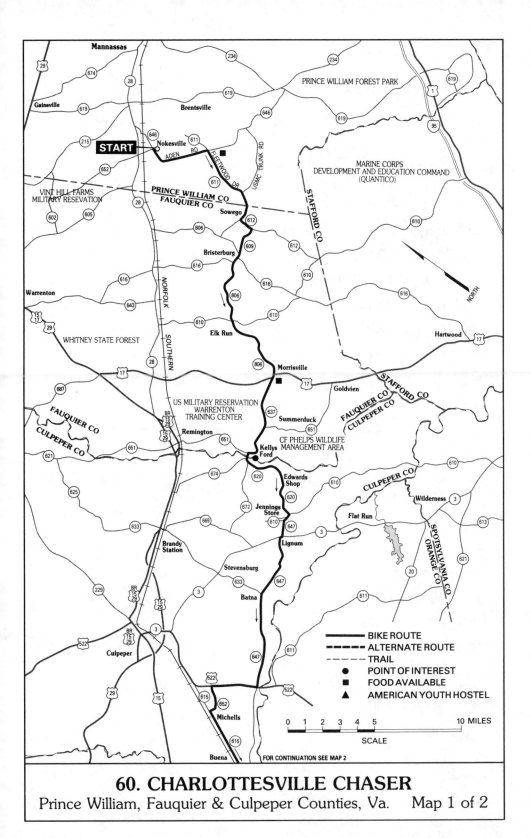

60. CHARLOTTESVILLE CHASER
Prince William, Fauquier & Culpeper Counties, Va.   Map 1 of 2

MAPS AND INFORMATION: Maps strongly advised: Culpeper, Orange and Albemarle Counties, Va. road maps. The Charlottesville Chamber of Commerce (804-438-7406), open weekdays 9 a.m. to 5 p.m., provides free brochures and information on Albemarle County and Charlottesville. It is located at the corner of Market Street and McIntire Road, west of the County Courthouse, to the right of Water Street at mile 83.0.

MILES   DIRECTIONS & COMMENTS

0.0   **Left** out of high school on **ADEN ROAD** (VA 646).

3.7   **Right** on **FLEETWOOD DRIVE** (VA 611) at Aden General Store.

7.2   **Right** to stay on **VA 611.**

9.0   **Left** on **VA 612.**

9.9   **Right** on **VA 609.**

11.7   **Left** on **VA 806.**

14.6   Cross US 17 in Morrisville. General store. **Straight** on **VA 637.**

18.0   **Right** on **VA 651.**

20.2   **Left** on **VA 620.** Cross Kellys Ford Bridge. Enter Culpeper County.

20.6   **Left** to stay on **VA 620.**

26.1   **Right** on **VA 610** at T. Richmond Respite (Tour 59) continues from here by turning left on VA 610.

26.7   **Left** on **VA 647**.

27.6   **Right** on **VA 3.**

27.8   **Immediate left** on **VA 647.**

37.2   **Right** on **US 522.**

39.8   **Left** on **VA 652.**

41.9   **Left** on **VA 615** (no sign). Turn before railroad crossing. [End of Map 1 instructions.]

46.7   **Bear left** to stay on **VA 615.** General stores on right at Rapidan, one block off route.

53.6   **Straight** on **SOUTH BUS VA 20** through Orange. Cross railroad tracks, then cross US 15. General store, inn and restaurants in Orange.

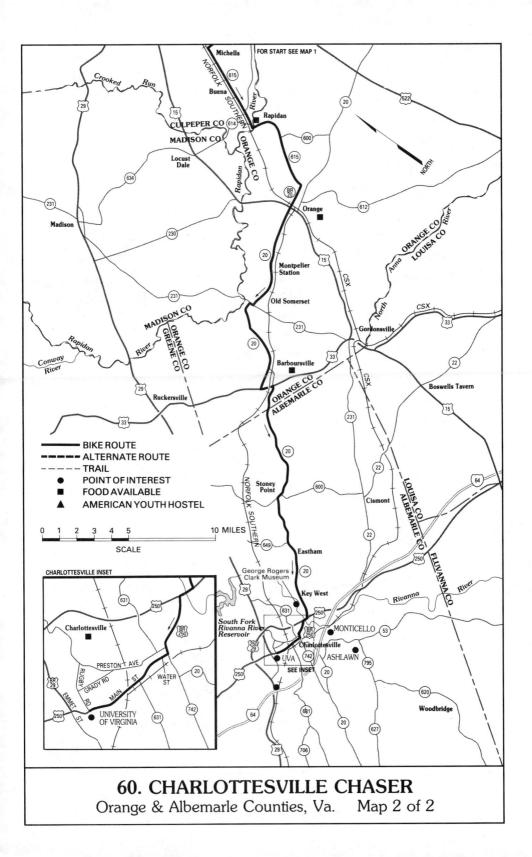

60. CHARLOTTESVILLE CHASER
Orange & Albemarle Counties, Va.   Map 2 of 2

60.2 **Straight** on **VA 20,** crossing VA 231.

65.9 **Left** on **US 33.** Cross railroad tracks.

66.5 **Right** on **VA 20** in Barboursville. Restaurant in town.

73.8 **Left** to stay on **VA 20.** Climb hills.

80.1 George Rogers Clark Museum on right.

81.6 **Right** on **VA 20/US 250.** Becomes **BUS US 250.** Enter Charlottesville. Heavy traffic.

82.8 **Left** on **BUS US 250.**

83.0 **Bear right** on **WATER STREET** (US 250). Becomes **MAIN STREET,** then **UNIVERSITY AVENUE.** Albemarle County Courthouse at corner of Park and Jefferson Streets.

84.5 **Arrive** at **ROTUNDA,** University of Virginia.

61. YORKTOWN YONDER

Bicycle along country roads from Coatesville, Va. through Jamestown and the colonial town of Williamsburg to Yorktown. The route follows portions of the Bikecentennial Transamerica Trail. It also visits Civil War battlefield sites in the Richmond area and passes by old Virginia plantations along the James River.

Coatesville at the start of the tour is a small town 22 miles northwest of Richmond. This tour can be combined with Tour 59 (Richmond Respite) or mixed for a route that best suits your cycling interests. See Richmond Respite to begin your itinerary from Washington to the Colonial Triangle.

John D. Rockefeller largely restored the colonial town of Williamsburg in the 1920s. This former capital of Virginia takes you back in time to colonial life, complete with craft demonstrations, fife and drum parades, cobblers and wool-spinning maidens in period costumes and much more. For additional information, contact the Williamsburg Information Center.

Yorktown marks the site of the final defeat of the British in the American Revolutionary War. One-third of all British forces in North America surrendered to General George Washington in October 1781. The National Park Service conducts tours of the battlefield from the town's Victory Center.

Jamestown, the third point of the Colonial Triangle, lays claim as the first permanent English settlement in the New World. See the Jamestown Loop (Tour 44) for details on its attractions.

START: Intersection of VA 738 and 671 in Coatesville, Va. From the Capital Beltway, take I-95 South and exit onto VA 639 West. Continue for four miles and turn onto VA 738 South (toward Beaverdam). Tour begins at the junction of VA 738 and 671. Coatesville is 64 miles south of the Capital Beltway.

LENGTH: 115.5 miles.

TERRAIN: Hilly.

POINTS OF INTEREST: Scotchtown at start, home of Patrick Henry (1719); Randolph Macon College at 13.0 miles; battle sites at 32.0 miles; Chickahominy River at 40.0 miles; Malvern Hill Battlefield at 52.6 miles; Richmond National Battlefield Park (804-226-1981) at 56.1 miles; Berkeley Plantation (804-829-6018) at 32.0 miles, home of President William Henry Harrison (open daily 8 a.m. to 5 p.m.) and location of the first official Thanksgiving observance in 1619; College of William and Mary (1693) at 100.6 miles, the second oldest college in the country with Sir Christopher Wren building and Sunken Garden; and Royal Governor's Palace at 101.0 miles. In Williamsburg, Bikesmith of Williamsburg (804-229-9858) and Abby Aldrich

Rockefeller Folk Art Center. In Yorktown, Colonial National Historic Park (804-898-3400), Yorktown Victory Center (804-877-1776), Battlefield (804-898-4000), "On the Hill" Cultural Arts Center (804-898-3076) and Watermen's Museum (804-877-2641).

FOOD: Markets at 13.0, 25.4 and 64.5 miles. Restaurants at 13.0 and 56.4 miles. Many food options in Williamsburg and Yorktown.

LODGING: In the Williamsburg area, campgrounds include Twin Oaks, Williamsburg Campsites (804-564-3101), and Jamestown Beach Campsites (804-229-7609). Call the local Chamber of Commerce (804-229-6511) for a brochure of area campsites, or Colonial Williamsburg Foundation (804-229-1000) for other lodging information.

MAPS AND INFORMATION: *Bike Map: Historic Triangle* from Williamsburg Information Center (800-HISTORY) or Virginia Department of Transportation; Hanover, Henrico, Charles City and James City Counties, Va. road maps. For National Park Service tours of Yorktown battlefields, call the Yorktown Visitor Center (804-898-3400).

MILES   DIRECTIONS & COMMENTS

0.0   **Left** to go southeast on **VA 738** in Coatesville. At approximately 5.0 miles, a 3.5-mile **SIDE TRIP** takes you to Scotchtown by turning right on VA 685.

6.8   **Right** after Hanover Academy, on **VA 667.** The tour follows Bikecentennial's Transamerica Trail for next 20 miles -- look for "Route 76" bike signs.

11.8   Enter Ashland corporate limits (signed). Bike shop in town.

12.8   **Bear left** onto **WEST PATRICK STREET** (no sign).

13.0   **Right** on **NORTH CENTER STREET** just before railroad tracks. This passes Randolph Macon College and becomes **SOUTH CENTER STREET.** Restaurant and general store in Ashland.

14.6   **Left** on **VA 667** (Bikecentennial Route 76).

17.7   Cross **LEWISTON ROAD** (VA 802). (For campgrounds, turn right and follow Lewiston Road 0.3 miles then left on Frontage Road for 0.3 miles.)

19.5   **Right** on **VA 656** (Bikecentennial Route 76).

21.0   **Left** on **VA 637** (Bikecentennial Route 76).

25.0   **Left** on **US 301.** Pass under railroad bridge.

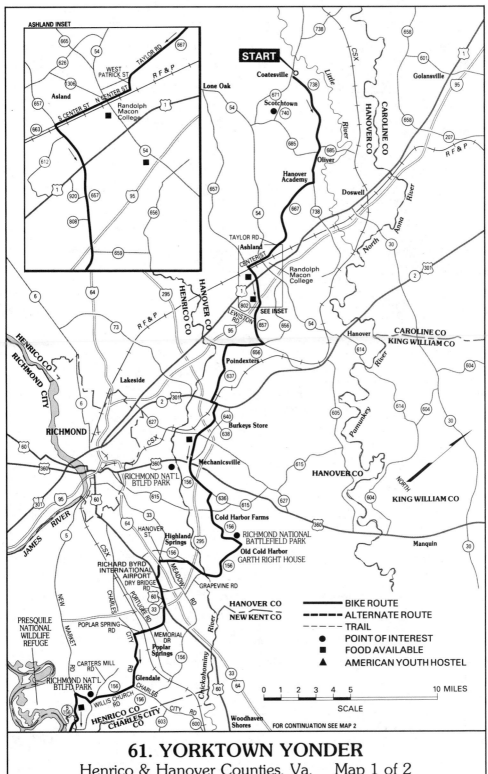

61. YORKTOWN YONDER
Henrico & Hanover Counties, Va.   Map 1 of 2

25.4   **Right** on **VA 638.** Market.

29.5   Enter Mechanicsville. **Straight** on **VA 156,** crossing US 360 (Cold Harbor Road).

32.0   **Right** to stay on **VA 156.** Watch for turns in road. Pass several Civil War battlefields from the Peninsula Campaign.

40.0   Cross Chickahominy River.

42.8   **Left** on **GRAPEVINE ROAD** (VA 33/US 60). Then **left** again to stay on **GRAPEVINE ROAD** (VA 33/US 60).

46.5   **Right** on **MEMORIAL DRIVE,** after passing under I-295.

48.0   **Straight** on **POPLAR SPRING ROAD,** crossing Portuguee Road.

49.0   **Left** on **CHARLES CITY ROAD** at T.

52.6   **Straight** on **VA 156 SOUTH** (Willis Church Road). Pass through Malvern Hill Battlefield.

56.1   Pass Richmond National Battlefield Park.

56.4   **Left** to stay on **VA 156/5** (New Market Road). Cafe on corner. [End of Map 1 instructions.]

61.8   **Straight** on **VA 5.** VA 156 turns right here.

64.5   Cross dirt road. Grocery and Berkeley Plantation on right.

71.1   Enter Charles City.

84.4   Cross Chickahominy River.

88.8   Cross river, *then* **right** on **VA 614.** Do not turn on unpaved VA 614!

90.8   **Right** on **VA 31** (VA F-665). Camping on right. **Left** on **VA 359** into Jamestown.

91.1   **Left** on **COLONIAL PARKWAY** to Williamsburg.

100.3 **Right** on **NEWPORT AVENUE RAMP** before tunnel, following signed bike route. *Caution: no bicycles allowed in tunnel.*

100.4 **Right** on **NEWPORT AVENUE.**

100.6 **Right** on **SOUTH HENRY STREET.** Pass College of William and Mary.

100.9 **Right** on **PRINCE GEORGE STREET.** Enter Colonial Williamsburg.

101.0 **Left** on **PALACE GREEN** to Royal Governors Palace. **Bear right** at **PALACE.**

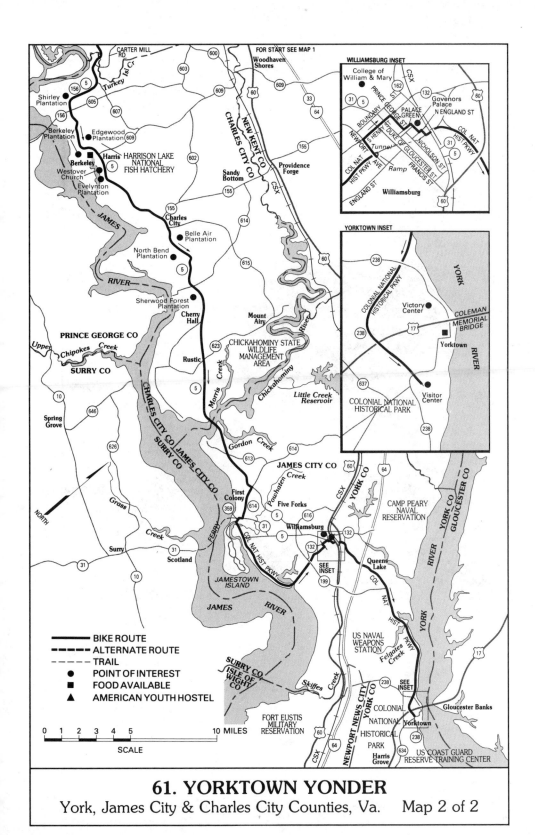

MARKING LEGEND

— BIKE ROUTE
--- ALTERNATE ROUTE
- - - TRAIL
● POINT OF INTEREST
■ FOOD AVAILABLE
▲ AMERICAN YOUTH HOSTEL

0 1 2 3 4 5   10 MILES
SCALE

61. YORKTOWN YONDER
York, James City & Charles City Counties, Va.   Map 2 of 2

Map labels:

CARTER MILL RD
Turkey Isl Cr
156
5
600
603
Woodhaven Shores
FOR START SEE MAP 1
609
609
60
33
64
NEW KENT CO
CHARLES CITY CO
605
607
Shirley Plantation
156
Edgewood Plantation
609
Berkeley Plantation
Berkeley
Harris
HARRISON LAKE NATIONAL FISH HATCHERY
602
Sandy Bottom
155
Providence Forge
CSX
Westover Church
Evelynton Plantation
155
Charles City
614
Belle Air Plantation
North Bend Plantation
5
615
60
Sherwood Forest Plantation
Cherry Hall
Mount Airy
JAMES RIVER
PRINCE GEORGE CO
Upper
Chipokes Creek
SURRY CO
623
Rustic
CHICKAHOMINY STATE WILDLIFE MANAGEMENT AREA
Little Creek Reservoir
Morris Creek
Chickahominy River
10
646
Spring Grove
626
Gordon Creek
613
614
James City Co
CHARLES CITY CO / JAMES CITY CO
SURRY CO
Grass Creek
First Colony
359
614
Powhatan Creek
Five Forks
JAMES CITY CO
60
CAMP PEARY NAVAL RESERVATION
CSX
YORK CO
64
Surry
31
Scotland
31
10
31
616
5
Williamsburg
132
SEE INSET
199
JAMESTOWN ISLAND
COL NAT HIST PKWY
FERRY
Queens Lake
JAMES RIVER
YORK RIVER
YORK CO / GLOUCESTER CO
NORTH
US NAVAL WEAPONS STATION
Felgates Creek
COL NAT HIST PKWY
SURRY CO / ISLE OF WIGHT CO
Skiffes Creek
NEWPORT NEWS CITY / YORK CO
238
COLONIAL NATIONAL HISTORICAL PARK
Yorktown
238
Gloucester Banks
17
FORT EUSTIS MILITARY RESERVATION
60
64
CSX
Harris Grove
634
US COAST GUARD RESERVE TRAINING CENTER

WILLIAMSBURG INSET:
College of William & Mary
CSX
162
31
5
132
60
Govenors Palace
N ENGLAND ST
PRINCE GEORGE ST
PALACE GREEN
BOUNDARY ST
NEWPORT AVE
S HENRY ST
DUKE OF GLOUCESTER ST
NICHOLSON ST
COL NAT HIST PKWY
5
Tunnel
Ramp
FRANCIS ST
ENGLAND ST
60
Williamsburg

YORKTOWN INSET:
238
COLONIAL NATIONAL HISTORICAL PKWY
Victory Center
17
COLEMAN MEMORIAL BRIDGE
YORK RIVER
238
Yorktown
637
Visitor Center
COLONIAL NATIONAL HISTORICAL PARK
238

101.1 **Left** on **NORTH ENGLAND STREET. Right** down **RAMP** to **COLONIAL PARKWAY. Left** to Yorktown.

113.5 Enter Yorktown.

115.5 **Arrive YORKTOWN VISITOR CENTER.**

V. Off the Road

62. MOUNT VERNON TRAIL

A well-travelled route along the Potomac River, the Mount Vernon Trail takes bicyclists, joggers and hikers from Roosevelt Island near Key Bridge to George Washington's home in Mount Vernon (now Fairfax County), Va.

Intrinsic to Washington, D.C.'s premier trail system, the Mount Vernon Trail receives heavy usage, especially on weekends. It takes bicycle commuters into the city from the south and also provides an escape from downtown Washington. The Mount Vernon Trail connects to the Rock Creek Trail (Tour 63) to the north, the C&O Canal Towpath (Tour 65) to the northwest, and the W&OD Trail (Tour 64) to the west via Arlington's Custis Trail or Four Mile Run Trail.

Ride with caution, as highway ramp crossings and weekend bicycle congestion require attentive cycling.

START: Theodore Roosevelt Island on the Potomac River in Rosslyn, Va. By car, Roosevelt Island is accessible only by travelling north on the George Washington Memorial Parkway from Roosevelt Bridge (I-66/US 50) or points further south. Accessible from downtown Washington, D.C. via the Roosevelt Bridge. [Rosslyn is within the Capital Beltway.] **METRO STARTS:** Rosslyn Metro station (Orange and Blue Lines) is near start; National Airport Metro station (Blue and Yellow Lines), Arlington Cemetery Metro station (Blue Line), King Street Metro station (Yellow Line) and Braddock Road Metro station (Yellow Line) are along trail.

LENGTH: 19.0 miles.

TERRAIN: Level with three hills. Well-maintained asphalt; boardwalk in swamp areas. Narrow in some places.

POINTS OF INTEREST: Navy-Marine Memorial (1934) at 2.5 miles, dedicated to Americans who served at sea; Gravelly Point at 3.5 miles, with good view of the Potomac River and spectacular view of National Airport's busy main runway; Daingerfield Island at 6.3 miles, with Washington Sailing Marina, food, bike shop (open Sundays), sailing and fishing facilities; Old Town Alexandria at 8.1 miles, with Torpedo Factory art galleries, parks, shops, food, museums; Jones Point Lighthouse at 10.2 miles, once southernmost tip of the District of Columbia; Belle Haven at 11.7 miles, a 1730s tobacco warehouse that is now a picnic area; Dyke Marsh at 11.7 miles, a 240-acre wetland with more than 250 bird species; Fort Hunt Park at 16.2 miles, with 156 acres; and Mount Vernon (703-780-2000) at end, historic home of George Washington (fee charged for tour).

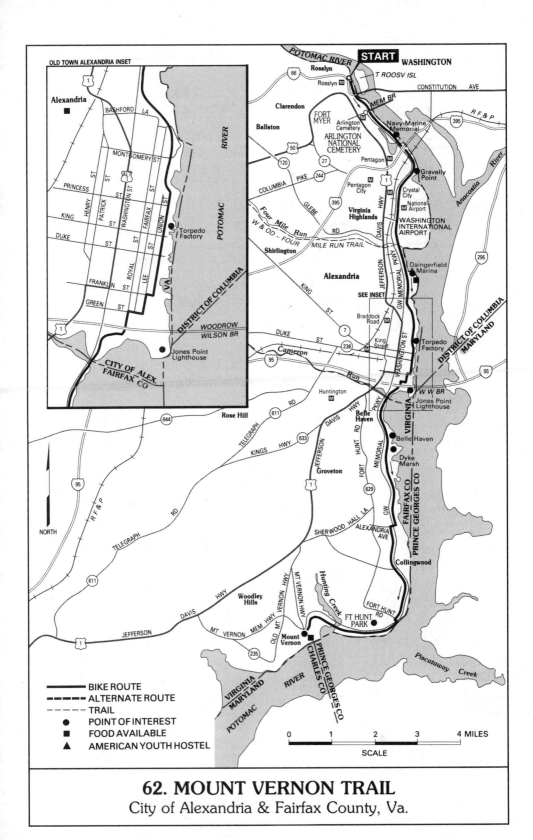

OLD TOWN ALEXANDRIA INSET

Alexandria

BASHFORD LA

MONTGOMERY ST

PRINCESS ST

KING ST

DUKE ST

HENRY ST · PATRICK ST · ALFRED ST · WASHINGTON ST · FAIRFAX ST · ROYAL ST · LEE ST · UNION ST

ALT 1

● Torpedo Factory

POTOMAC RIVER

VA

DISTRICT OF COLUMBIA

FRANKLIN ST

GREEN ST

WOODROW WILSON BR

CITY OF ALEX. FAIRFAX CO

● Jones Point Lighthouse

START WASHINGTON

POTOMAC RIVER

Rosslyn

66

Rosslyn Ⓜ

T ROOSV ISL

CONSTITUTION AVE

Clarendon

FORT MYER

Arlington Cemetery

MEM BR

Navy-Marine Memorial

R F & P

395

Ballston

ARLINGTON NATIONAL CEMETERY

50

120

27

244

COLUMBIA PIKE

GLEBE RD

Pentagon Ⓜ

1

Gravelly Point ●

Anacostia River

Pentagon City

395

Virginia Highlands

Four Mile Run

W & OD - FOUR MILE RUN TRAIL

Crystal City Ⓜ

National Airport Ⓜ

WASHINGTON INTERNATIONAL AIRPORT

295

Shirlington

DAVIS HWY

JEFFERSON PKWY

Daingerfield Marina ■

Alexandria

KING ST

SEE INSET

GW MEMORIAL PKWY

Braddock Road Ⓜ

DUKE ST

7

236

Cameron

95

Run

King Street Ⓜ

WASHINGTON ST

● Torpedo Factory

DISTRICT OF COLUMBIA MARYLAND

95

Huntington Ⓜ

RD

DAVIS HWY

FORT HUNT RD

MEMORIAL PKWY

Belle Haven

W W BR

● Jones Point Lighthouse

VIRGINIA

Belle Haven ●

Rose Hill

644

TELEGRAPH RD

611

633

KINGS HWY

JEFFERSON

Groveton

1

629

Dyke Marsh

FAIRFAX CO PRINCE GEORGES CO

95

611

TELEGRAPH RD

RF & P

SHERWOOD HALL LA

GW

ALEXANDRIA AVE

Collingwood

NORTH

Woodley Hills

DAVIS HWY

MT VERNON HWY

OLD MT VERNON HWY

Hunting Creek

FORT HUNT PARK

FT HUNT RD

Piscataway Creek

JEFFERSON

1

MT VERNON MEM HWY

MT VERNON HWY

Mount Vernon ■

235

PRINCE GEORGES CO CHARLES CO

VIRGINIA MARYLAND

POTOMAC RIVER

LEGEND

—— BIKE ROUTE

- - - ALTERNATE ROUTE

– – – TRAIL

● POINT OF INTEREST

■ FOOD AVAILABLE

▲ AMERICAN YOUTH HOSTEL

0 1 2 3 4 MILES

SCALE

62. MOUNT VERNON TRAIL
City of Alexandria & Fairfax County, Va.

FOOD: Markets at 8.1 miles. Restaurants at 6.3, 8.1 and 19.0 miles. Picnic areas at 6.3 and 11.1 miles.

MAPS AND INFORMATION: *Mount Vernon Trail Official Guide* available from the National Park Service, Turkey Run Park, McLean, VA 22101 (703-285-2601).

MILES DIRECTIONS & COMMENTS

0.0   Theodore Roosevelt Island. Go **south** (downriver) on **TRAIL.** Note connection with Arlington's Custis Trail to the north (upriver) via the bicycle bridge over the George Washington Memorial Parkway into Rosslyn.

1.5   Pass under Memorial Bridge. Narrow crossing!

2.5   Navy-Marine Memorial on left. Narrow passage over "Humpback Bridge" with poor protection from cars.

3.5   Gravelly Point. Soccer field. Good view of jet operations on National Airport's busy main runway; very noisy. Pass National Airport. *Caution: dangerous intersections with airport ramps.*

5.4   Connection to W&OD Trail via Arlington's Four Mile Run Trail, by bearing left through underpass under highway and railroad tracks. NOT MARKED, but just before bridge. **Keep right** to remain on Mount Vernon Trail.

6.3   Daingerfield Island (Washington Sailing Marina). Restaurant, water, bike shop, toilets, picnic facilities.

8.1   Enter Alexandria. Alternate routes through the city -- just keep heading south. Torpedo Factory, museums, restaurants, markets, shops.

10.2   Jones Point Lighthouse. Cross under Wilson Bridge (Capital Beltway).

11.7   Belle Haven picnic area. Separate trail to Dyke Marsh.

16.2   Fort Hunt Park on right.

19.0   **Arrive** at **MOUNT VERNON** parking lot and bike racks.

63. ROCK CREEK TRAIL

The scenic and popular Rock Creek Trail winds 25 miles from the Lincoln Memorial in Washington, D.C. to Lake Needwood Park in Montgomery County, Md. The Algonquin Indians, the area's original settlers, fished from Rock Creek, hunted bison and deer, raised crops and quarried quartzite for weapons and tools. Later, European settlers built grist mills and a saw mill on the creek, where farmers brought corn, wheat, buckwheat and rye to be ground into flour or meal.

Today the park and trail provide a refreshing escape to a more natural setting without leaving the city. However, the trail's popularity and narrow width make the Washington section highly congested, especially in fair weather and on weekends. Cyclists should observe caution, particularly at the dangerous car ramp intersections and the many sharp turns with short sight distances. On weekends and holidays, the National Park Service closes Beach Drive to motor traffic from Broad Branch Road to the Maryland line (a few stretches remain open to shared use with cars).

The Montgomery County section is less congested, wider and better maintained. It winds through woods, parks and residential neighborhoods, generally buffered from traffic and suburban sprawl. Similar to the Washington portion, cyclists should expect toddlers, pets and other distractions along the path.

The beginning of this route connects to the Mount Vernon Trail (Tour 62) just across the Memorial Bridge. Together, the two trails provide a tri-state 44-mile bicycling artery through the heart of the Washington area, with additional connections into Virginia via the Arlington's Custis Trail to the north and Four Mile Run Trail to the south, both of which connect further west to the W&OD Trail (Tour 64). Also, the C&O Canal Towpath (Tour 65) starts at 1.1 miles.

START: Bank of the Potomac River on the west side of the Lincoln Memorial below Memorial Bridge in Washington, D.C. Parking in Potomac Park, south of start. [The starting point is within the Capital Beltway.] **METRO STARTS:** Foggy Bottom Metro station (Blue and Orange Lines) is near start, on 23rd and I Streets NW (go south on 23rd Street NW to the Mall and the Lincoln Memorial); Woodley Park-Zoo Metro station (Red Line) is near the 4.0-mile cue (from the elevator, go south two blocks on Connecticut Avenue NW, then south into park from 24th Street NW, where the trail crosses the entrance road); Grosvenor Metro station (Red Line) is at 17.1 miles (go south one block on Rockville Pike, then left on Grosvenor Lane, then bear right on Beach Drive to intersection of trail and Franklin Street); Silver Spring Metro station (Red Line) is near 11.4 miles (1.7 miles east of trail). **ALTERNATE START:** At 10.8 miles. Meadowbrook Recreation Center (Candy Cane City), Silver Spring, Md.

From the Capital Beltway, take Connecticut Avenue south for one mile and exit, turning left onto East-West Highway (MD 410). Go one mile, then turn right onto Beach Drive. Center is on left, at traffic light.

LENGTH: 25.0 miles. From **ALTERNATE START:** 14.2 miles.

TERRAIN: Level. 6-8 feet wide asphalt trail, some roadway.

POINTS OF INTEREST: Lincoln Memorial near start; Kennedy Center at 0.6 miles (bike racks located on front plaza); Thompson's Boat House (202-333-4861) at 1.0 miles, with bike and boat rentals; Old Stone House, 3051 M Street NW, three blocks off the trail at 1.1 miles in Georgetown (open Wednesday-Sunday); National Zoo at 3.7 miles, with more than 2,000 animals from around the world, including pandas from China; Pierce Mill at 5.4 miles, a restored 18th-century grist mill; Art Barn at 5.4 miles, an old carriage house exhibiting local art (closed Mondays, Tuesdays and holidays); Miller's Cabin at 7.5 miles; Meadowbrook Recreation Center and Candy Cane City playground at 10.8 miles; riding stable at 11.1 miles; Mormon Temple at 12.9 miles; and Lake Needwood Park at end.

FOOD: Markets, fast food and restaurants at 1.1 miles (take Pennsylvania Avenue NW exit), 4.2 miles (Porter Road NW exit, turn right up hill to Connecticut Avenue NW) and 22.8 miles (turn right on Baltimore Road to Bauer Drive). Water fountains along trail. Snack vendors (seasonal) near start and at 3.7 miles.

MAPS AND INFORMATION: *Rock Creek Park Official Guide* available from National Park Service Rock Creek Park Headquarters, 5000 Glover Road NW, Washington, DC 20015-1098 (202-426-6832); *Rock Creek Hiker-Biker Trail* available from MD-NCPPC Community Relations, 8787 Georgia Avenue, Silver Spring, MD 20910-3760 (301-495-4600); *ADC's Washington Area Bike Map; Lower Montgomery County Bicycle Route Map.*

MILES   DIRECTIONS & COMMENTS

0.0   From underneath Memorial Bridge, go **north** (upriver) on **TRAIL.** Trail is accessible by sidewalk from Mall or southwest side of Lincoln Memorial.

0.6   Pass Kennedy Center terrace.

1.0   Thompson's Boat House on left. *Use caution crossing car ramps.*

1.4   C&O Canal Towpath begins on left. (Exit here by car ramp to Georgetown eateries, Old Stone House.)

2.4   Exercise course begins on left.

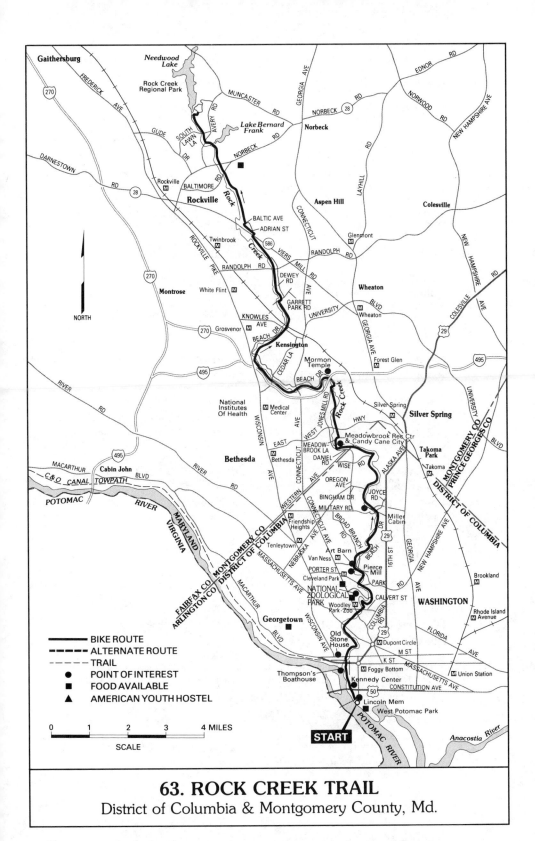

63. ROCK CREEK TRAIL
District of Columbia & Montgomery County, Md.

3.1   Cross Calvert Street NW ramp. *Caution: cars do not slow for bicycles.* Choose trail to right after crossing road.

3.4   **Left** around tunnel (you may also walk bicycle through tunnel on narrow sidewalk).

3.7   Intersection with road to National Zoo on left. Food, toilets, bike parking. *Note: bicycles are prohibited within Zoo grounds.*

4.2   Bike ramp on left to Porter Street NW, Connecticut Avenue NW groceries and restaurants just after bike bridge.

5.4   Pierce Mill and Art Barn on left, mill spillway on right.

5.7   **Straight** on **BEACH DRIVE** (closed to cars on weekends and holidays). *Caution crossing Broad Branch Road.* Parallel bike path to left after street crossing.

7.3   Park Police Substation on right.

7.4   **Straight** on **BEACH DRIVE**. Alternate on signed bike trail. (Another trail goes left on Joyce Road.) Miller's Cabin on left at 7.5 miles.

8.1   **Straight** on **BEACH DRIVE,** as bike path goes left on Bingham Drive. Path becomes steep and poorly maintained, but continues to Wise Road, as an alternate route. Share road with cars for 0.7 miles on weekends.

9.4   Pass Wise Road on left. Share road with cars for 0.1 miles on weekends. **Bear left** to stay on **BEACH DRIVE.** Cars again at Maryland line.

10.2 Maryland line.

10.8 **Right** over bridge at traffic light to enter **MEADOWBROOK RECREATION CENTER** and Candy Cane City. Go **north** through recreation center parking lot on **MEADOWBROOK LANE.** ALTERNATE START begins here.

11.1 **First left** to stay on **MEADOWBROOK LANE.** Riding stable on left. Bike path is two-way on road shoulder.

11.4 Cross East-West Highway at traffic light to return to off-road portion of trail. **Bear left** on **TRAIL.** Silver Spring Metro station 1.7 miles to right. Connection to Baltimore (Tour 52).

12.7 Cross Jones Mill Road.

12.9 Trail shares shoulder briefly. **Left** to stay on **ROCK CREEK TRAIL** at Beach Drive. Mormon Temple to right after turn.

13.3   Pass exercise course.

14.2   Cross under Connecticut Avenue. Alternate at-grade crossing to right.

15.0   Cross Cedar Lane at traffic light. Bike route to National Institutes of Health goes left.

16.4   **Stay left** at fork.

16.7   **Stay left** at fork.

17.1   Cross Knowles Avenue at traffic light. (Grosvenor Metro station 0.9 miles away: left on Grosvenor Lane, then right on Rockville Pike.)

18.1   Cross Garrett Park Road. Veirs Mill Park offices on right.

18.8   **Bear right** to stay on **TRAIL** at fork.

19.1   Trail forks. **Bear right** and follow sidewalk to traffic light at Randall Road. Cross Dewey Road and **continue** on **TRAIL.**

19.5   **Bear left** to stay on **TRAIL** at fork with drinking fountain. Immediately cross bridge, then **sharp right** up hill.

21.0   Cross Veirs Mill Road. **Left** on **ADRIAN STREET,** then **right** on **BALTIC AVENUE.**

21.1   **Left** on **ACCESS ROAD TO TRAIL.**

22.8   Cross Baltimore Road. (For pizzeria and market, turn right on Baltimore Road to Bauer Drive.)

23.1   Trail junction with Norbeck Road.

23.9   Cross parking lot and Avery Road.

24.3   Cross South Lawn Lane.

25.0   **Arrive** at Rock Creek Regional Park, **LAKE NEEDWOOD.**

64. W&OD TRAIL

One of the Washington area's great bicycling resources, the Washington and Old Dominion (W&OD) Railroad Regional Park takes bicyclists through Northern Virginia west from Shirlington Village in Arlington to Purcellville, Va., just nine miles east of the Blue Ridge Mountains.

The W&OD Trail takes its name from the railroad that ran along the right-of-way for nearly 100 years. Also named the "Virginia Creeper" after the pervasive vine growing along the corridor (and because of its reputed slow service!), the train transported residents of Washington to the Northern Virginia countryside, where they escaped the hot city summers in country resorts established along the rail line. The corridor was abandoned for train travel in 1968, and later put to new use by the Northern Virginia Regional Park Authority. Today the W&OD Trail is one of the country's most popular and successful rail-trails and one of the most heavily used parks in Virginia.

The town of Purcellville, a business center for surrounding cattle farms and villages, was incorporated in 1908. In its early days, a bicyclist was fined a hefty $2.50 for riding on the wooden sidewalks.

For a rewarding westward extension to this tour, combine it with Virginia Creeper to Bear's Den (Tour 54).

START: Shirlington Village, eastern terminus of the W&OD Trail at the intersection with Four Mile Run Drive and Shirlington Road in Arlington, Va. Shirlington Village is north of the Shirlington exit of I-395. The W&OD Trail is also accessible from the Mount Vernon Trail (Tour 62), at the southern tip of National Airport, by way of the Four Mile Run Trail to the intersection of South Glebe Road and West Glebe Road, then reverse cues in Arlington History Ride (Tour 37) from 20.7 miles to 19.6 miles. [Arlington is within the Capital Beltway.] **METRO STARTS:** From Ballston Metro station (Orange Line), take North Fairfax Drive west (to the right from the Metro elevator) to the I-66 Custis Trail, then go left (west) two miles to the W&OD Trail at Bon Air Park at mile 3.6; the East Falls Church Metro station (Orange Line) is adjacent to the W&OD Trail, at the Arlington line; National Airport Metro station (Blue and Yellow Lines) is closest to the Four Mile Run Trail to Shirlington; West Falls Church Metro station (Orange Line) is near mile 7.6.

LENGTH: 45.0 miles.

TERRAIN: Level, smooth asphalt surface.

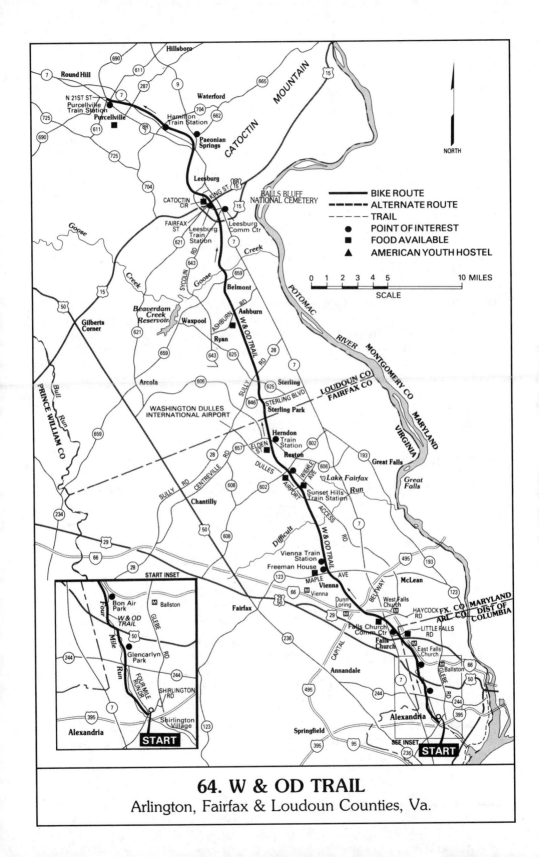

64. W & OD TRAIL
Arlington, Fairfax & Loudoun Counties, Va.

POINTS OF INTEREST: Glencarlyn Park at 1.7 miles; Bon Air Park at 3.5 miles, with beautiful rose garden; Falls Church Community Center at 5.7 miles; Historic Freeman House at 11.8 miles; Vienna railroad station and train museum at 12.0 miles; Lake Fairfax Park at 17.0 miles; Sunset Hills railroad station at 18.0 miles; Herndon railroad station at 20.0 miles; Leesburg Community Center at 33.7 miles; Leesburg train station at 34.5 miles; Work Horse Museum at 39.5 miles; Hamilton train station at 41.1 miles; and Purcellville train station at 44.4 miles. Many bicycle shops on or near the trail.

FOOD: Markets at 5.6, 18.1, 27.7, 35.0 miles and at end. Fast food at 7.2, 11.8, 17.0, 20.0 miles. Restaurants at 34.5 miles (south of trail on King Street and Catoctin Circle) and at end. Water at 2.5, 3.3, 3.9, 11.6, 16.6 and 20.0 miles.

LODGING: In Leesburg, Laurel Brigade Inn (703-777-1010) on 20 West Market Street, three blocks north of the trail, near intersection with US 15 at 35.8 miles. In Purcellville, Purcellville Inn (703-338-2850) on Main Street (VA 7). Also see Virginia Creeper to Bear's Den (Tour 54).

MAPS: *W&OD Railroad Regional Park Trail Guide,* a detailed book of strip maps and information available for $4 postpaid from Northern Virginia Regional Park Authority, 5400 Ox Road, Fairfax Station, VA 22039 (703-352-5900).

MILES   DIRECTIONS & COMMENTS

0.0   Go **west** on **TRAIL** from Shirlington Road and Four Mile Run Drive. Bike shop in Shirlington Village. Arlington Community Center is northwest of start, on South Monroe Street.

1.0   Pass through Arlington County parks.

1.7   Glencarlyn Park on right.

3.5   Bon Air Park with rose garden.

3.6   Junction with I-66/Custis Trail. Water fountain.

5.6   East Falls Church Metro station on right. Convenience store near Lee Highway (US 29) crossing.

5.7   Falls Church Community Center is two blocks south of here, on Little Falls Road.

7.2   City of Falls Church. Bicycle overpass over West Broad Street (VA 7), scheduled for completion in October 1992. Fast food and bike shop on West Broad Street to left.

7.6   West Falls Church Metro station (off trail) north on Haycock Road, approximately 0.5 miles.

9.0   Cross over Capital Beltway.

11.8   Town of Vienna. Fast food and bike shop on Maple Avenue (VA 123) to left. Historic Freeman House beside the trail on Church Street.

12.0   Vienna railroad station and train museum on left. Note bright red caboose!

17.0   Fast food on right at Wiehle Avenue. Lake Fairfax Park is one block north.

18.0   Sunset Hills railroad station and ranger station, in Reston, on right. Convenience store on left. Bike shop in Reston Town Center.

20.0   Herndon railroad station and fast food. Bike shop is four blocks northeast, on Elden Street.

21.4   Enter Loudoun County.

22.5   Bike shop on left.

27.7   Convenience store on Ashburn Road on left.

30.3   Cross over Goose Creek.

33.0   **Small detour** around **VA 7/15,** entering Leesburg.

33.7   Leesburg Community Center on Sycolin Road on right.

34.5   Leesburg Train Station and bike shop on Fairfax Street on left, off King Street. Restaurants south of trail on King Street and Catoctin Circle.

35.8   Laurel Brigade Inn three blocks north of trail, near intersection with US 15.

38.5   Historic stone arch.

39.5   Residential hamlet of Paeonian Springs, location of the Work Horse Museum.

41.1   Hamilton train station on right.

44.4   Purcellville train station on left.

45.0   Trail ends in Purcellville at North 21st Street. Inn, restaurants and groceries in Purcellville.

65. C&O CANAL TOWPATH

Running along the Chesapeake and Ohio (C&O) Canal amidst woodland and wildlife, the 184-mile C&O Canal Towpath serves both cycling and hiking interests in the Washington area. The C&O Canal played a part in the history of the national competition to open the western frontier (in the early 19th century the "frontier" was Wheeling, W.Va. on the Ohio River). On the same day that the C&O Canal Company began construction of its water route to Cumberland (which would then connect to Wheeling by road), the B&O Railroad began its westward push. The railroad ultimately won the race to the West.

The canal-building industry suffered from high land costs and persistent trouble in obtaining land titles. The B&O Railroad obtained land rights at Point of Rocks, Md., and secured an injunction against canal passage there for four years. The canal finally reached Cumberland in 1850, eight years after the railroad. Plans for further extensions to the west were abandoned.

The C&O Canal contains 74 lift locks and 11 stone aqueducts over Potomac tributaries. It was used until 1924, when a flood destroyed it for the second time. The Towpath is now surfaced with earth and crushed stone and ribbed with tree roots. Heavy rains can cause temporary washouts -- call the C&O Canal Park Headquarters in Sharpsburg before setting out on a trip. Most of the Towpath is impassable on light touring or racing bicycles; a mountain bike or one-speed clunker with heavy-duty tires is recommended.

For additional rides from Harpers Ferry, see Between the Hills to Harpers Ferry (Tour 55), Washington to Harpers Ferry Hostel (Tour 51), and Harpers Ferry 3-State Tour (Tour 34).

START: Rock Creek Trail at the corner of Pennsylvania Avenue NW ramp and Rock Creek Parkway near Georgetown in Washington, D.C. [The starting point is within the Capital Beltway.] **METRO START:** From Foggy Bottom Metro station (Orange and Blue Lines), go north one block on 23rd Street NW to Washington Circle, and go 270 degrees counterclockwise around Washington Circle to Pennsylvania Avenue NW toward Georgetown. Go three blocks to Rock Creek Parkway ramp, on left, before the Four Seasons Hotel.

LENGTH: 184.5 miles.

TERRAIN: Level. Packed dirt and crushed stone surface, 6-8 feet wide. Outside of the Capital Beltway, the surface is not suitable for thin bicycle tires.

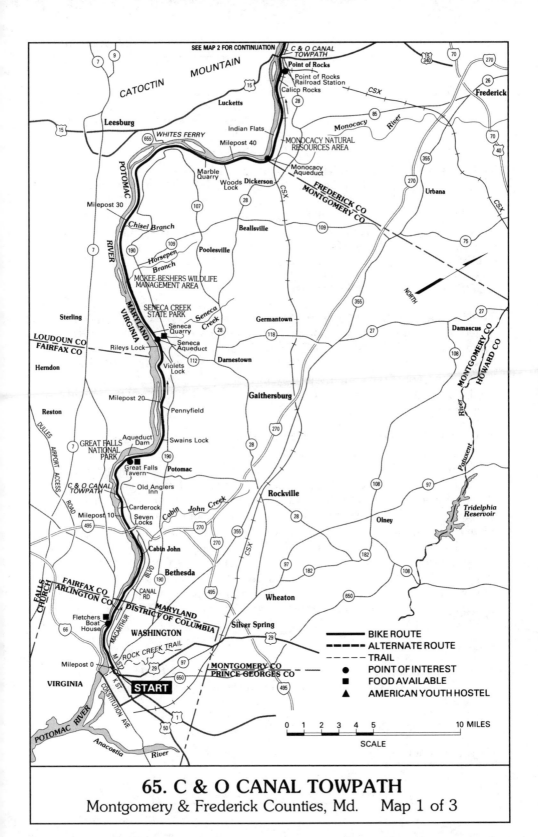

65. C & O CANAL TOWPATH
Montgomery & Frederick Counties, Md.   Map 1 of 3

POINTS OF INTEREST: Thompson's Boat House (202-333-4861) and Tidal Lock 0.3 miles south of start (on Rock Creek Trail), with bike rentals; old locks and gate houses at 0.3 through 14.3 miles; Fletcher's Boat House (202-244-0461) at 3.1 miles, with canoe and bike rentals; Great Falls Tavern and C&O Canal Museum and visitor center at 14.3 miles; Point of Rocks at 47.8 miles, with restored 19th century railroad station; Harpers Ferry at 60.7 miles (see also Tour 55); C&O Canal Park Headquarters (301-432-2231) at 76.6 miles in Sharpsburg; Williamsport (301-223-7711) at 99.0 miles, a classic C&O Canal town; Fort Frederick State Park (301-842-2155) at 112.5 miles, including the last remaining British stone fort in the U.S.; Paw Paw Tunnel at 155.2 miles; and Cumberland at 180.7 miles, featuring a scenic steam-powered train ride round-trip from Cumberland to Frostburg.

FOOD: Markets and restaurants along the route.

LODGING: On the towpath, campsites are located every five miles, with pit toilets, picnic tables, fire grills and water in most cases. Near Harpers Ferry, Harpers Ferry AYH-Hostel, 19123 Sandy Hook Road, Knoxville, Md. (301-834-7652); and Hilltop House (800-338-8319), on Ridge Street, 10 blocks from C&O Canal Towpath. In Cumberland area, bed-and-breakfasts include the Inn at Walnut Bottom, 120 Green Street (301-777-0003) and the Casselman Inn in Grantsville (301-895-5055).

MAPS AND INFORMATION: *C&O Canal Official Guide* available from the National Park Service at C&O Canal, P.O. Box 4, Sharpsburg, MD 21782-0004 (301-739-4200). Maps also available from Potomac Area Council AYH and some local stores. *Chesapeake and Ohio Canal,* a detailed handbook on the history of the canal, is available at a few visitor centers along the trail. The Allegany County, Md. Chamber of Commerce operates a pedestrian and bicycle shuttle bus on weekends between Cumberland and the Paw Paw Tunnel. A $2 fee entitles bicyclists to ride all day between any points on the route (Western Maryland Station, North Branch, Spring Gap, Oldtown and Paw Paw Tunnel). The bus departs southbound from Cumberland's Western Maryland Station at noon and 4 p.m., and northbound from Paw Paw Tunnel at 1:05 p.m. and 5:05 p.m. For more information call 301-722-2820.

MILES   DIRECTIONS & COMMENTS

0.3   Go **west** from Rock Creek Trail on **TOWPATH.** [Note: C&O Canal mileage is traditionally measured from Tidal Lock, 0.3 miles south of here.]

3.1   Fletcher's Boat House on left, through tunnel.

14.3   Great Falls Tavern (C&O Canal Museum) on right.

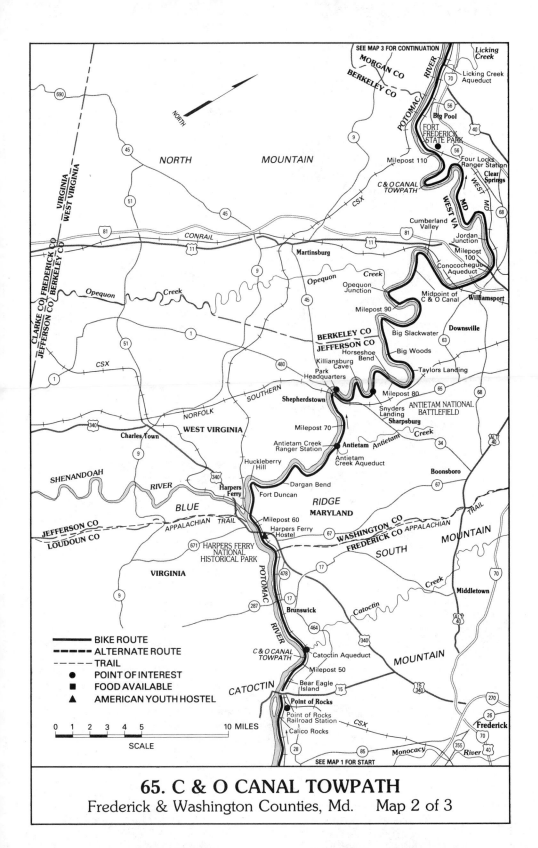

65. C & O CANAL TOWPATH
Frederick & Washington Counties, Md.   Map 2 of 3

22.8   Seneca Aqueduct. Stonemill ruins.

42.2   Monocacy Aqueduct. [See Aqueduct Ride (Tour 4) for connections.]

47.8   Point of Rocks railroad station. [End of Map 1 instructions.]

51.3   Catoctin Aqueduct.

60.7   Cross Appalachian Trail. Harpers Ferry AYH-Hostel to right. Harpers
        Ferry to left.

69.4   Antietam Creek Aqueduct. *Caution: walk bike.*

76.6   Snyders Landing. Road north to Sharpsburg and Park Headquarters.

99.0   Pass Williamsport, a classic C&O Canal town.

112.5   Fort Frederick State Park on right.

118.0   [End of Map 2 instructions.]

155.2   Paw Paw Tunnel.

176.0   C&O Canal boat replica at North Branch.

180.7   Evitts Creek Aqueduct, entering Cumberland area.

184.5   **End** of Towpath.

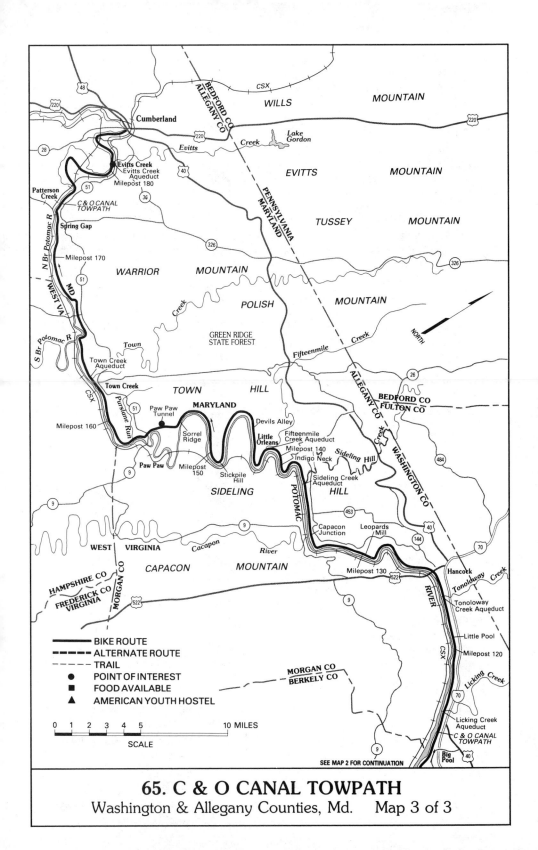

65. C & O CANAL TOWPATH
Washington & Allegany Counties, Md.   Map 3 of 3

66. BALTIMORE AND ANNAPOLIS TRAIL

The Baltimore and Annapolis (B&A) Trail travels through refreshing stands of tulip poplar and expansive open space, offering you a relaxing bicycle trip within one mile of half of Anne Arundel County, Md.'s population. This 112-acre linear park is the county's most popular and lies near quiet residential homes, schools, offices and a variety of shops.

The B&A Trail runs between Glen Burnie and historic Annapolis, first settled in 1649. Parking, restrooms, food and information are easy to find along the entire length of the trail. The trail is patrolled by park rangers and maintained with safety in mind.

START: Park and Ride lot on MD 450 in Annapolis, Md. From the Capital Beltway, take US 50 East (toward Annapolis) and exit onto MD 450 South (toward Naval Academy; first exit after Severn River Bridge). Stay in right lane; parking lot is immediately on the right. Annapolis is 33 miles west of the Capital Beltway.

LENGTH: 13.3 miles.

TERRAIN: Level, smooth asphalt surface.

POINTS OF INTEREST: United States Naval Academy and Museum (410-263-6933) near start; Maryland State House (410-974-3400) also near start, the oldest U.S. State house (1772) in continuous legislative use with exhibits of Annapolis colonial life; Severna Park at approximately 6.0 miles. Many historic sites and museums in Annapolis, including Banneker-Douglass Museum, 84 Franklin Street (410-974-2893) and Museum of African-American Art and Culture.

FOOD: Market at 9.0 miles. Restaurants at 1.0, 7.0, 9.0, 9.5, 10.0, 12.0 and 13.0 miles. Other options frequent along the route.

LODGING: No lodging next to trail, but many places available along Ritchie Highway and in Annapolis. In Annapolis, inns include Charles Inn (410-268-1451), Prince Georges Inn (410-263-6418), Green Street Inn (410-263-6631) and Historic Inns at Annapolis (410-263-2641). For more information on lodging, contact the Annapolis and Anne Arundel County Visitor Bureau (410-268-TOUR).

MAPS AND INFORMATION: B&A Trail map available from B&A Trail Headquarters, P.O. Box 1007, Severna Park, MD 21146-8007 (410-222-6244). City of Annapolis Office of Tourism (410-263-7940); Annapolis Visitor's Center (410-268-8687).

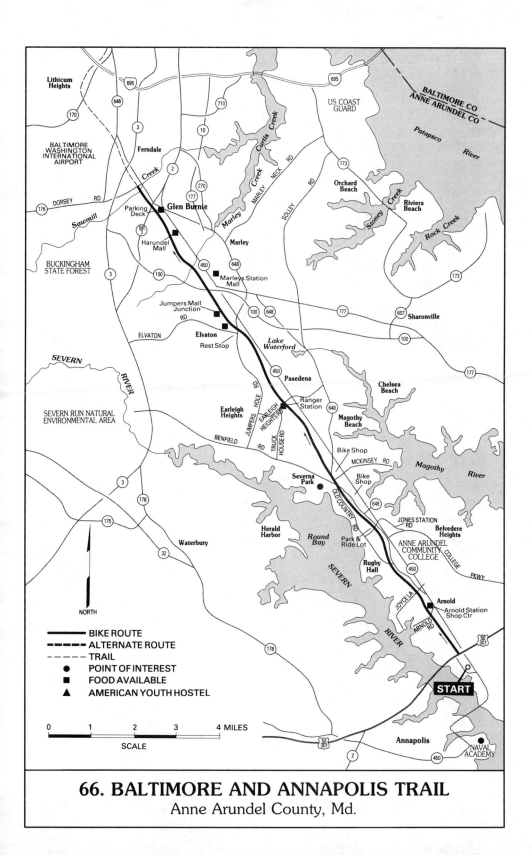

66. BALTIMORE AND ANNAPOLIS TRAIL
Anne Arundel County, Md.

MILES DIRECTIONS & COMMENTS

0.0   Go **north** out of the parking lot on the **TRAIL.**

1.0   Cross Arnold Road. Arnold Station Shopping center on right with bike shop, food and water.

3.0   Pass the Power House, once a power generation station for the railroad, now the B&A Trail's maintenance building. Restrooms and water available.

3.5   Park and Ride at Jones Station road.

5.0   Cross McKinsey Road. Water fountain on left. Bike shop on north side of McKinsey Road to the right.

7.0   Cross Earleigh Heights Road. Ranger station on left. Restrooms, food, water, parking and first aid available.

9.0   Rest stop on left. Food store is behind rest stop, across the street (on Elvaton Road).

9.5   Jumpers Mall Junction on left. Food, restrooms in mall area.

10.5 Cross MD 100. Marley Station Mall on right. Food, restrooms and other amenities available.

12.0 Harundale Mall with restrooms and food on right.

12.7 Cross BUS MD 3.

13.0 Enter Glen Burnie. Parking garage deck with restrooms and restaurants on right.

13.3 Trail ends at Dorsey Road (MD 176).

67. NORTHERN CENTRAL RAILROAD TRAIL

An exemplary rails-to-trails conversion, the Northern Central Railroad Trail offers you a bicycle tour with few cross streets in a pastoral off-road setting. Canopied by trees and following the meandering Gunpowder Falls, the trail promises a relaxing excursion into the Baltimore County countryside, separated from the traffic of nearby roads.

The Northern Central Railroad once transported both passengers and freight between Baltimore and York, Pa. One of the oldest rail lines in the country, it ran for 134 years until 1972 when Hurricane Agnes dealt the last destructive blow to its financially unstable owner. Later, the Maryland Department of Natural Resources converted the corridor into a trail which opened to the public in 1984. Today, hundreds of people enjoy the trail daily by bicycle, foot and horse. The trail also provides boating and fishing access to the popular Gunpowder River and Loch Raven watershed.

START: Parking lot on Ashland Road in Ashland, Md. From the Baltimore Beltway, take I-83 North and exit onto Shawan Road (exit 20). Go east and turn right onto York Road. Turn left onto Ashland Road and continue 0.5 miles to parking lot (do not bear left on Paper Mill Road). Ashland is approximately 40 miles northeast of the Capital Beltway.

LENGTH: 20.0 miles.

TERRAIN: Level, smooth crushed stone surface.

POINTS OF INTEREST: Villages of Corbett and Monkton at 6.0 and 7.5 miles, both on the National Register of Historic Places; and restored Monkton train station at 7.5 miles, now a visitor center with concessions, bike rental, first-aid station and restrooms. Historic railroad structures along the trail, as well as scenic rock outcrops, spring wildflowers, Gunpowder Falls, Beetree Run and other natural beauties.

FOOD: Market at 7.5 miles.

MAPS AND INFORMATION: *Guide to the Northern Central Rail Trail,* available for $6.50 (postpaid) from Howling Wolf Publications, 8630 Fenton Street, Silver Spring, MD 20910 (301-589-9455); *Baltimore Area Bike Map;* Baltimore County, Md. road map.

MILES   DIRECTIONS & COMMENTS

0.0   Go **north** out of parking lot on **TRAIL.**

2.0   Community of Phoenix. Parking, portable toilet and phone on left.

4.0   Town of Sparks. Parking.

6.0   Victorian village of Corbett at crossroads.

7.5   Town of Monkton. Restored train station with parking on left. Restroom, telephone, food available.

9.2   Community of Bluemont.

10.8   Community of White Hall. Parking lot, telephones on left.

12.9   Town of Parkton.

15.7   Bentley Springs. Portable toilet.

16.0   Community of Beetree. Look for interesting 19th century brick viaducts at intervals along Beetree Run.

18.0   Community of Freeland. Parking at trail intersection with Freeland Road. Restrooms.

20.0   Maryland State Line. The rail corridor continues into Pennsylvania.

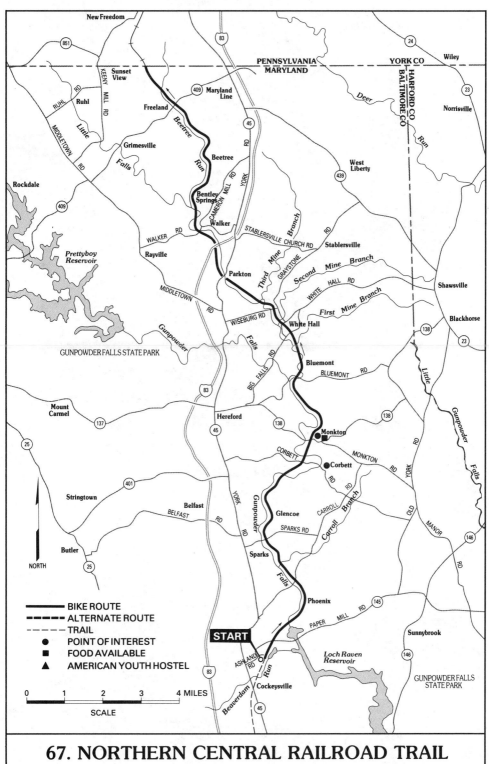

Legend

- —— BIKE ROUTE
- - - - ALTERNATE ROUTE
- – – – TRAIL
- ● POINT OF INTEREST
- ■ FOOD AVAILABLE
- ▲ AMERICAN YOUTH HOSTEL

START

0 1 2 3 4 MILES
SCALE

NORTH

67. NORTHERN CENTRAL RAILROAD TRAIL
Baltimore County, Md.

VI. Mountain Bike Rides

68. MOUNT GILEAD TO HAMILTON TREK

Featuring vistas of vineyards, mountains and horse farms, plus a few spectacular downhill runs, this very scenic ride takes you through the Mount Gilead area of Loudoun County, Va. The loop also passes through the communities of Hamilton and Goose Creek.

The ride can also be started in Hamilton, which is near the Purcellville terminus of the W&OD Trail.

START: Junction of VA 621 and VA 771 in Loudoun County, Va. From the Capital Beltway, take I-66 West for seven miles and exit onto US 50 West (toward Fair Oaks Mall). Continue 12 miles and turn right onto VA 659. Continue one mile and turn left onto VA 621 (Evergreen Mills Road) at Arcola. Go six miles and turn left onto VA 771 (The Woods Road). Park on the shoulder of VA 771. The starting point is 27 miles west of the Capital Beltway.

LENGTH: 34.2 miles.

TERRAIN: Rolling hills.

POINTS OF INTEREST: Hamilton at 12.3 miles. Goose Creek and Beaverdam Creek cross at many places along the route.

FOOD: Market at 12.3 miles.

MAPS: Loudoun County, Va. road map.

MILES	DIRECTIONS & COMMENTS
0.0	**Straight** (north) on **VA 771** (The Woods Road).
1.9	**Right** on **VA 650** (Gleedsville Road).
2.5	**Left** on **VA 651** (Mountain Gap Road).
3.3	**Right** on **US 15**.
3.5	**Left** on **VA 651** (Hogback Mountain Road).
5.5	**Left** on **VA 797** (Mount Gilead Road).
6.4	**Right** on **VA 662** (Loudoun Orchard Road).
8.1	**Bear right** to remain on **VA 662**.
10.3	**Left** on **VA 707** (Canby Road).
11.8	**Right** on **VA 704** (Hamilton Road).

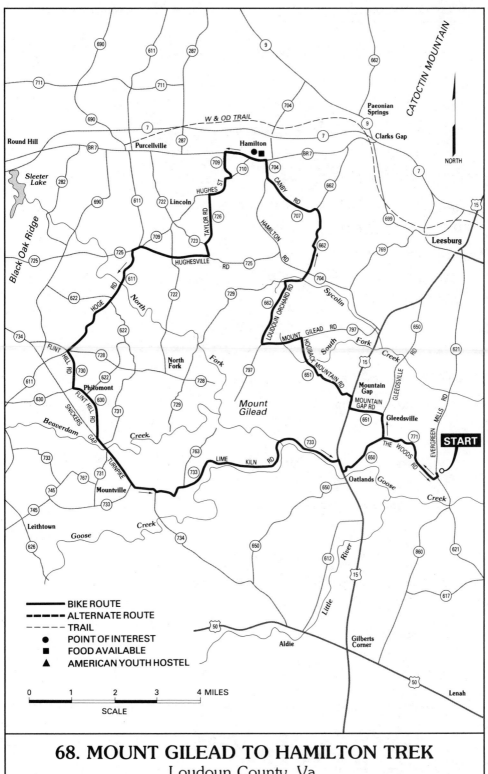

68. MOUNT GILEAD TO HAMILTON TREK
Loudoun County, Va.

12.3   **Left** on **BUS VA 7** into Hamilton. General store.

12.9   **Left** on **VA 709** (Hughes Street).

13.7   **Left** on **VA 726** (Taylor Road).

15.9   **Left** on **VA 723** (still Taylor Road).

16.2   **Right** on **VA 725** (Hughesville Road).

17.9   **Left** on **VA 611** (Hoge Road).

20.9   **Left** on **VA 730** (Flint Hill Road).

21.8   **Left** on **VA 630** (still Flint Hill Road).

23.1   **Left** on **VA 734** (Snickers Gap Turnpike).

25.0   **Left** on **VA 733** (Lime Kiln Road). Very nice riding here.

30.7   **Right** on **US 15**.

30.9   **Left** on **VA 650** (Gleedsville Road).

32.3   **Right** on **VA 771** (The Woods Road).

34.1   **Left** on **VA 621** (Evergreen Mills Road).

34.2   **Right** to **PARKING AREA.**

69. LEESBURG-WATERFORD-HAMILTON DIRT RIDE

Sporting a number of long steep hills with panoramic views of the neighboring countryside, this scenic loop takes you primarily on gravel and dirt roads. The towns of Waterford and Hamilton provide small-town diversions, with plenty of historic landmarks along the way.

START: Loudoun County High School on Dry Mill Road (VA 699) in Leesburg, Va. From the Capital Beltway, take VA 7 West for 28 miles to Leesburg. At the Leesburg city limits, continue straight to remain on BUS VA 7, and turn left onto Catoctin Circle. At the third traffic light turn right onto Dry Mill Road (VA 699) and continue 200 yards; school parking lot is on right. Leesburg is 31 miles northwest of the Capital Beltway.

LENGTH: 32.1 miles.

TERRAIN: Rolling hills.

POINTS OF INTEREST: Leesburg at start; Waterford at 6.9 miles; W&OD Trail at 18.6 miles; and Hamilton at 19.6 miles. Historic landmarks and hillside views along the route.

FOOD: Market at 19.6 miles.

MAPS: Loudoun County, Va. road map.

MILES   DIRECTIONS & COMMENTS

   0.0   **Left** on **DRY MILL ROAD** (VA 699) [paved]. Cross W&OD Trail.

   0.7   **Right** on **CORNWALL STREET** [paved].

   0.8   **Left** on **MEMORIAL DRIVE** [paved].

   0.9   **Right** on **GIBSON PLACE** [paved].

   1.1   **Left** on **OLD WATERFORD ROAD** (VA 698) [paved and unpaved].

   6.9   **Right** on **VA 665** (Taylorstown Road) [paved]. Waterford.

   8.4   **Left** on **VA 662** (Old Mill Road) [unpaved].

  11.0   **Right** on **VA 698** (Old Wheatland Road) [unpaved].

  14.0   **Left** on **VA 9** (Charles Town Pike) [paved].

  14.7   **Right** on **VA 738** (Hampton Road) [unpaved].

  16.4   **Left** on **VA 711** (Picketts Bottom Road) [unpaved].

16.9   **Bear left** to remain on **VA 711.**

18.6   **Right** on **VA 704** (Hamilton Station Road) [paved]. Cross W&OD
       Trail.

19.0   Cross VA 7 Bypass.

19.6   **Right** on **BUS VA 7** [paved]. Hamilton. General Store.

19.7   **Left** on **VA 704** (Hamilton Station Road) [paved].

20.2   **Left** on **VA 707** (Canby Road) [unpaved].

21.7   **Right** on **VA 662** (Loudoun Orchard Road) [unpaved].

23.3   **Straight** to remain on **VA 662** [unpaved].

24.4   Cross VA 704 (Hamilton Station Road).

25.0   **Left** to remain on **VA 662** [unpaved and paved].

26.7   **Left** on **VA 797** (Mount Gilead Road) [unpaved].

28.5   **Left** on **VA 770** (Dunlops Mill Road) [unpaved].

29.3   **Left** on **VA 704** (Hamilton Station Road) [paved].

29.6   **Right** on **VA 769** (Woodburn Road) [unpaved and paved].

31.6   **Right** on **VA 699** (Dry Mill Road) [paved].

32.1   **Left** into **PARKING LOT.**

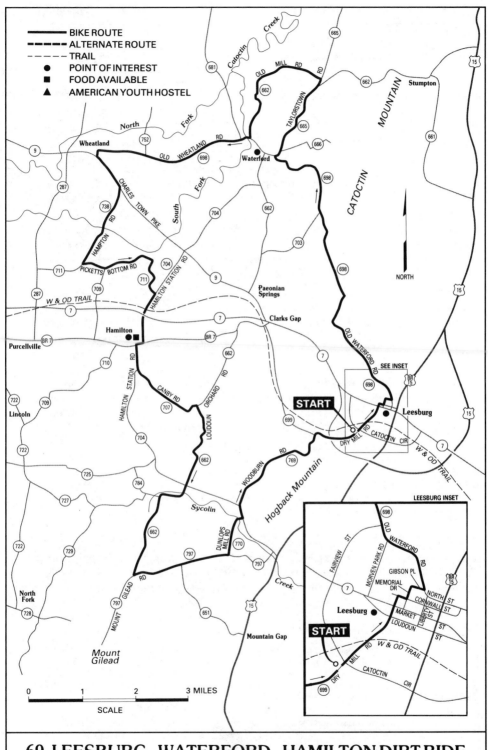

LEGEND

━━━━━━ BIKE ROUTE
┅┅┅┅┅ ALTERNATE ROUTE
┄┄┄┄┄ TRAIL
● POINT OF INTEREST
■ FOOD AVAILABLE
▲ AMERICAN YOUTH HOSTEL

NORTH

SEE INSET

START

LEESBURG INSET

START

69. LEESBURG - WATERFORD - HAMILTON DIRT RIDE
Loudoun County, Va.

70. POINT OF ROCKS EXPLORER

A panorama of terrain and countryside, this tour loops through Waterford, Va. and Point of Rocks, Md. on predominantly gravel and dirt roads. The first half in Virginia contains some long, steep hills, but the Maryland portion on the C&O Canal Towpath is level. The Towpath may be impassable with mud after heavy rains, so plan accordingly.

This tour includes a side trip to Balls Bluff National Cemetery. In October 1861, Union General George McClellan ordered a probe of Confederate defenses in Loudoun County. At Balls Bluff, the Union troops were trapped against the high banks of the Potomac River and forced to choose between deadly Confederate gunfire and a suicidal leap to the waters below. Nearly 1,000 died, a bloody omen of the coming years. The defeat was an enormous blow to the Union. For days afterward, blue-clad corpses were sighted downstream in Georgetown. Among the wounded was Oliver Wendell Holmes, Jr., a recent Harvard College graduate and future Supreme Court Justice. Today, the Balls Bluff site remains an undeveloped national cemetery and quiet testimony to American history's most violent and emotional chapter.

START: Loudoun County High School on Dry Mill Road (VA 699) in Leesburg, Va. From the Capital Beltway, take VA 7 West for 28 miles to Leesburg. At the Leesburg city limits, continue straight to remain on BUS VA 7, and turn left onto Catoctin Circle. At the third traffic light turn right onto Dry Mill Road (VA 699) and continue 200 yards; school parking lot is on right. Leesburg is 31 miles northwest of the Capital Beltway.

LENGTH: 36.0 miles.

TERRAIN: Rolling hills.

POINTS OF INTEREST: Leesburg at start; Point of Rocks on the Potomac River at 17.7 miles, with restored 19th century railroad station; C&O Canal, from 17.8 to 30.6 miles; Whites Ferry (301-349-5200) at 30.6 miles, the only continually operating ferry on the Potomac River ($0.50 for bicycles, 7 days a week); Balls Bluff National Cemetery.

FOOD: Markets at 14.9 and 17.7 miles.

MAPS: Loudoun County, Va. and Montgomery County, Md. road maps.

MILES   DIRECTIONS & COMMENTS

    0.0   **Left** on **DRY MILL ROAD** (VA 699) [paved]. Cross W&OD Trail.

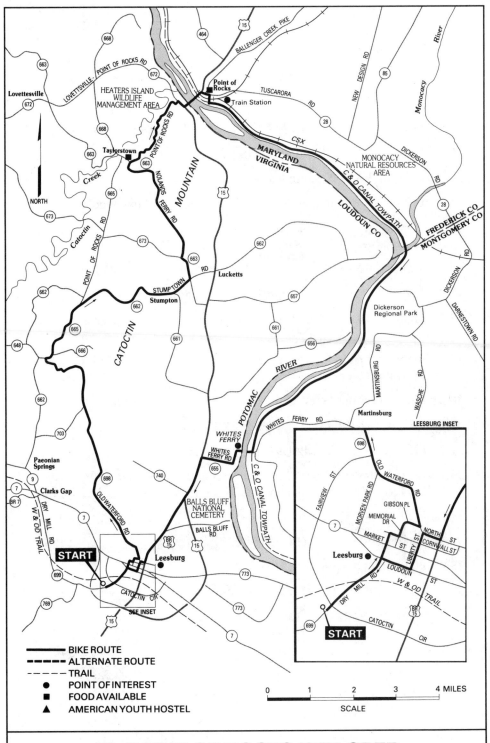

LEESBURG INSET

BIKE ROUTE
ALTERNATE ROUTE
TRAIL
● POINT OF INTEREST
■ FOOD AVAILABLE
▲ AMERICAN YOUTH HOSTEL

0   1   2   3   4 MILES

SCALE

70. POINT OF ROCKS EXPLORER
Loudoun County, Va. & Montgomery & Frederick Counties, Md.

0.7   **Right** on **CORNWALL STREET** [paved].

0.8   **Left** on **MEMORIAL DRIVE** [paved].

0.9   **Right** on **GIBSON PLACE** [paved].

1.1   **Left** on **OLD WATERFORD ROAD** (VA 698) [paved and unpaved].

6.9   **Right** on **VA 665** (Point of Rocks Road) [paved].

8.3   **Right** on **VA 662** (Stumptown Road) [paved].

11.4 **Left** on **VA 663** (Nolands Ferry Road) [paved and unpaved].

14.9 **Right** on **VA 665** (Point of Rocks Road) [unpaved]. [Note: store in Taylorstown, 0.2 miles ahead on VA 663.]

17.3 **Right** on **VA 672** (Lovettsville-Point of Rocks Road) [paved].

17.4 **Left** on **US 15**. Cross Potomac River into Maryland.

17.7 **Right** on **MD 28** (Tuscarora Road) [paved]. Point of Rocks. General store one block on left.

17.8 **Right** at first driveway to go **left** (downriver) on **C&O CANAL TOWPATH** [unpaved].

30.6 **Right** to **Whites Ferry.** Cross Potomac River into Virginia on ferry.

30.6 Continue **straight** on **WHITES FERRY ROAD** (VA 655) [paved].

31.8 **Left** on **US 15** [paved]. Use road shoulder.

33.1 **Bear right** on **BUS US 15** [paved] to Leesburg. For SIDE TRIP to Balls Bluff, bear left here to stay on US 15 and turn left on Balls Bluff Road.

34.7 **Right** on **NORTH STREET** [paved].

34.9 **Left** on **LIBERTY STREET** [paved].

35.0 **Right** on **LOUDOUN STREET** [paved].

35.4 **Left** on **DRY MILL ROAD** (VA 699) [paved].

36.0 **Right** into **PARKING LOT.**

71. FORT CIRCLE TRAIL

Following a wonderful greenway between Fort Stanton and Fort Mahan, this 4.6-mile tour takes you on a challenging gravel path through forested terrain. The tour is perhaps the only urban mountain bike route in the United States, and is essentially impassable without a mountain bike.

The tour connects a series of historic forts that still dot the Washington region. During the Civil War, a formidable ring of 74 forts and 22 batteries were erected around Washington by Union troops, protecting the 100-square mile diamond of the original District of Columbia.

The National Park Service still owns many of these fort sites. They range from vacant lots to ruins to parks to one reconstructed fort. Perhaps the most notable is Fort Stevens, where President Abraham Lincoln witnessed a skirmish in July 1864 -- the only Civil War military action in Washington.

Originally planned for a scenic road, the National Park Service purchased land in the 1920s to form a connecting corridor between the fort sites. The Park Service never built the road and eventually planned a pedestrian and bicycle trail along the route as a Bicentennial project. By 1971, the Park Service completed the portion east of the Anacostia River and dedicated it as a National Recreational Trail. Budget shortfalls and other priorities have limited expansion of the route, although modest improvements to the existing trail continue and completion of the entire 27-mile crescent remains a possibility.

*The trail is easy to follow, and most road crossings are well marked. The forts were set on high hills, so expect extreme climbs and descents as well as numerous narrow and single-track sections. While the trail is remote, it is in a high-crime part of the city. Cyclists should remain aware of their surroundings, particularly at city street crossings. Allow plenty of daylight to complete this route -- it takes much longer than the distance implies! This trail is **not** recommended to novice mountain bicyclists.*

*[**Note:** mileage is approximate.]*

START: Fort Stanton Park near the Anacostia Museum at 1901 Fort Place SE in Washington, D.C. [The starting point is within the Capital Beltway.] **METRO STARTS:** Fort Mahan at 4.2 miles is between Minnesota Avenue and Benning Road Metro stations (Orange Line); Fort Stanton is near Anacostia and Congress Heights Metro stations (Green Line).

LENGTH: 4.6 miles.

TERRAIN: Steep hills, gravel surface. Mountain bikes required. Not for novices.

POINTS OF INTEREST: Frederick Douglass Memorial Home near start; Anacostia Museum (202-357-2700) near start; Fort Stanton near start; Fort Baker at 0.5 miles; Fort Davis at 2.0 miles; Fort Dupont at 2.6 miles; Fort Chaplin at 3.7 miles; and Fort Mahan at 4.2 miles.

FOOD: Available along the route near major crossroads.

MAPS: *ADC's Washington Area Bike Map.*

MILES   DIRECTIONS & COMMENTS

0.0   From the Anacostia Museum, cross Fort Place SE and follow path up hill to a **left** onto the **TRAIL.** Continue down steep hill, over bridge. **Left** at fork.

0.5   Cross Good Hope Road SE. Enter Fort Baker Park.

0.9   Cross Naylor Road SE.

1.1   **Jog left** on **28TH STREET SE**. (Off-road path along road on west side.)

1.6   **Left** along **PARK DRIVE SE** for one block. Cross Branch Avenue SE.

2.0   Cross Pennsylvania Avenue SE. Enter Fort Davis Park.

2.5   Cross Fort Davis Drive SE. Path is asphalt here.

2.6   Cross Massachusetts Avenue SE. Enter Fort Dupont Park. **Bear left** at fork. (Go right here for side trip to Fort Dupont.) **Two left turns** approaching Ridge Road SE to remain on **TRAIL.**

3.3   **Diagonal left** over Ridge Road SE and Fort Davis Drive SE (Texas Avenue SE).

3.7   **Jog right** at C Street SE. Trail starts before Burbank Street SE. *Caution: trail may be hard to find; overgrown vegetation and no sign on west side.* Enter Fort Chaplin.

3.9   **Diagonal left** at East Capitol Street. Continue to climb hill on diagonal.

4.1   **Straight** on **ASPHALT PATH** for approximately 30 feet, then **right** onto **GRAVEL PATH** again. **Straight** on **41ST STREET NE** to end.

4.2   Cross Benning Road NE. Enter Fort Mahan Park. Go up **UNMARKED EMBANKMENT** to asphalt path. **Right** on **PATH,** which curves to the left to parallel 42nd Street NE.

4.6   Trail **ends** at **42ND STREET NE** and **GRAND STREET NE.** (Go left on Grand Street NE to the Minnesota Avenue Metro station.)

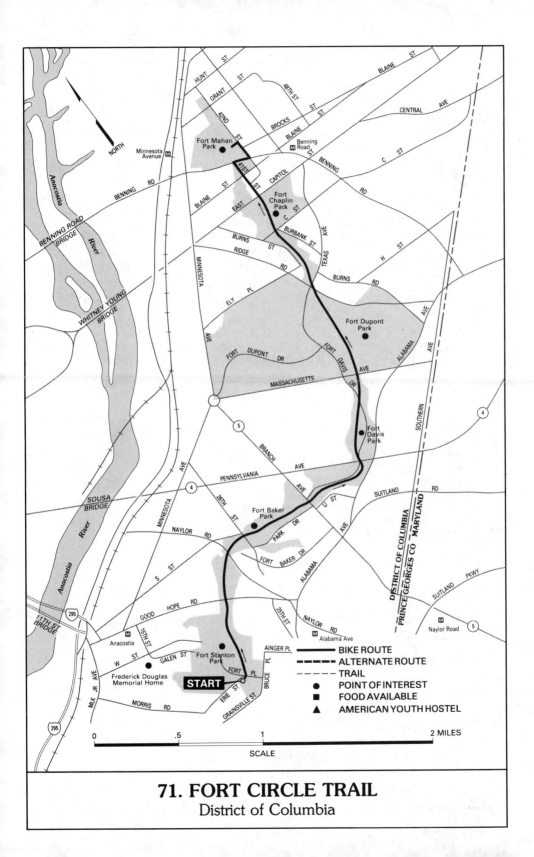

71. FORT CIRCLE TRAIL
District of Columbia

Appendix

WHERE TO ORDER ADDITIONAL MAPS

Do you want additional detail on the areas where you are touring? State, regional and local maps complement the maps in this atlas. You may find it helpful to request order forms first, which contain details on map size, scale and cost. The Washington Area Bicyclist Association (WABA) also distributes many maps for a nominal fee, via mail or pick-up. Contact WABA for a price list. All prices and availability are subject to change.

Bike Maps and Guides

Regional

ADC's Washington Area Bike Map (1992). A table-sized map showing bike paths and on-road bikeways in the Washington area. Alexandria Drafting Company, 6440 General Green Way, Alexandria, VA 22312, 703-750-0510. $7, available in many convenience stores including most 7-Elevens.

Delaware

Delaware Maps for Bicycle Users. Delaware DOT, P.O. Box 778, Dover, DE 19903-0778, 302-739-4318. Very comprehensive.

District of Columbia

Getting Around Washington By Bicycle (1983). Eight section maps covering Washington, D.C. in fine detail. D.C. Office of Documents, 1350 Pennsylvania Avenue NW, Washington, DC 20004-3094, 202-727-6561. $3 postpaid.

Rock Creek Park Official Guide. A map of the NPS portion of the Rock Creek Park and Trail. National Park Service, 5000 Glover Road NW, Washington, DC 20015-1098, 202-426-6829. Free; send a self-addressed stamped business-size envelope.

Maryland

Baltimore Area Bike Map (1984). Commuting and touring routes in the Baltimore region. Baltimore Regional Planning Council, 2225 North Charles Street, Baltimore, MD 21218-5767, 410-333-4881. $2.50 + $2 shipping.

Bicycle Tours of Frederick County, Maryland. Nine tours in Frederick County. Tourism Council of Frederick County, 19 East Church Street, Frederick, MD 21701-5401, 301-663-8687. $5.25 postpaid.

C&O Canal Official Guide. A map of the 185-mile C&O Canal. C&O Canal National Park, P.O. Box 4, Sharpsburg, MD 21782-0004, 301-739-4200. Free; send a self-addressed stamped business-size envelope.

A Frederick Cycling Guide. Frederick County Tourism Council, 19 East Church Street, Frederick, MD 21701-5401, 301-663-8687. $3.75 postpaid.

Guide to the Northern Central Rail Trail. Howling Wolf Publications, 8630 Fenton Street, Silver Spring, MD 20910, 301-589-9455. $6.50 postpaid.

Hiker/Biker/Equestrian Trails. A guide to Maryland's trails. MD-NCPPC, 14741 Governor Oden Bowie Drive, Upper Marlboro, MD 20772-3090, 301-952-3522.

Lower Montgomery County Bicycle Route Map (1985). Shows nearly 250 miles of recreational and commuting routes. Montgomery County DOT, Office of Transportation Planning, 101 Monroe Street, Rockville, MD 20850-2580, 301-468-4065. $1.75.

Rock Creek Hiker-Biker Trail. A map of the Montgomery County portion of the Rock Creek Trail. MD-NCPPC Community Relations, 8787 Georgia Avenue, Silver Spring, MD 20910-3760, 301-495-4600.

Pennsylvania

Bicycle Trails in Berks County. P.O. Box 6677, Reading, PA 19610, 215-374-4085. Free.

Blue Marsh Lake Hiking/Mountain Biking Trails. Berks County U.S. Army Corps of Engineers, Route 1, Box 1239, Leesport, PA 19533, 215-376-6337.

Guide to Bicycle Touring Routes Between Hostels in Eastern Pennsylvania and New Jersey. Detailed strip maps. Delaware Valley Council AYH, 38 South Third Street, Philadelphia, PA 19106, 215-925-6004. $6 postpaid.

Lancaster County Bicycle Tours. A 35-map series including many through Amish areas and a county map. Lancaster Bicycle Club, P.O. Box 535, Lancaster, PA 17603, 717-394-8220. $8.50 postpaid.

Pennsylvania Bicycle Guide. 22"x36" color state map. PennDOT Map Sales, P.O. Box 2028, Harrisburg, PA 17105-2028, 717-787-6746. Free. More detailed quadrants are $1.25 each.

Virginia

Arlington County Bikeway Map and Guide (1991). Extensive detail of Arlington's bikeway system, plus safety tips, mileage charts and bicycle laws. Arlington County DPW, 1 Courthouse Plaza, Suite 717, Arlington, VA 22201-5430, 703-358-3681. Free.

Historic Triangle Bike Map: Yorktown, Jamestown, Williamsburg. Four recommended tours in the Colonial Triangle. Virginia DOT, 1401 East Broad Street, Richmond, VA 23219-2040, 804-786-2964. Free.

Mount Vernon Trail Official Guide. A map of the 19-mile trail. National Park Service, Turkey Run Park, McLean, VA 22101, 703-285-2601. Free; send a self-addressed stamped business-size envelope.

TransAmerica Trail Guide (BC-1543). Bikecentennial's 370-mile easternmost segment (from Yorktown to Christianburg) of the historic transcontinental route. Bikecentennial, P.O. Box 8308, Missoula, MT 59807-8308, 406-721-1776. $6.95.

Virginia Loop Bicycle Trail. Strip maps of 600-mile loop tour through hilly Virginia countryside, beginning in Washington, D.C. Bikecentennial, P.O. Box 8308, Missoula, MT 59807-8308, 406-721-1776. $8.95.

W&OD Railroad Regional Park Trail Guide (1991). Guide and strip maps of the trail. Northern Virginia Regional Park Authority, 5400 Ox Road, Fairfax Station, VA 22039-1022, 703-352-5900. $4 postpaid.

State and County Road Maps

Delaware

Delaware DOT, P.O. Box 778, Dover, DE 19903-0778, 302-739-4318. $3 per county.

District of Columbia

D.C. DPW Maps, 2000 14th Street NW, 6th floor, Washington, DC 20009-4484, 202-929-8115. Free with a self-addressed 7x10 envelope with $1.21 postage.

Maryland

Maryland Maps Distribution, 2323 West Joppa Road, Brooklandville, MD 21022, 410-321-3518. $1.20 per county plus postage.

Pennsylvania

Pennsylvania DOT Sales Store, P.O. Box 2028, Harrisburg, PA 17105-2028, 717-787-6746. $0.75 per county.

Virginia

Virginia DOT, 1401 East Broad Street, Richmond, VA 23219-2040, 804-786-2963. County maps are $0.25 or $2.50 (for large scale) plus postage. $26 for a book of county maps.

West Virginia

Maps Section, West Virginia Department of Highways, 1900 Washington Street East, Charleston, WV 25305, 304-348-2868. Variable prices for county maps.

Books

Chuck and Gail's Favorite Bike Rides, Cycleways Publications, P.O. Box 5328, Takoma Park, MD 20913-5328, by Chuck and Gail Helfer. $16.95.

Cycling Historical Landscapes: Sugarloaf Regional Trails, Maryland National Capital Parks and Planning Commission (MD-NCPPC), 8787 Georgia Avenue, Silver Spring, MD 20910-3760. $2. Thirteen short routes in historic areas of Montgomery and Frederick Counties.

Have Bike, Will Tour, Baltimore Bicycle Club, P.O. Box 5906, Baltimore, MD 21208-0906. $5 postpaid. Over 40 tours in the Baltimore area.

Rivers and Trails, Outdoor Press, P.O. Box 266, Knoxville, MD 21758-0266. $4.95. Maps of bike routes, hiking trails and rivers in the mid-Atlantic region.

BICYCLE AND RELATED ORGANIZATIONS

Regional

American Youth Hostels/Potomac Area Council
1108 K Street NW
Washington, DC 20005
202-783-0717
Co-publisher of this Atlas, Potomac AYH is the Washington area office of the American Youth Hostels, a national outing and low-cost travel organization. Potomac AYH sponsors weekend and summer bicycling, hiking, camping, skiing and equestrian trips for all ages, as well as cultural and educational programs through its network of 10 hostels in the mid-Atlantic region. Potomac AYH's travel shops carry bicycle equipment, maps and guide books. Potomac AYH also operates the Washington International AYH-Hostel at 1009 11th Street NW (202-737-2333).

Armed Forces Cycling Association
P.O. Box 6137
Arlington, VA 22206-0137
703-820-1991
Open to active, retired and reserve members of the Armed Forces and National Guard.

Coalition for the Capital Crescent Trail
1400 Sixteenth Street NW, Suite 300
Washington, DC 20036-2222
202-234-4874
An advocacy group dedicated to the conversion of the abandoned Georgetown Branch Line into a bicycle trail between Georgetown in Washington, D.C. to Silver Spring in Montgomery County, Md.

Coalition for the Metropolitan Branch Trail
1819 H Street NW, Suite 640
Washington, DC 20006-3603
202-986-4870
An advocacy group dedicated to the conversion of an abandoned railroad on the former Metropolitan Branch right-of-way into a bicycle trail between Union Station in Washington, D.C. and Silver Spring in Montgomery County, Md., with a connection east from the Fort Totten Metro into northern Prince Georges County, Md.

National Capital Velo Club
P.O. Box 14004
Washington, DC 20044-4004
301-779-1310
A racing club.

Potomac Pedalers Touring Club
P.O. Box 23601
Washington, DC 20026-3601
202-363-TOUR
The nation's largest local bicycle touring club offers rides almost every day of the year to riders of all ages and abilities.

Urban Nomads
P.O. Box 3493
Alexandria, VA 22302-0493
703-379-8785
A regional organization interested in off-road mountain bike use in the metropolitan Washington, D.C. area.

Washington Area Bicyclist Association
1819 H Street NW, Suite 640
Washington, DC 20006-3603
202-872-9830
Co-publisher of this Atlas, WABA is one of the nation's oldest, largest and most effective local bicycle advocacy groups. A non-profit membership organization, WABA works with volunteers and community and government agencies and officials to improve bicycling conditions for transportation and recreation. WABA's programs range from facility creation and improvement to policy and planning. WABA's Bicycle Helmet Safety Institute is internationally renowned for providing reliable and current information on helmet safety and testing.

Washington Women Outdoors
P.O. Box 301
Garrett Park, MD 20896-0301
301-864-3070
A local club offering one-day and overnight outing trips for women.

National

American Youth Hostels
P.O. Box 28607
Washington, DC 20038-8607
202-783-4943
AYH organizes national and international bicycling trips for all ages, promotes low-cost travel through 41 regional councils (of which Potomac AYH is one) and more than 300 hostels. The hostels provide dormitory lodging for a nominal price. AYH is a member of the International Youth Hostel Federation which manages more than 5,000 hostels in 62 countries.

Bicycle Federation of America
1818 R Street NW
Washington, DC 20009-1692
202-332-6986
A national non-profit non-membership organization that promotes bicycle use and serves as a clearinghouse for bicycling information and statistics.

Bicycle Institute of America
P.O. Box 53406
Washington, DC 20009-9406
A national trade group for bicycling transportation issues.

Bikecentennial
P.O. Box 8308
Missoula, MT 59807-8308
406-721-1776
A national member-supported service organization for recreational bicycling.

International Mountain Bicycling Association
Route 2, Box 303
Bishop, CA 93514
619-387-2757
A national membership advocacy organization concerned with mountain bike access issues.

League of American Wheelmen
190 West Ostend Street #120
Baltimore, MD 21230-3731
410-539-3399
A national membership organization of state and local bicycle clubs and individuals, founded in 1880 to protect the rights and promote the interests of bicyclists.

Rails-to-Trails Conservancy
1400 Sixteenth Street NW, Suite 300
Washington, DC 20036-2222
202-797-5400
A national membership organization to promote the conversion of abandoned railroad corridors into recreational and commuter greenways.

U.S. Cycling Federation
1750 East Boulder Street, Suite 4
Colorado Springs, CO 80909
719-578-4581
The governing body of American amateur bicycle racing.

Women's Cycling Coalition
PO Box 281
Louisville, CO 80027
303-666-0500
The WCC's two objectives are to be an active voice for women in the sport of cycling and to encourage women to get involved and stay involved in cycling.

Maryland

Baltimore Bicycle Club
P.O. Box 5906
Baltimore, MD 21208-0906
410-484-0306
A large touring club sponsoring rides at all levels in Maryland.

Capital Cycle Challenge Club
14 Newbury Court
Gaithersburg, MD 20882-4005
301-253-5819

College Park Area Bicycle Coalition
P.O. Box 1035
College Park, MD 20741-1035
301-441-2740
An active bicycle advocacy group focusing on north Prince Georges County.

College Park Bicycle Club
4360 Knox Road
College Park, MD 20740-3171
301-779-4848
A racing club.

Eastern Shore Velo Club
P.O. Box 393
Centreville, MD 21617-0393
410-778-4881

Frederick Pedalers Bicycle Club
P.O. Box 1293
Frederick, MD 21701-0293

Oxon Hill Bicycle Club
P.O. Box 81
Oxon Hill, MD 20750-0081
301-839-4270

Salisbury Bicycle Club
708 Walnut Street
Pocomoke City, MD 21851-1525
410-957-3089

WB&A Trail Association
9430 Lanham-Severn Road
Seabrook, MD 20706-2642
410-459-7090
An advocacy group promoting the establishment of a bicycle trail on the abandoned Washington Baltimore & Annapolis Railroad right-of-way.

Virginia

Arlington County Bicycle Club
Arlington County Parks Department
300 North Park Drive
Arlington, VA 22203-2599
703-558-2871

Bicycle Organization of South Side (BOSS)
P.O. Box 36458
Richmond, VA 23235-8458
804-276-0934

Blue Ridge Bicycle Club
P.O. Box 13383
Roanoke, VA 24033-3383

Central Virginia Bicycle Club
P.O. Box 4344
Lynchburg, VA 24502-0344
804-528-1914

Emporia Bicycle Club
P.O. Box 631
Emporia, VA 23847-0631
804-634-2222

Fredericksburg Cyclists
P.O. Box 7844
Fredericksburg, VA 22404-7844
703-371-0398

Friends of the W&OD Trail
P.O. Box 5621
Arlington, VA 22205-0121
703-534-2511
A non-profit organization dedicated to preserving, protecting and improving the W&OD Trail.

Peninsula Bicycling Association
P.O. Box 5639
Newport News, VA 23605-0639

Rappahannock Bicycle Club
P.O. Box 682
Bowling Green, VA 22427-0682
804-633-6500

Reston Bicycle Club
P.O. Box 3389
Reston, VA 22090-1389
703-758-1000
A fast-growing, active touring club.

Richmond Area Bicycling Association
9013 Prestondale Drive
Richmond, VA 23294-5918
804-346-0242

Shenandoah Valley Bicycle Club
P.O. Box 1014
Harrisonburg, VA 22801-1014

Tidewater Bicycle Association
P.O. Box 12254
Norfolk, VA 23502-0254
804-425-9301

Whole Wheel Velo Club
9514 Main Street
Fairfax, VA 22031-4031
703-323-0500
A racing club.

Williamsburg Bicycle Association
P.O. Box 713
Williamsburg, VA 23187-0713

Winchester Wheelmen
1609 Van Couver Street
Winchester, VA 22601-3228
703-667-6703

GOVERNMENT DIGEST

The following information is subject to change without notice.

Regional

Council of Governments

Jon Williams
Metropolitan Washington Council of Governments
777 North Capitol Street NE, Suite 300
Washington, DC 20002-4201
202-962-3200

National Park Service

Richard Metzinger
NPS National Capital Region
1100 Ohio Drive SW
Washington, DC 20242-0001
202-523-5555

Delaware

State Parks

Delaware Division of Parks
89 Kings Highway
Dover, DE 19901-3816
302-739-4401

Tourism Office

Delaware Tourism Office
P.O. Box 1401
Dover, DE 19903-1401
800-441-8846
800-282-8667 in Delaware

Transportation Department

Bicycle Coordinator
Delaware DOT
P.O. Box 778
Dover, DE 19903-0708
302-739-3267

District of Columbia

Tourism Office

Washington D.C. Visitor Association
1212 New York Avenue NW
Washington, DC 20005-3992
202-789-7000

Transportation Department

D.C. DPW Bicycle Office
2000 14th Street NW, 7th Floor
Washington, DC 20009-4473
202-939-8016

Maryland

B&A Trail Park	B&A Trail Park P.O. Box 1007 Severna Park, MD 21146-8007 410-222-6244
Charles County	Robert Purcell Charles County Department of Planning P.O. Box B La Plata, MD 20646-0167 301-870-3000
Frederick County	James Gugel Frederick County Planning Commission 12 East Church Street Frederick, MD 21701-5402 301-694-1144
Gaithersburg	Don Stickle Gaithersburg Planning Department 31 South Summit Avenue Gaithersburg, MD 20877-2325 301-258-6325
Greenbelt	Harry Irving Greenbelt Department of Recreation 25 Crescent Road Greenbelt, MD 20770-1891 301-474-6878
Howard County	Clara Gouin Howard County Department of Parks 3300 North Ridge Road Ellicott City, MD 21043-3383
Montgomery County Parks	Joe Anderson MD-NCPPC 8787 Georgia Avenue Silver Spring, MD 20910-3760 301-495-4525
Montgomery County DOT	Bob Simpson Montgomery County DOT 101 Monroe Street, 10th Floor Rockville, MD 20850-2540 301-217-2145
Prince Georges County Parks	Bruce Hancock MD-NCPPC 14741 Governor Oden Bowie Drive Upper Marlboro, MD 20772-3050 301-952-3530

State Parks   Maryland Department of Natural Resources
                                    Tawes State Office Building
                                    580 Taylor Avenue
                                    Annapolis, MD 21401-2397
                                    410-974-3771

Takoma Park   Lisa Schwartz
                                    City of Takoma Park
                                    7500 Maple Avenue
                                    Takoma Park, MD 20912-4998
                                    301-270-1700

Tourism Office   Maryland Office of Tourism Development
                                    217 East Redwood Street
                                    Baltimore, MD 21202-3316
                                    800-543-1036
                                    410-333-6611

Transportation Department   Steve King
                                    Maryland State Highway Administration
                                    707 North Calvert Street, Suite 218
                                    Baltimore, MD 21202-3615
                                    800-252-8776 weekdays 8:30 a.m. to 4 p.m.

Pennsylvania

State Parks   Pennsylvania Bureau of State Parks
                                    P.O. Box 8551
                                    Harrisburg, PA 17105-8551
                                    800-63PARKS

Tourism Office   Pennsylvania Bureau of Travel Development
                                    416 Forum Building
                                    Harrisburg, PA 17120
                                    717-787-5453

Transportation Department   Bicycle Coordinator
                                    Pennsylvania DOT
                                    917 Transportation Building
                                    Harrisburg, PA 17120
                                    717-787-1251

Virginia

Arlington County   Ritch Viola
                                    Arlington County DPW
                                    1 Courthouse Plaza, Suite 717
                                    Arlington, VA 22201-5430
                                    703-358-3699

Alexandria   Buffy Brownstein
                                    Alexandria Department of Parks
                                    1108 Jefferson Street
                                    Alexandria, VA 22314-3924
                                    703-246-4649

Falls Church

Howard Herman
Falls Church Recreation Department
223 Little Falls Street
Falls Church, VA 22046-4304
703-241-5077

Fairfax City

Lisa Burke
City of Fairfax Planning Department
3730 Old Lee Highway
Fairfax, VA 22030-1806

Fairfax County

David Marshall
Fairfax County Office of Comprehensive Planning
4050 Legato Road
Fairfax, VA 22033-4003
703-246-1263

Loudoun County

Milt Herd
Loudoun County Office of Planning
18 North King Street
Leesburg, VA 22075-2818
703-777-0252

Prince William County

Tim Goodwin
Prince William County Department of Planning
1 County Complex Court
Prince William, VA 22192-9201

State Parks

Virginia Division of State Parks
203 Governor Street, Suite 306
Richmond, VA 23219-2010
804-786-5045

Tourism Office

Virginia Division of Tourism
101 North Ninth Street
Richmond, VA 23219
804-786-4484

Transportation Department

Richard Lockwood
Virginia DOT State Bicycle Coordinator
1401 East Broad Street
Richmond, VA 23219-2040
804-786-2964

Vienna

Gregory Hembree
Vienna Planning Department
127 Center Street South
Vienna, VA 22180-5719
703-255-6341

W&OD Trail

Paul McCray
Northern Virginia Regional Park Authority
5400 Ox Road
Fairfax Station, VA 22039-1022
703-689-1437

West Virginia

Tourism Office	West Virginia Tourism Division Capitol Complex Charleston, WV 25305 800-CALL-WVA
State Parks	West Virginia Parks & Recreation Division Capitol Complex Charleston, WV 25305 800-624-8632
Transportation Department	Bicycle Coordinator West Virginia DOT 1900 Washington Street East Charleston, WV 25305

AREA HOSTELS

Are you interested in low-cost overnight lodging specially suited to cyclists? American Youth Hostels operates nine hostels in the mid-Atlantic region that are conveniently located to many tour routes in this atlas. They are:

BALTIMORE INTERNATIONAL AYH-HOSTEL is a comfortably restored 19th century brownstone mansion centrally located in the downtown district. Near Harborplace and the Baltimore Orioles baseball stadium at Camden Yards, the hostel has two common rooms, ping-pong, dining room, kitchen, laundry facilities, secure bicycle storage, and separate dormitory facilities for men and women. Cost: $13 per night ($10 for AYH members). Closed daily between 10 a.m. and 5 p.m. For information, call 410-576-8880. For reservations, send name and first night's deposit to: 17 West Mulberry Street, Baltimore, MD 21201-4440.

BEAR'S DEN AYH-HOSTEL is located on the Appalachian Trail about 15 miles west of Leesburg in Bluemont, Va., just off VA 601 South. Near extensive roads and trails for hiking and biking, the hostel has a common room with fireplace, kitchen, laundry facilities, outdoor bicycle storage, separate dormitory facilities for men and women, and a room for couples and families. Cost $12 per night ($9 for AYH members). Closed daily between 9:30 a.m. and 5 p.m. For information, call 703-554-8708. For reservations, send name and first night's deposit to: Route 1, Box 288, Bluemont, VA 22012-9502.

BOWMANSVILLE AYH-HOSTEL is a former post office and general store, now the oldest hostel in the United States. Nestled in the heart of Pennsylvania Dutch country, the hostel has a common room, kitchen, laundry facilities, bicycle rentals, outdoor bicycle storage, separate dormitory facilities for men and women, and a summer cabin for couples and families. Cost: $11 per night

($8 for AYH members). Closed daily between 9:30 a.m. and 5 p.m. For information, call 215-445-4831. For reservations, send name and first night's deposit to: 1252 Reading Road, Bowmansville, PA 17507.

GETTYSBURG INTERNATIONAL AYH-HOSTEL is located in the downtown historic district, within easy cycling distance of the Gettysburg National Historic Park. The hostel features a comfortable common room, kitchen, laundry facilities, indoor bicycle storage, separate dormitory facilities for men and women, and rooms for couples and families. Cost: $11 per night ($8 for AYH members). Closed daily between 9:30 a.m. and 5 p.m. For information, call 717-334-1020. For reservations, send name and first night's deposit to: 27 Chambersburg Street, Gettysburg, PA 17325.

HARPERS FERRY AYH-HOSTEL stands high on a bluff overlooking the Shenandoah and Potomac Rivers in Knoxville, Md. About two miles from the Harpers Ferry National Historic Park, the hostel has a common room with fireplace, kitchen, laundry facilities, outdoor bicycle storage, separate dormitory facilities for men and women and a room for couples and families. Cost: $12 per night ($9 for AYH members). Closed daily between 9:30 a.m. and 5 p.m. For information, call 301-834-7652. For reservations, send name and first night's deposit to: 19123 Sandy Hook Road, Knoxville, MD 21758-1330.

SANGRAAL-BY-THE-SEA AYH-HOSTEL is situated on 18 acres of land bordering the Chesapeake Bay. Just 30 miles from historic Colonial Williamsburg and 13 miles from Urbanna, Va., the hostel features kitchen facilities, outdoor bicycle storage, laundry facilities, and separate dormitory facilities for men and women. Cost: $13 per night ($10 for AYH members). Closed daily between 9:30 a.m. and 5 p.m. For information, call 804-776-6500. For reservations, send name and first night's deposit to: P.O. Box 187, Urbanna, VA 23175-0187.

SHIREY'S AYH-HOSTEL is located in Pennsylvania Dutch country near Geigertown, close to the BikeCentennial (Maine to Virginia) Bicycle Route and the Horse Shoe Trail. The hostel has a common room, kitchen, laundry facilities, outdoor bicycle storage, and separate facilities for men and women. Cost: $11.25 per night ($8.25 for AYH members). Closed daily between 9:30 a.m. and 5 p.m. For information, call 215-286-9537. For reservations, send name and first night's deposit to: Box 49, Geigertown Road, Geigertown, PA 19523.

WASHINGTON INTERNATIONAL AYH-HOSTEL is a newly renovated, 250-bed facility located in Washington, D.C.'s central business district. Within walking distance of the White House and Smithsonian museums, the hostel features a commons room, game room, dining room, kitchen, laundry facilities, indoor bicycle storage, separate dormitory facilities for men and women, and couples rooms for two or more people (limited availability). Cost $17 per night ($14 for AYH members). Closed daily between 11 a.m. and 12 noon. For information, call 202-737-2333. For reservations, send name and first night's deposit to: 1009 11th Street NW, Washington, DC 20001-4401.

YE LANTERN INN AYH-HOSTEL is located on the shores of the Chesapeake Bay in Betterton, Md. Just two blocks from sandy Betterton Beach, the hostel features kitchen facilities, outdoor bicycle storage, and separate dormitory facilities for men and women. Private bed and breakfast-style rooms are available at an additional cost. Cost: $15 per night ($12 for AYH members). Closed daily between 9:30 a.m. and 5 p.m. For information, call 410-348-5809. For reservations, send name and first night's deposit to: P.O. Box 29, Betterton, MD, 21610-0029.

American Youth Hostels is expanding its network of hostels in Maryland and Virginia. If cycling takes you to Annapolis, Charlottesville or Williamsburg, call AYH at 202-783-0717 for the latest information on projected opening dates.

MOUNTAIN BIKING TIPS

Are you planning to take a mountain bike tour on your next cycling adventure? Mountain bikes now account for the majority of sales of new bicycles in the United States. Well-suited to Washington's terrain, they are immensely popular.

Most mountain bike enthusiasts eschew asphalt and head for fire roads, power line rights-of-way, hiking paths and even remote sections of urban areas. The mountain bike is the perfect exploratory vehicle: mobile, rugged, durable, practical. So if you master the dirt road rides in this atlas, head for the hills! Cycling in remote areas does require some extra planning however; if you break down halfway up a mountainous fire road, you have significantly fewer options than your suburban counterpart. Remember to take along a few extras such as food, water, tools and weather gear.

Maryland offers plenty of mountain biking opportunities. Most of these routes are on fire roads or hiking trails in the Maryland state park system. Call the Maryland Department of Natural Resources at 410-974-3771 for details. Virginia generally prohibits off-road mountain biking in its state parks.

Enjoy your trip, but always remember the six rules of off-road riding, adapted from the International Mountain Bicycle Association (IMBA):

1. Ride on open trails only; do not trespass.

2. Leave no trace.

3. Control your bicycle.

4. Always yield the trail.

5. Never spook animals.

6. Always plan ahead.

For more information mountain biking opportunities, read the *Mountain Bike Action Kit*, available for $2 from the Bicycle Federation of America, 1818 R Street NW, Washington, DC 20009-1692, 202-332-6986. For IMBA membership information, write to them at Route 2, Box 303, Bishop, CA 93514.

CROSSING THE CHESAPEAKE BAY BRIDGE

Does your cycling take you to the other side of the Chesapeake Bay Bridge? Many of the most spectacular rides in this atlas are on Maryland's historic Eastern Shore. Flat terrain, beautiful countryside and quaint villages make the peninsula a bicycling paradise.

Bicycling is prohibited on the Chesapeake Bay Bridge, the sole passage between Washington and the Eastern Shore. Fortunately, there *are* ways to cross the Bay Bridge with your bicycle.

The Maryland Transportation Authority offers free van rides to bicyclists, when available. However, there is a risk. Vans accommodate only two bicycles at a time, and bicyclists are at the bottom of the priority list. Nevertheless, this option may be worth a try. If you are traveling east to the Eastern Shore, cycle to the bridge administration building and request transport from the on-duty police officer. If you are traveling west toward Washington, you must call 410-974-0341 ahead of time to make arrangements.

A more dependable (but costly) way is to use Kent Island Taxi Service (410-643-2361). This commercial carrier costs $15 total for one or two cyclists; an additional rider is $5. Payment is required *before* the ride in cash or traveler's checks *only*. The cabs carry a maximum of three cyclists. A larger capacity van is available, but you need to arrange this at least two hours beforehand. If you are traveling east from Washington to the Eastern Shore, stop at the McDonald's at Saint Margaret's Road (MD 179) and US 50, about one mile before the bridge. If you are traveling west from the Eastern Shore to Washington, stop at the Texaco station and "Conveniently Yours" store at the intersection of MD 18 and MD 8, just north of the last US 50 exit before the bridge. *You must use one of these locations to call!* Waiting time averages 15 minutes. Both locations offer food, phones and toilets.

BIKE-ON-METRO

Trying to escape the city to start your ride? Get a Bike-on-Rail permit and let Washington's Metrorail whisk you beyond the city line! Washington is one of the few U.S. cities with a bike-on-rail transit program, an invaluable resource to commuter and recreational cyclists alike.

The Bike-on-Rail program was instituted after years of advocacy by the Washington Area Bicyclist Association. With a Bike-on-Rail permit, you and your bicycle may use Metrorail after 7 p.m. on weekdays, and all day weekends and holidays (except Independence Day). You pay the normal fare. A maximum of four bicycles are allowed per train, and bicyclists can use only the first and last doors of the last subway car. Other safety rules also apply.

To obtain your Bike-on-Rail permit, you must take a short test on the program's rules and regulations. Metro offers the test Mondays at 12 noon and Tuesdays at 8 a.m. at the Office of Marketing, 600 Fifth Street NW in Washington, 202-962-1116 (closest Metro station is Metro Center). From April to October, the test also is given the first Wednesday of the month between 4:30 p.m. and 6:30 p.m., and the first Saturday of the month between 10 a.m. and 12 noon. Allow about 30 minutes. A permit costs $15 and is valid for three years.

BIKE ON PLANE

Checking your bicycle as luggage on a commercial airline flight to Washington? Most airlines charge between $15 and $50 to transport your bicycle, and will not guarantee its intact arrival. In fact, despite the fee, airlines do *not* provide special treatment for your precious cargo, and even require that you sign a damage waiver. (If this seems ridiculous to you, write a letter of objection to your airline!)

You can pack your bicycle for airline shipment in several different ways:

- Special bicycle luggage (both hard shell and soft shell) is highly protective but expensive. You may be able to rent it from your bike shop.

- Cardboard bike boxes are available from almost any bike shop (call first!). Most airlines also provide bike boxes. Call the ticket agent counter at your departure airport, not the toll-free reservation number of your airline. Getting your bike into a box requires rotating the handlebars and removing the pedals. Remember to have tools handy at departure and arrival.

- Airline bags are more convenient than boxes, but less available. Bags are made of thick, transparent plastic; the bike is highly visible inside the bag. While bags offer little true protection, the baggage carriers seem to handle them more gently since they can see the bicycle; this may be the safest mode of transport.

Regardless of your packing method, your front fork is especially vulnerable to collapse when the front wheel is removed. Lodge a piece of wood between the prongs of the fork when you pack your bike.

Three major airports serve the Washington metropolitan area. *National Airport* is the most convenient to Washington, located across the Potomac River in Arlington, Va. It has its own Metrorail station, served by the Yellow and Blue Lines. While the Mount Vernon Trail traverses the airport property (see Tour 62), bicycling on the terminal grounds is illegal. Walk your bike to the trail at the north end of the airport, which is to the right from the terminal area.

Dulles International Airport is located about 20 miles northwest of the city in western Fairfax and eastern Loudoun Counties, Va. Bicycle access to Dulles is extremely limited. Your best bet is to take a limousine, taxi (expensive!) or bus from the airport to the West Falls Church Metro station, which is near the W&OD Trail (see Tour 64). If you must cycle, exit the airport grounds on the Dulles Access Road to VA 28 (bicycles are not allowed on the Dulles Access Road, but they are permitted as far as VA 28). Take VA 28 (Sully Road) north to VA 846 (Sterling Boulevard), about two miles. Turn right on VA 846. You will intersect the W&OD Trail in less than a mile. Turn right on the W&OD Trail and proceed to Washington.

Baltimore Washington International Airport (BWI), located south of Baltimore near Severn, Md., is served by train, limousine and taxi. From the airport terminal, *walk* your bicycle to the right until the sidewalk ends, then ride 0.5 miles on Elm Road to the stoplight at MD 170 (Camp Meade Road). Turn right (north) on MD 170, then left on Hammonds Ferry Road. At the intersection with West Nursery Road, pick up cues of the Washington to Baltimore Tour (Tour 37) beginning at mile 35.7. Follow cues to Baltimore, or reverse cues to Washington.

Acknowledgements

The editors and publishers gratefully thank everyone who made this book a reality. The kind, hardy souls who checked rides, donated time, read drafts, and above all offered moral support include Chip Andrews, Joe Anshein, George Baughman, Helen Baughman, Andy Clem, Robin Dean, Paul De-Long, Bob Doyle, Jennifer Farnsworth, Steven Fondriest, Kindy French, Sharon Gang, Marcy Goldstein, Peter Harnik, Kevin Hein, Ed Kearney, Linda Keenan, Peter Keenan, Kit Keller, Stuart Kipnis, Janice Knutson, Kathy Kranzfelder, Aron Livingston, Robin Miller, Keith Murphy, Tom Pendleton, Dick Shorten, Barbara Swart, Randy Swart, Dianne Vandivier, Chris Vick, Morris Warren and Gina Wright.

This fourth edition of the *Greater Washington Area Bicycle Atlas* also owes much to its earlier editions, which date back nearly two decades to 1974, and to the editors of those editions.

PHOTO CREDITS: Potomac Area Council of American Youth Hostels (Rides 1, 16, 24 and 61); Northern Virginia Regional Park Authority (Ride 37); Washington Area Bicyclist Association (Ride 13).

CHARLES BAUGHMAN is a member of the Potomac Pedalers Touring Club, the Potomac Appalachian Trail Club and the Sierra Club.

BONNIE NEVEL is the Director of the Washington Area Bicyclist Association. She is the co-author of *Railroads Recycled: How Local Initiative and Federal Support Launched the Rails-to-Trails Movement.*

BILL SILVERMAN is President of the Washington Area Bicyclist Association and Friends of the W&OD Trail.

Index

C

G

H

Hains Point . . . . Tour 13
Hamilton, Va. . . . . Tours 68, 69
Hanover County, Va. . . . . Tours 59, 61
Harborplace . . . . Tour 52
Harford County, Md. . . . . Tour 20
Harpers Ferry, W.Va. . . . . Tours 14, 34, 51, 55, 65
Harpers Ferry AYH-Hostel . . . . .Tours 3, 14, 34, 51, 55, 65; Appendix
Harpers Ferry National Park . . . . Tours 34, 55, 65
Henrico County, Va. . . . . Tours 59, 61
Herndon, Va. . . . . Tour 64
Hirshhorn Museum and Sculpture Garden . . . . Tour 13
Holocaust Museum . . . . Tour 13
Hooper Island, Md. . . . . Tour 30
House Office Buildings . . . . Tour 13
Howard County, Md. . . . . Tours 11, 12, 21, 22, 52
Hugh Mercer's Apothecary . . . . Tour 56

I

Ingleside Plantation . . . . Tour 57

J

J. Edgar Hoover Building . . . . Tour 13
James City County, Va. . . . . Tour 61
James Monroe Museum . . . . Tour 56
James River . . . . Tour 61
James River Ferry . . . . Tour 44
Jamestown, Va. . . . . Tours 44, 58, 61
Jamestown Festival Park . . . . Tour 44
Jefferson County, W.Va. . . . . Tours 3, 34
Jefferson Memorial . . . . Tour 13
John Marshall home . . . . Tour 45
Jones Point Lighthouse . . . . Tour 62

K

Kellys Ford . . . . Tours 59, 60
Kenmore House . . . . Tour 56
Kennedy Center . . . . Tour 63
Kent County, Md. . . . . Tours 28, 53
King Street Metro station . . . . Tour 62

L

Lafayette Park . . . . Tour 13
Lake Fairfax Park . . . . Tour 64
Lake Needwood Park . . . . Tour 63
La Plata, Md. . . . . Tour 26
Laytonsville, Md. . . . . Tour 10
Lancaster County, Pa. . . . . Tours 16, 24
Leesburg, Va. . . . . Tours 14, 64, 69, 70
Lexington Market . . . . Tour 52
Library of Congress . . . . Tour 13

M

N

T

Ride Listings

Rides by Length (in miles)

Rides of Civil War Interest

3. ANTIETAM BATTLEFIELD LOOP
13. MONUMENTS MEANDER
14. POTOMAC RIVER RAMBLE
25. NONEXISTENT NOTTINGHAM
26. PORTSIDE PACER
34. HARPERS FERRY 3-STATE TOUR
37. ARLINGTON HISTORY RIDE
40. MANASSAS MAULER
50. WARRENTON WANDERLUST
51. WASHINGTON TO HARPERS FERRY HOSTEL
55. BETWEEN THE HILLS TO HARPERS FERRY
56. FIT FOR A PRINCE
57. FREDERICKSBURG TO SANGRAAL HOSTEL
59. RICHMOND RESPITE
61. YORKTOWN YONDER
65. C&O CANAL TOWPATH
70. POINT OF ROCKS EXPLORER
71. FORT CIRCLE TRAIL

Rides With Metrorail Access

10. GAITHERSBURG GETAWAY
13. MONUMENTS MEANDER
36. GREAT FALLS VIRGINIAN
37. ARLINGTON HISTORY RIDE
51. WASHINGTON TO HARPERS FERRY HOSTEL
52. WASHINGTON TO BALTIMORE
62. MOUNT VERNON TRAIL
63. ROCK CREEK TRAIL
64. W&OD TRAIL
65. C&O CANAL TOWPATH
71. FORT CIRCLE TRAIL

Rides for the Family

13. MONUMENTS MEANDER
37. ARLINGTON HISTORY RIDE
62. MOUNT VERNON TRAIL
63. ROCK CREEK TRAIL
64. W&OD TRAIL
65. C&O CANAL TOWPATH
66. BALTIMORE AND ANNAPOLIS TRAIL
67. NORTHERN CENTRAL RAILROAD TRAIL

Rides Off-Road for Mountain Bike Enthusiasts

65. C&O CANAL TOWPATH
68. MOUNT GILEAD TO HAMILTON TREK
69. LEESBURG-WATERFORD-HAMILTON DIRT RIDE
70. POINT OF ROCKS EXPLORER
71. FORT CIRCLE TRAIL

Rides by Starting State and County

District of Columbia

Washington, D.C.	13. MONUMENTS MEANDER
	51. WASHINGTON TO HARPERS FERRY HOSTEL
	52. WASHINGTON TO BALTIMORE
	63. ROCK CREEK TRAIL
	65. C&O CANAL TOWPATH
	71. FORT CIRCLE TRAIL

Maryland

Anne Arundel County	66. BALTIMORE AND ANNAPOLIS TRAIL
Baltimore County	17. PRETTYBOY PRANCE
	18. SHAWAN SHAKE
	19. LOCH RAVEN LOOP
	20. SWEET AIR SWING
	21. ELLICOTT CITY LOOP
	67. NORTHERN CENTRAL RAILROAD TRAIL
Cecil County	27. DELAWARE-MARYLAND FLATLAND
Charles County	26. PORTSIDE PACER
Dorchester County	30. BLACKWATER WILDLIFE REFUGE RIDE
Frederick County	1. THREE COVERED BRIDGES
	2. FREDERICK ICE CREAM
	3. ANTIETAM BATTLEFIELD LOOP
	34. HARPERS FERRY 3-STATE TOUR
Kent County	28. ROCK HALL RAMBLE
Montgomery County	4. AQUEDUCT RIDE
	5. POOLESVILLE - LEESBURG LOOP
	6. BACK OF SUGARLOAF
	7. SENECA - POOLESVILLE LOOP
	8. SENECA TOUR
	9. SENECA SANDSTONE TRAIL
	10. GAITHERSBURG GETAWAY
	11. TRIADELPHIA TROT
	12. AWAY TO OLNEY
	14. POTOMAC RIVER RAMBLE
	15. MONOCACY MADCAP
	22. HOWARD'S HILLS
Prince Georges County	25. NONEXISTENT NOTTINGHAM
Queen Anne's County	53. QUEENSTOWN TO YE LANTERN INN
Somerset County	23. NASSAWANGO NATURAL
	32. FERRY FLAT TOUR
Talbot County	29. ST. MICHAELS SCRAMBLE

Pennsylvania

Lancaster County	16. PENN DUTCH TREAT
	24. EPHRATA EFFERVESCENCE

Virginia

Accomack County	31. GHOST TOWN GAMBOL
Albemarle County	43. BLUE RIDGE BREAKAWAY
Arlington County	36. GREAT FALLS VIRGINIAN
	37. ARLINGTON HISTORY RIDE
	62. MOUNT VERNON TRAIL
	64. W&OD TRAIL
Clarke County	33. SHENANDOAH VALLEY VENTURE
Fairfax County	40. MANASSAS MAULER
	41. GUNSTON HALL TOUR
Fauquier County	35. VINEYARD VISIT
	38. WARRENTON WANDERER
	45. ZAP THE GAP
	47. PEDALING THE PIEDMONT
	48. MIDDLEBURG MEANDER
	49. RESPLENDENT RAPPAHANNOCK
	50. WARRENTON WANDERLUST
Hanover County	61. YORKTOWN YONDER
James City County	44. JAMESTOWN LOOP
Loudoun County	46. VIRGINIA HUNT COUNTRY
	54. VIRGINIA CREEPER TO BEAR'S DEN
	55. BETWEEN THE HILLS TO HARPERS FERRY
	68. MOUNT GILEAD TO HAMILTON TREK
	69. LEESBURG-WATERFORD-HAMILTON DIRT RIDE
	70. POINT OF ROCKS EXPLORER
Middlesex County	58. SANGRAAL HOSTEL TO YORKTOWN
Prince William County	39. HILL HATERS HALF HUNDRED KILOMETERS
	42. PRINCE WILLIAM PARK
	56. FIT FOR A PRINCE
	59. RICHMOND RESPITE
	60. CHARLOTTESVILLE CHASER
Stafford County	57. FREDERICKSBURG TO SANGRAAL HOSTEL

Membership Applications

SUPPORT WABA AND HELP IMPROVE BICYCLING IN THE WASHINGTON AREA

A good place to bicycle is a resource we can't take for granted. If you ride in the Washington area, you benefit from the hard work of the Washington Area Bicyclist Association (WABA), which has energetically advocated bicycle transportation and recreation since 1972. WABA's many accomplishments include:

- ☞ A network of off-road bicycle paths and on-street bicycle lanes.
- ☞ The weekend closing of Beach Drive to automobiles.
- ☞ A bicycle bridge over the George Washington Memorial Parkway and bicycle-safe sidewalks on Key Bridge.
- ☞ Bicycle offices in every jurisdiction in the Washington area.
- ☞ Bicycle parking facilities in new retail and commercial buildings.
- ☞ The Bike-on-Metro program and bike-to-Metro facilities.
- ☞ Helmet safety programs and the nationally acclaimed *Consumer's Guide to Bicycle Helmets*.

WABA needs your help to continue its successful program of bicycle advocacy! By joining WABA you add your voice to an ever-growing number of people who want to improve and enjoy bicycling in the Washington area, for recreation and transportation.

Among the many benefits of joining WABA are:

- ✓ Discounts on bikes, accessories and repairs at 50 area bike shops.
- ✓ Access to a wealth of information on bicycle safety, laws, events, maps and publications, as well as discounts on t-shirts, buttons, maps, guide books, and more.
- ✓ Legal assistance for bicyclists involved in traffic accidents or unfair ticketing.
- ✓ *Ride On!*, a monthly newletter covering the latest news about bicycling in the area, articles on current issues and proposals, a calendar of upcoming events, and notices about WABA activities.
- ✓ The opportunity to volunteer to participate in bicycling issues in your region.
- ✓ Personalized bicycle commuting assistance.

To join, complete the membership application on the reverse side.

WABA MEMBERSHIP APPLICATION

Name _____

Address _____

City_____State_____Zip_____

Additional Names (family memberships only)_____

_____

Phone H-(   )_____ W-(   )_____

Occupation_____

How do you get to work?_____

_____

WABA needs volunteers! Please indicate below if you are interested in assisting in any of the following categories:

___Mailing parties	___Legislation & testifying
___Membership recruitment	___Newsletter
___Bike-a-Thon	___WABA table @ events
___Safety and education	___Graphic art
___Facilities	___Telephone calls
___Computer	___Special events
___Bike shop liaison	___Accounting
___Advisory board liaison	___Other

ONE YEAR MEMBERSHIPS
___$15 Low income
___$20 Individual
___$30 Family
___$75 Sustaining
___$150 Patron
___$300 Life

TWO YEAR MEMBERSHIPS
___$35 Individual
___$55 Family

___Other Contribution of $_____

Memberships expire on the 15th of the month one/two year(s) from application. Dues and contributions are tax deductible. Please add $5 **per year** and check here for first class receipt of the newsletter:____

TOTAL ENCLOSED:_____

NEW____   RENEWAL____

Mail application to: Washington Area Bicyclist Association
1819 H Street NW, Suite 640
Washington, DC 20006
202-872-9830

10 good reasons to join AYH.

1. **Use of more than 5,000 hostels in 67 countries worldwide.** Whether vacationing in Europe or cycling to Harpers Ferry, your AYH card is your key to clean, friendly accommodations for as little as $5 per night.

2. **Free copy of the *Hosteling North America* handbook.** Packed with maps, special attractions and more than 300 U.S. and Canadian hostel listings, this handbook helps you get the most out of your travels across America.

3. **Free use of the Travel Resource Center.** Use this reference library of travel brochures, maps and individual tips to plan your trip to more than 70 countries worldwide!

4. **Big discounts at all AYH Travel Shops.** Discover a wide range of guidebooks, travel gear, and backpacks—all at special member discounts. Plus Eurailpasses and airline tickets.

5. **Free subscription to the *AYH Calendar of Events*, the monthly event listing of Potomac AYH.** This activity-filled newsletter is your guide to the more than 200 programs and events that are sponsored annually by AYH.

6. **Great weekends on AYH outings across the Potomac region.** Enjoy our regular schedule of day and overnight trips for adults. . . cycling, hiking, horseback riding, rafting, canoeing, sailing and more!

7. **Fun evening at social events and travel programs.** Your AYH card gives you instant access to travel seminars, international dinners, foreign films, outdoor activities, plus interesting people like you!

8. **Great community volunteer opportunities.** Work with others to benefit our community. Volunteer for one-day neighborhood spruce-up projects, weekend outings with disadvantaged kids, and more!

9. **Low prices on international airline tickets.** Going abroad? If you are a student, a recent graduate or under 26 years old, you can buy an airline ticket on a scheduled airline at a low, low price.

10. **Free copy of the *Budget Travel Source Guide*, the AYH sourcebook for international travel.** Get all the basics of foreign travel and the best sources for finding out more. Find out the best buys in budget travel!

Join AYH and get the benefits!

For membership, complete the application on the reverse side.

HOSTELLING INTERNATIONAL®

**American Youth Hostels
Potomac Area Council**
P.O. Box 28607, Central Station
Washington, DC 20038
202/783-4943

Membership Application

☐ **Yes!** I want to join AYH, the outdoor recreation and international travel organization. Sign me up today!

Name _____

Address _____

_____

City_____ State _____ Zip _____

Home Phone # (_____)_____

Birth Date _____ / _____ / _____
　　　　　　　　DAY　　　　　　　MONTH　　　　　　　YEAR

Please check the appropriate membership category:

☐ Life $250
☐ Adult (18-54) $25
☐ Youth (under 18) $10
☐ Senior Citizen (over 54) $15

* Annual membership, amount over $25
　is tax deductible.

☐ Family (children under 18) $35
☐ Supporting* $50
☐ Sustaining* $100
Contribution—help hosteling! . . $_____
Postage & handling　　　　　$2.50
TOTAL . . . .$_____

*Join by mail, or visit one of our convenient
AYH Travel Shops for on-the-spot service:*

1108 K Street, N.W.
Washington, DC 20005
(202) 783-4943

*"One block from
Metro Center"*

17 West Mulberry St.
Baltimore, MD 21201
(301) 576-8880

*"Four blocks from
Harborplace"*

7420½ Baltimore Ave.
College Park, MD 20740
(301) 209-8544

*"At the University
of Maryland"*